GW00787850

LETTERS FROM MOSCOW

LETTERS FROM MOSCOW 1982–5

by

RICHARD OWEN
Moscow correspondent of
The Times

LONDON
VICTOR GOLLANCZ LTD
1985

First published in volume form in Great Britain 1985
by Victor Gollancz Ltd,
14 Henrietta Street, London WC2E 8QJ

British Library Cataloguing in Publication Data
Owen, Richard
Letters from Moscow.
1. Soviet Union—Social life and customs—1970–
I. Title
947.085'4'0924 DK287

ISBN 0–575–03766–0

Typeset at The Spartan Press Ltd,
Lymington, Hants,
and printed in Great Britain by St Edmundsbury Press,
Bury St Edmunds, Suffolk

CONTENTS

LETTERS FROM MOSCOW

INTRODUCTION

"JUST LOOK AROUND you," my predecessor said when I arrived in Moscow. "Everywhere you look you will find the most extraordinary things — on the street, on the beach, in the shops." The scale of the place seems vast at first: the eight- and ten-lane boulevards and the weird Stalin Gothic skyscrapers not made for human beings but for some new race of men, drawn perhaps from the pages of Edwardian science fiction rather than Marx or Engels. There was a Jules Verne quality to many Moscow objects, one felt, from the hydrofoils on the river to the design of radio sets. It was like stepping into another dimension as well as into a foreign country. "The past is like a foreign country: they do things differently there." Russia is doubly strange, being both alien and in some curious way set in a different time zone, with twentieth-century symbols (plate-glass tower-blocks, modernized Cyrillic signposts) at odds with an agrarian and Asian culture, symptoms of a poor Third World economy vying with modernity and power. As we shot off in the office "Zhiguli" (one of the few standard makes of Soviet car — made under licence from Fiat) and I was initiated into the unfamiliar Moscow road system, another author sprang to mind: Kafka. There are (paradoxically) no left turns in the Moscow street system, or very few legal ones: to get to where you want to go you have to start by facing the opposite direction and make a series of right turns, doubling back on yourself in underpasses and making U-turns at designated points in the stream of traffic. It occurred to me more than once in the months that followed that this convoluted way of doing things had an internal logic to which one, in the end, became accustomed, and which in some way reflected Russian national character and thinking. It was, surely, a sort of metaphor both for Byzantine Kremlin politics and the business of daily living and survival in the Soviet state.

It also crossed my mind in September 1983, during the Korean airliner crisis, that that tragedy was partly a clash between cultures and time zones as well as between two superpowers. It was rather like the shock of seeing an electric lift in the Royal Palace in the film *Nicholas and Alexandra* — a modern device in a backward or developing setting. All societies have their clashes and contradictions, and different ways of resolving them. Many of the baffling aspects of Russia, I felt, came from the unacknowledged tug between the 1890s and the 1980s. "Everywhere you look you will find the most extraordinary things."

I arrived at the beginning of June 1982, six months before Brezhnev's death, and left in October 1985, just over six months after Gorbachov had come to power. In between came a series of Red Square funerals, Kremlin power politics, East-West crises, spy expulsions, KAL Flight 007, the breakdown of the Geneva arms talks and their resumption a year and a half later. Yet in all this political whirl it was ordinary life which tended to fascinate us. It is, in a way, absurd to live in a foreign country for three and a half years and presume to peer through centuries-old layers of secrecy and alien ways in order to pass instant judgement on what you see for Western readers. Russia is not some menagerie, full of curious specimens to be loftily examined in the patronizing manner Westerners tend automatically to adopt. Russia has a long, proud and ancient history and culture, and will go its own way long after Western reporters have departed with their notebooks and tape-recorders.

But the challenge was inescapable, and exciting: it was, I found, rather like reporting from the moon or some distant planet. Every time I descended to Earth for a brief period of home leave (we called them, appropriately enough, "breathers", suggesting that the oxygen-masks we wore on Kutuzovsky Prospekt could come off — do Russians feel the same about London or New York?), I found that what *Times*' readers really wanted to know was how the Russians lived, what they did to amuse themselves, what they thought, what they were taught, what they read or saw on television. However many times I repeated what I had seen and heard, it still appeared to be a revelation from the sky, travellers' tales from another galaxy.

I made a list of the things that struck me as odd as we were settling in, struggling with daily problems such as how to get milk from Finland, where to find cockroach powder and how the buses and Metro worked:

— many stores are full of nothing but tinned fish, row upon fish row;
— the stamps have wonderful designs but terrible glue and don't stick properly;
— the water carts which clean the streets still operate when it's raining (or indeed snowing, I later found);
— all performers at concerts and meetings get the same red carnations in cellophane;
— government limousines are all black and all have curtains at the back;
— dress-shop assistants hold customers back behind crash-barriers even though there is nothing to buy, and few customers inside;
— people stand for three hours in a queue to get a railway ticket and think nothing of it;
— goods vehicles just say "Bread", "Milk";
— the people who appear to be looking for contact lenses under dusty city trees are in fact mushroom-hunting;
— all restaurants have bands which play at deafening volume, making conversation impossible;
— Russians put an all-purpose mysterious green ointment on ailing children, so they look like spotted Martians;
— the number of taxis in Moscow is a state secret, and so is the number of planes in the Aeroflot fleet;
— all Russians stare at foreign cars, and Russian drivers stare at your mud flaps—something most Russian cars do not have;
— books and newspapers all smell of cheap paper;
— foreign air-crashes are reported but not Russian ones, giving the impression disasters don't happen here, although everyone knows this is not true (yet nobody says so);
— foreign plastic bags are a status symbol;
— tv advertises speedboats and crystal chandeliers at prices equivalent to a lifetime's wages, yet nobody seems in the least resentful;
— residental districts are uncannily quiet, with subdued

voices and few radios blaring (I did not notice this strange lack of self-assertion at first);
— no heads ever turn in the street, even though many Russian girls are pretty and well dressed;
— all babies are tightly swaddled and overdressed;
— there are vast numbers of traffic policemen, most of whom seem to exist to stop the traffic to let government limousines sail past.

Some of these still strike me as odd, but many now seem perfectly normal.

I was, I suppose, as well prepared as I could have been, and better prepared than most, with a degree in Russian, postgraduate degrees in politics, even a brief study trip to Russia fourteen years before. And yet I scarcely knew what to expect, and continued to be surprised, infuriated and occasionally delighted. It is partly that Russia has always been, for West Europeans, an isolated and remote land, even though it is not all that far away geographically.

It is a nation compounded of patriotism, endurance in the face of apparently inevitable hardship, a millennial belief in the perfectibility of man (derived partly from the Orthodox Church tradition, partly from Marxism), and a secret police mentality of suspicion and betrayal. All this is difficult to penetrate, since — as Robert Byron observed in *First Russia, Then Tibet* in the 1930s — Russians tend to regard the foreigner "either as a subject for propaganda of the most tedious kind, or a heretic to be regarded with profound suspicion". Russia's relative isolation also means that its people do not really believe what they hear about the outside world, and if the Moscow shops were suddenly to become as abundantly stocked as the average high street supermarket many Russians would probably refuse to accept that this had been normal in the West for decades, and would be convinced that Russia had achieved another "first".

It seems to us an Asian nation of gloom and unpredictability, of onion domes and vast, immeasurable forests and steppe, whose inhabitants confuse us by dressing in Western costume and claiming to share the heritage of Western culture, even though the Renaissance and Reformation both passed them by. "I do not blame Russians for being what they are, I blame them for pretending to be what we are," wrote that irascible but perceptive traveller, the Marquis de Custine, in 1839.

The exotic nature of the Russians is compounded of course — as many writers on Russia have noted — by the great post-war ideological divide. Trying to report objectively and find out what is going on behind the Kremlin wall, the correspondent in Moscow is at the sharp end of the struggle of systems and ideas, whether he likes it or not, and is subject to various pressures, among them the incessant outpouring of TASS propaganda, with no relief, no escape and no alternative viewpoint. It was entertaining to find that stock phrases used by TASS, in its strangely Martian English (and no less stilted Russian), such as "as is well known", or "it is no coincidence that", or "they in Washington and London must realize", were invariably followed by some quite outrageous assertion or whopping untruth. Even TASS men made light of it, after a glass or two of vodka. But it was nonetheless — as one Western colleague put it — rather like Chinese water torture.

The Russians — not unlike participants in Middle Eastern and other explosive religious or national conflicts — seemed to me obsessed with proving their case, often as not in the face of reason or fact, with a determination which we found wearying but of which they never ever tired. They had more stamina, although we had humour and scepticism. It never stopped, never let up day or night; and criticisms or counter-arguments tended to be taken personally ("What's the matter, don't you like us?"). Dialogue, that panacea much beloved of many well-intentioned Westerners appalled by the East-West divide and anxious to bridge it, seemed to us in the end not so much pointless as a ritual in which both sides vented their feelings and made their case, but in which the cause of mutual understanding was scarcely advanced, if at all. I cannot think of a single case of a discussion with a Russian — official or unofficial — which ended with an evolution of thought. The best one could do, I decided, was to try and portray the Russians as they really were, or as they really seemed to a Western-educated observer, neither worse nor better, with wishful thinking pushed to one side.

The Times has a long tradition of portraying ordinary Russian life as well as politics and diplomacy, from Donald Mackenzie Wallace and Dudley Disraeli ("Braham") in the nineteenth century and George Dobson at the turn of the century to Kyril Tidmarsh, David Bonavia and Michael Binyon more recently.

These "Letters" seek to continue the tradition by offering vignettes from all over the Soviet Union, but above all from Moscow, including our own district, on Kutuzovsky Prospekt (named after the hero of the 1812 Patriotic War) near the Moscow river. At first sight (and to some extent at second sight) it is a depressing area of high-rise blocks for Russians and foreigners alike (the latter guarded by police), with the ridiculous but magnificently rococo Ukraine Hotel as the local landmark. In some ways it is not much of an advance on the Dorogomilovsky slum district it replaced in the Forties and Fifties.

But look a little closer: there is the river embankment (Donald Maclean, the traitor, lived close by until his death in 1983); the stores, from the hire shop and the drapers to the bakery (where customers abuse each other and the stolid shop assistant while prodding the bread with a metal spatula) and the huge toy shop, all hidden behind window displays so unprepossessing you might drive by and not realize these shops were there at all; the local peasant market, often a sea of mud, with the haunting smell (repellent at first) of pickles, and absurdly pricy fruit, flowers and vegetables; the Russian bath house, all chipped ceramic tiles and down-at-heel furnishings, but with a relaxed and friendly atmosphere and a never-ending display of grotesque shapes through the steam; and the Kiev Railway Station, lines to the Ukraine and beyond, which hardly seems to have changed since it was built just before the Revolution and which my wife Julia always said reminded her of the opening chapter of *Anna Karenina*, with vast patient crowds of peasants and soldiers with shapeless bundles ("I hope the architect got his money from the Bolsheviks", Julia remarked). A recently installed electronic map at the station advises the traveller to change at Chop for Rome and Athens, destinations which for the old women with their bursting string bags and the fresh-faced soldiers with their cardboard suitcases might as well be on the moon.

In some ways, I think, it helps to approach the place as Russia rather than the Soviet Union — not putting Marxism–Leninism on one side (no chance of that), but still regarding Russia as the same country described by Dobson and Mackenzie Wallace from St Petersburg, with an ideology of proletarian socialism (and a mission of world revolution) grafted on. This makes it a country at once hostile and hospitable, baffling and fascinating, infuriating and delightful. In the debate over whether Communism is imposed on Russia (as it is in Eastern Europe, or even the minority Soviet republics) or is indigenous, I incline to the view that the system springs on the whole from Russian tradition and character, both good and bad aspects, and draws on a capacity for conformism, social envy, xenophobia.

The Russians, with their penchant for self-congratulation, often struck me as self-satisfied, although they have relatively little to be self-satisfied about — and yet the reverse side of this bluster and complacency is an inferiority complex of epic proportions and a fear that foreigners will find them backward. Many Russians I met claimed to be better informed about the West than the West is about them — and yet when it comes to it they can be remarkably incurious about life "over there", a life so remote that it bears no relation to the daily and time-consuming business of survival in Soviet society, in which every purchase, every permit is a minor victory, won with effort and ingenuity. Power in the Soviet Union stems from the control of access to something desirable, and everybody controls access to something, from the doorman who only keeps one door open and the ticket clerk who makes you wait for hours to the ministers and party officials who control rather more important things. Everybody has a stake in the system of control, which is essentially self-policed.

I once watched a Soviet official who had boarded the Moscow-bound British Airways flight in London in jeans and a leather jacket disappear in mid-flight to the lavatory, returning in the standard ill-fitting Soviet bureaucrat's suit for the descent to Sheremetyevo, in order to be back in character for arrival at Moscow. All Russians are consummate actors ("*Koshmar!*" [Nightmare] our housekeeper used to exclaim at every minor upset, squeezing the maximum dramatic value out of it) and play many parts. The traditional image of the Russian mystery wrapped inside an enigma is the Matryoshka doll, placed one inside another almost *ad infinitum*; or the layers of an onion. I was reminded of the theatre: "Russia", one of our colleagues used to remark almost daily with sardonic wit, "is the theatre of the absurd put on every day for our entertainment". But of course, as he knew, it was not for our entertainment at all: there were 270 million lives on stage. One mask after another peels off, and still you cannot be sure which is the real face underneath.

When Anglo-Soviet relations plummeted from relatively cordial to relatively chilly in the spring of 1985 after a series of tit for tat expulsions, Soviet officials who had previously been friendly and affable with the British Ambassador suddenly switched to a cool and distant manner until the political barometer crept up again.

Because of this role-playing — the only way to survive in an authoritarian state perhaps — Russians seem to be able to hold two or three contradictory ideas in their heads and believe them all. (Orwell once said this was the mark of an intelligent man, but that is another matter.) The same official or well-connected person who has just given you a stern lecture on the iniquities of capitalism and imperialism will ask, without pausing for breath, whether you can get him a girlie calendar or a Sony Walkman next time you go to the West. The standard Moscow joke is that if Russia ever overran the Western world, it would have to keep Switzerland independent in order to have somewhere to buy desirable and well-made goods.

Thus you find on the one hand overweening pride and confidence, and on the other profound insecurity of the kind which instinctively prompts the Kremlin to forbid "alien" ideas, films and books, without giving ordinary Russians a chance to draw their own conclusions and make up their minds. Because of the education system, many Russians would probably have difficulty thinking for themselves in any case, even if they did have access to "forbidden" material. "The Soviet people are indignant," commentators often used to say on television, discussing some East-West row or other.

No Russian of my acquaintance — or at least comparatively few — found it strange that "the people" had never been asked whether they were indignant or not. It never even occurred to them to formulate the question.

When I arrived in Moscow, a man at the Customs with short hair and a long black leather coat (he never gave his rank) confiscated thirty of my books after a careful two-hour search of my belongings. We discussed, amicably enough, why he had singled out the thirty books (they were all in English, and theoretically his action was a violation of the Helsinki Agreement). The officer was not much of a literary critic, but he knew which books might undermine the Russian State. He gave me back a Penguin edition of Plato's *Symposium* when I pointed out that Plato was (a) Greek and (b) dead, but kept the Maxim Gorky (oddly), the Sakharov and the Solzhenitsyn (less oddly). "These you will never get back," he said solemnly as we parted, I to begin my life in Russia, he to bring the Index of forbidden literature up to date. "Some books are so dangerous to our society you may not take them out of the country." He was completely serious. I spent a long time trying to fathom this puzzling line of thought, but gave it up in the end, although it presumably has some internal logic for the border guards, the Interior Ministry and the KGB on Dzerzhinsky Square in their imposing yellowstone building (formerly the Rossya Insurance Company) which tourist guides never point out, and which Russians try not to look at as they hurry past towards Detski Mir, the children's store, or the Berlin Hotel (formerly the Savoy).

I always found the officials with whom I had to deal unfailingly courteous, polite and helpful, even when they were being subtly (or unsubtly) obstructive. Ordinary citizens are subjected to humiliations and indignities every day, but foreigners are in a privileged category. Officials were always apologetic about having to help you through the tangled thicket of Soviet bureaucracy, as if all the form-filling, letter-writing and stamping were as much a burden to them as to us (which no doubt it is). On the other hand, the Kremlin's attitude to the Western press is necessarily adversarial: the Soviet view of the press is that it should relay the government's instructions and wishes (if domestic) and foster good international and bilateral relations (if foreign). Russian officials take the view that a journalist is a guest in their country, and must observe the house rules: no mention of the leader's health, and don't talk to undesirables (dissidents). Naturally this leads to tensions, since Western journalists do both. *Izvestiya* and *Pravda* men in London or Washington give their readers a totally slanted view of Western society, in line with Party propaganda, and are not attacked or harassed by Western authorities. But then they are operating within Western rules, and can say what they like.

I took the view — I think rightly — that Russia had to be reported as if it were any other foreign country. If there is relatively little in this volume about dissidents, this is because in contrast to the Sixties and Seventies, when they dominated Western news from Moscow, there are hardly any left, thanks to the subtle and ruthless policies of Yuri Andropov.

Since Russian history tends to be cyclical, no doubt this will change, and dissident intellectuals will spring to the fore again despite repression. In my time, the only leading dissident thinker was Roy Medvedev, and the only major group of dissidents (though they did not call themselves that) were the unofficial peace activists, most of whom bravely held meetings and illegally circulated documents in the dismal suburban tower blocks where they lived.

I was only publicly attacked once, and the article which offended the Kremlin was not about dissidents at all, but about how foreigners live in Moscow, and the authorities' attempts to restrict contact with local citizens by issuing warnings about foreign spies. This was an attitude which pre-dated Soviet times, I suggested, and went back to Ivan the Terrible. The Soviet press reacted with a long *ad hominem* attack entitled "A Guest with a Stone in His Bosom", a colourful reference to the Soviet argument that journalists are welcomed into the Russian family on trust, and must not abuse Russian hospitality by throwing stones at the windows. The attack had no lasting effect, I am glad to say, and evidently gave vent to Kremlin irritation: other Western reporters were also taken to task at about the same time, and afterwards. Twice in my time the Russians threw out a Western journalist on trumped-up charges: in each case the reaction of those remaining was determination to carry on as before.

We were, of course, watched, bugged and surveilled methodically, though it is difficult to know what the unseen listeners could possibly have made of our household conversations.

There is no direct censorship — newspaper offices have their own telexes — and reporters no longer have to take their copy to the Telegraph Office on Gorky Street to confront the State censor, as they used to have to do. Correspondents observe the normal rules of courtesy and objectivity. But in my experience it is a myth that Moscow correspondents pull their punches for fear of punishment by the authorities. We were harassed in minor ways, and to be told that an article has "displeased" the authorities is a form of psychological pressure, since behind it lies the ultimate threat of expulsion. In one case, an article I had written about an unorthodox theatre run on a shoe-string was resurrected by Soviet television over a year after it had appeared, and the theatre director was warned, even though my article had quoted accounts of the theatre in the Soviet press. But for every such incident there was an act of kindness or generosity by ordinary Russians to restore one's faith in human nature, or a word of praise from a colleague to bolster morale. In general we assumed that if the Kremlin singled you out for attack you were probably on the right track.

The resulting portrait makes no claim to be comprehensive — far from it. I am conscious of the omissions: Siberia, for example, that vast tract of inhospitable land which the Russians have developed in the face of adverse conditions (and where they still send their political prisoners); the national passion for chess, and the very unsocialist pastime of betting on horses at the Hippodrome; the open-air swimming-baths, which operate in winter but not in summer, when they are closed for disinfection; the Stalin Gothic hotels (we had a daily view of the Ukraine Hotel from our window), which Malcolm Muggeridge once described as somebody's idea of Victorian luxury seen from the outside rather than from inside, as by an urchin with his nose pressed against the windowpane; and the sheer, all-pervading smell of Russia, instantly recognizable. Fitzroy Maclean, one of the greatest of all writers on Russia, described it in the 1930s as a potent mixture of black bread, sheepskin, vodka and unwashed humanity (the odour of Tsarist Russia) with a Soviet admixture of cheap petrol, disinfectant, and the "clinging, cloying smell of Soviet soap". Fifty years later it is still the same.

In short, the Moscow presented here is my Moscow, and others will have different impressions. The themes perhaps reflect my own preoccupations as much as the Russians': the persistence of crime and privilege in a society which claims to be abolishing both; the challenge posed by videos and computers to the authoritarian and secretive State; the gap between the real and the ideal, between the pretence that Russia is a popular democracy of high living standards and the dismal, observable reality of housing and shops; and the gaps in official historical memory, again in the face of what Russians actually remember, with a consequent deleterious effect on national consciousness and intellectual development.

I should record that, as several architectural historians wrote to tell me, William Walcott, the Englishman who designed the Metropole Hotel, is not "little known": he was born in Odessa of Anglo-Russian parentage and designed a number of well-known buildings in London, dying by his own hand in Britain in 1943. I should record also that since the "Letters" first appeared in *The Times* (not all of these pieces appeared under that heading, but all were in the same style), some things have changed.

The stationery store was closed for refurbishment recently, and as I write is undergoing transformation into a more modern shop called "*Voskhod*" (Sunrise); Mr Ryzhkov, the young and dynamic opponent of bureaucracy, has been brought into the Politburo by Mr Gorbachov; the Pasternak *dacha* at Peredelkino has at last been taken over by the State in the shape of the Writers Union, and the Pasternak family have been evicted. On the whole the first two seem to me to be improvements, the third not. As Lenin used to say, two steps forward, and one step back.

I am grateful to *The Times* for allowing me to reprint published pieces. I should like to take this opportunity to thank the Editor of *The Times*, Charles Douglas-Home, for sending me to Moscow, and for unfailingly supporting me; all our friends, mostly artists and writers but also some "ordinary people", for their warmth, spirit and hospitality on many evenings over tables laden with food and drink, often the kitchen table (the heart of every Russian home): the Press Department of the Foreign Ministry, and other Soviet officials, for tolerating what I know they regard as bourgeois propaganda; and my colleagues in the Moscow foreign press corps, one of the most perceptive and resilient bands of men and women in international journalism.

Above all, I thank my wife, Julia, who brought all the above-mentioned qualities to our life in Moscow, and who somehow managed to offer support, conduct research, do battle with the ancient telex and share the hardships and exhilarations while at the same time running a household and bringing up our twin daughters, Isabel and Eleanor, who were born during our Moscow assignment. This book is dedicated to her, and to them.

FIRST IMPRESSIONS

A peep behind the cosmetic façade

"SO IT'S TRUE what they say about Moscow," said a friend just out from England. "Drab, monumental buildings, endless queues in shops with nothing worth buying, rude and authoritarian officials, militia all over the place. . . . "

We were standing on a bend of the Moscow River, on a tree-lined boulevard, with people fishing off the embankment. Around the corner, twinkling in the July sun, were the spectacular golden domes of the Kremlin. Cheerful groups of youngsters in Western jeans strolled in groups, eating the high-quality ice-cream which only the Russians still seem to make.

There is a tendency for visitors from the West to assume that the tourist Russia they are shown — Red Square, the ballet — is a cosmetic façade, a kind of Potemkin village "wheeled out by Intourist for the benefit of foreigners", while the drab and authoritarian Russia they glimpse behind the cracks is the real one, the one that Russians themselves have to endure.

It is certainly true that Moscow is a city of shortages, of monumentality, and of stifling bureaucracy, not to mention rudeness. For the latter at least I can quote no less an authority than President Brezhnev, who complained to the Young Communist League in May about the "rude treatment of customers" in shops.

He was presumably speaking from second-hand reports rather than experience, since the Soviet leadership (like foreign residents) does its shopping in special stores stocked with goods hidden from the general public.

All the same, frank public criticisms of the shortcomings of Soviet life are much more frequent than is imagined. One Moscow paper recently launched into a devastating tirade about having to queue for hours to buy a railway ticket.

Far from being drab and conformist, Moscow is a vital, colourful city with as much nineteenth-century elegance as Stalinist architecture, full of remarkable characters finding ingenious ways to beat the system and get hold of the numerous goods which happen to be *defitsitny* (unobtainable).

Perhaps precisely because Soviet society is so strictly controlled, individuals within it lead intense and varied lives. Even food is adequate, if not plentiful, once you dig under the surface. The state stores have hopelessly inefficient production and distribution. But go down to the market where peasants come in from the countryside to sell their produce, and a world of flowers, fruit and vegetables opens up, with even that rare commodity, meat, on display.

Prices are high, but somehow most Russians seem to find the money. And that is another of Moscow's surprises: although the average wage is low, most people have quite a few more roubles than they know what to do with.

Beneath the surface of the state system a parallel economy is at work. You need a refrigerator, or a fashionable blouse, or perhaps one of those smart Zhiguli cars? Well, you could put your name down and wait, of course, with millions of others. But the chances are you have a friend who has a friend who needs a favour, such as access to your *dacha* some time, and in return . . . it is called doing business *na levo*, literally "on the left". And, of course, a bottle or two of vodka helps the process along.

The world of officialdom is never far away, it is true. From the window of *The Times* flat I can see a sign strung along the top of a building a mile away and illuminated at night, proclaiming "Long live the Communist Party of the Soviet Union!" But the slogans are surprisingly few, and most have a rather faded and neglected look.

Muscovites have good reason to be grateful to the tourists, at least in one important respect: almost all the improvements in the antiquated procedures you encounter in shops, hotels and restaurants stem from the influx of foreigners into Moscow for the Olympic Games in 1980.

There are other signs too of the spread of Western influence, with even home-grown pop music sounding not unlike its counterpart in London or Paris, from sophisticated jazz rock to bouncy tunes of the Abba variety. There is an Art Deco restaurant just around the corner from the KGB secret police headquarters on Dzerzhinsky Square. You can forget the privations and shortcomings by dancing the night away to the strains of Glenn Miller reproduced impeccably by a Saturday night dance band of Conservatoire students making money on the side.

Moscow
21 July 1982

ZONES OF LEISURE:

HOLIDAYS AND TRAVEL

Changing cars behind the Curtain

THE MOSCOW OFFICE of *The Times* has a new car. Not a particularly noteworthy event, you might say, and you would be right, except that all transactions in Russia are noteworthy, and the buying or selling of cars seems to arouse strong emotions in the hearts of Soviet bureaucrats.

Or perhaps it is simply money. Foreigners in the Soviet Union can buy Soviet cars only with "hard currency" such as dollars or pounds. When the time comes to sell, however (most last only three or four winters; most cars, that is, not foreigners), the authorities will pay out only roubles. Roubles cannot be transferred back into what we tend to call here "real money" and can be used only in Russian shops, where there is nothing worth buying. Selling to Soviet citizens or even other foreigners is strictly forbidden, and the penalties are severe.

So roubles it is. The procedure, for once, is relatively straightforward. You take your clapped-out vehicle to the government garage, where they give you a "take it or leave it" price based on annual devaluation and wear and tear. There is then a pause of three months or so while the government sells the car to someone else (pocketing the difference), and transfers the agreed trade-in price to your bank account (in roubles). Straightforward, that is, unless the office car happens to be registered in the name of your predecessor, which it invariably is. He, of course, has been posted elsewhere and has long since left the country. It would no doubt have been sensible to have transferred the registration before he left — except that under Soviet regulations that is not possible. It therefore takes a series of stamped and signed declarations, witnessed and double-checked, to persuade the state bank, the police and the Customs to hand over the money.

No matter: phase one is completed, and you have learned something in the process about how Russia works. Now to buy a new car, preferably one built to handle icy roads for most of the year and muddy roads for the rest. Foreigners at least have a choice (unlike Russians, who can only buy Soviet ones, and even then there is a long waiting list). Diplomats, businessmen and journalists can either buy Soviet vehicles (for hard currency), or imported ones (ditto).

Since Soviet prices have recently gone up and are not all that different from foreign ones, more and more foreign residents are going for imports with Saab and Volvo leading the field. The best Soviet car is the tough and chunky Niva Land-Rover, but it is noisy and lacks the engineering and finish of Scandinavian competitors. And so to Helsinki, capitalist Mecca for all foreigners in the Soviet Union, where Saab had despatched their latest 900 GL, equipped with metal-studded winter tyres. After Customs formalities in Helsinki (all of three hours) your correspondent drove to the Soviet-Finnish border, into the Soviet Union, and back to Moscow by way of Vyborg and Novgorod.

Of the journey, suffice it to say I was thankful for the chunky winter tyres and the Saab's roadholding, especially since Russian road clearance is less efficient than Finnish. Driving on packed snow with ice underneath while overloaded ramshackle lorries come pounding at you from the other direction in the middle of the road can be unnerving. I was also glad I had stashed a large can of Finnish petrol in the boot, since the first (and last) petrol station I came to before Vyborg was six feet deep in snow, and totally deserted. I was also glad I had stocked up in Helsinki on antifreeze and oil (unobtainable in Russia) and windscreen wipers (which tend to get stolen on Moscow streets). Once in Moscow, there is the small matter of obtaining Soviet licence plates. (These are in code, incidentally — "D" for diplomat, "K" for correspondent and so on, followed by the number of the country. Britain, naturally, is number one, so that *The Times* licence number begins "K01", and all traffic policemen can pick it out at once. But I digress.) After the registration (one day) comes Customs clearance (one or two days), insurance (one day), and fixing the new plates (half a day). This is not intended to make life difficult for those who import, it is simply how Russia functions; pleasantly, correctly, but slowly.

Moscow
12 March 1983

The sticky rules of a Moscow summer

THIS BEING SUMMER, most of Moscow is heading either for the sunny south or for *dachas* (cottages) in the suburbs and on the banks of the Moscow River to swim, fish and laze about. For many Soviet citizens, a holiday means an organized outing to a trade-union rest home or resort, an extension of collectivism at work. But an escape to the *dacha* or the river is an escape to the relative freedom of the great outdoors.

Russia is an over-regulated society, with the emphasis on "*Niet*" rather than "*Da*". It all comes from the mores of a peasant society, in which the village atmosphere encourages everybody to poke their noses into everybody else's business.

But Russians enjoy themselves hugely, especially on the beach or river bank. Gargantuan women either wobble about in whalebone swimming costumes or strip unashamedly to voluminous underwear. Men tend to sunbathe standing up, striking attitudes as they face the sun. Later, instead of the western vacuum flask and sandwiches, a picnic of sausage, pickled gherkins and vodka is spread on the grass.

The "no you can't" mentality is never far away, though, and is reinforced by the official assumption that those in authority know what is good for you. Even a short journey beyond the city limits holds hazards for foreigners and for local residents. Foreigners are encouraged to go to the "diplomatic beach" (unless they are Americans, who have been barred from the beach in retaliation for the banning of Soviet diplomats from Long Island). But there is nothing to stop you going to the ordinary Russian beach, provided you are prepared to observe the rules.

One reason there is no unemployment in the Soviet Union is clearly that half the population is in uniform. The police are invariably polite and correct. They are sticklers for regulations, even when the rule appears to defy logic. On one recent weekend, I went with some Russian friends to a stretch of the Moscow River where you can hire rowing boats and swim or picnic. As we approached the shore road, with the sparkling blue water beckoning ahead, out popped a militiaman in his grey and blue uniform, sweating slightly in the heat and waving his white truncheon. The road was closed, he said. "Why?" we asked. Because it's Saturday, the policeman said, pointing to a sign which clearly bore him out. But Saturdays, we said, are precisely when people go to the river. The perspiring policeman said the Russian equivalent of "I don't make the rules, I just enforce them" and we joined a stream of uncomplaining Muscovites cheerfully trekking the last mile or two to the water.

Even when you reach the river, regulations lurk behind every blade of grass and ice-cream kiosk. If you plunge in and strike out for the farther shore, a militia boat comes hurtling up in a cloud of spray and informs you through a megaphone that it is dangerous to swim more than 20 metres from the bank (as indeed it is when a barge comes thundering downriver). It is also forbidden to go swimming when drunk, to dive from boats, or to have two people rowing at the same time side by side.

One foreign resident who took his windsurfing board to the river had scarcely clambered aboard when he was assailed by loud-hailers from all sides. "You can't do that here," said a disembodied voice from the police launch. "This is a zone of leisure." "But I am at leisure," protested the windsurfer. "That's as may be," came the reply, "but you can't do that here. Go downstream." Windsurfing, it seemed, was allowed only on strictly defined stretches of the river.

Perhaps the most significant aspect of that scene, however, was not that the windsurfer came up against the Russian mania for regulations, but that windsurfing is now an unremarkable sight in a Russian resort. The policeman's whistle and the dressing-down are all in the Russian tradition, pre-dating the Communist era, and presumably designed to keep citizens in line and make them justify their actions.

But within the limits, the Soviet Union is absorbing features of Western life which would have seemed unthinkable even ten years ago, from Pepsi-Cola and Western jeans to windsurfing. Not many Russians can afford the kind of windsurfing board found in California or Western Europe, nor, as yet, are many manufactured here. Russians make their own, and have fun with all the unconstrained enjoyment that comes from relatively unsophisticated, home-made entertainment.

Public transport to the river beaches is frequent and cheap and the countryside begins right on Moscow's doorstep. Only five miles upstream from the Kremlin large family groups are setting up camp in the woods by the water, cooking over fires (no regulations here, strangely enough), chatting, singing, listening to the radio, playing ball.

The quiet of the pine and birch woods, the lap of warm water and the tranquillity of fishermen on the banks are enough to make anyone — even policemen — forget the existence of man-made rules. In Russia, summer is brief, intense and enjoyed while it lasts.

Moscow
10 August 1982

"Wild ones" plague Yalta

ANTON CHEKHOV BUILT himself a villa here at Yalta. So did Nicholas II, and Soviet leaders come here to rest from the cares of the Kremlin. It is not hard to see why. Yalta, set on a superb stretch of Black Sea coast, offers sun, bathing and scenery comparable with the Italian or French Riviera. The Russians rather earnestly refer to Yalta's climatic properties and restorative powers, but we would simply say it is a first-class resort.

There is no topless sunbathing, and the usual fare of cabbage pies and chicken Kiev reminds you that you are still in the Soviet Union. But there are comparatively few propaganda slogans, and the atmosphere is relaxed.

"The Soviet Union is the bulwark of peace" seems a little absurd on a giant placard at the entrance to the Hotel Yalta, as if it had been placed by mistake on a corniche near Nice. The same is true of the portrait of Lenin next to the Beach Restaurant where Yalta's good-time girls gather in the warm, fragrant evening in search of hard currency tourists and entry to the magic world of foreign tourism.

The Hotel Yalta is the town's showpiece. Completed five years ago with Yugoslav help, it has 1,500 unusually clean and well-appointed rooms, a higher standard of service than normally found in Russia, and a lift straight down to the beach. On the Adriatic this might not seem remarkable but on the Black Sea it is a welcome surprise. The private beach is a babble of German, English, Finnish, and some Russian, since quite a few privileged

Soviet citizens seem able to take their families to the Hotel Yalta for their annual holiday.

The vast majority of Russians, though, go to Sanatoria and "houses of rest" run by their trade union or factory. Here conditions are more spartan, but on the other hand the *putyovkas* (vouchers) are very cheap and much in demand. In the Soviet Union you do not spend winter evenings flicking through colourful travel brochures (only tiny numbers ever travel abroad, in supervised groups). Instead you put your name down for a *putyovka* and pull as many strings as you can to ensure you get a place in a sanatorium or holiday centre at some desirable resort such as Yalta, Sochi or Sukhumi.

The voucher system is designed to ensure that workers and peasants have access to holiday places which were previously the preserve of the aristocracy, the merchant class and the intelligentsia, and on the whole it works very well. Flights are also cheap, and Russians feel that, despite the queues, congestion and shortages, they benefit from the Soviet rule. What worries the authorities, on the other hand, is the astonishing rise in the numbers of "wild" tourists, known in Russian as *dikari*, who cast aside the collective and just turn up on the Black Sea, often finding rooms in private flats.

Down at the Yalta quayside, where holidaymakers stroll and enjoy a lively fun-fair while the great steamers dock alongside, an old man taking ferry tickets grabbed me by the arm and fixed me with his mariner's eye. He said he was a retired naval officer, and complained that Yalta was becoming clogged up with wild tourists. "We haven't the facilities," he said. "Yalta budgets for two million visitors a year, but we're getting nearly three million."

The *Literary Gazette* recently reported that at the high season there are twice as many people in the Crimean resorts as they can cope with. Most of the *dikari*, it said, are in their teens and twenties, young Russians impatient with the restrictions of the pioneer camp or the house of rest. The paper suggested, without much hope that it would work, that police in the Crimea should be stationed at Black Sea resorts in a mass operation to keep the "wild ones" out.

Yalta
6 September 1984

Andropov breaks with the seaside routine

WHERE DO RUSSIAN leaders go in summer? The traditional answer is the Black Sea, although in this (as in other things) Mr Andropov seems to have a style of his own.

The first élite *dachas* at Sochi were built at the turn of the century. The Tsar's pseudo-Renaissance palace at Livadia, along the coast at Yalta, was completed in 1911. It served as the site of the 1945 Yalta conference, no doubt because Stalin liked the climate (even in February).

Khrushchev preferred palm-fringed Pitsunda, on the Georgian Black Sea coast, but Brezhnev moved the Kremlin's summer headquarters back to the Crimea, and spent many an August sailing, sunbathing and receiving foreign guests at Oreanda, looking for all the world like one of President Nixon's less savoury business companions, in his windcheater and dark glasses.

Each new Soviet leader always finds fault with his predecessor's summertime arrangements, so that the whole paraphernalia of presidential communications, including the hotline to the White House, has to be carted off to some new specially-equipped *dacha*.

Mr Andropov has full access to the Politburo Crimean *dachas*. But he seems to prefer to spend his leisure time (when he has any) in the mountains of his native Caucasus. Mr Andropov has a new and fully-equipped *dacha* just outside Moscow, so that he can enjoy the woods and the Moscow River while being able to dash down to the Kremlin in a convoy of black limousines if the need arises. He also has a presidential flat not far from the city centre, on the same street as *The Times* office, but does not often use it, possibly because it now bears a plaque saying: "Leonid Ilyich Brezhnev lived here." But when the sun sparkles above the mountain lakes and meadows of the Caucasus, Mr Andropov is drawn to the spa of Kislovodsk, about 3,000 feet above sea level. Kislovodsk is not far from the Soviet leader's birthplace in the Stavropol region.

It has long been a centre for the treatment of nervous and cardiac disorders, not to mention kidney complaints and diabetes, all of which sounds like a summary of Mr Andropov's last check-up.

The spa was founded in 1823, and produces the only drinkable Russian mineral water, called *Narzan*. At the exclusive sanatorium at Red Stones (so named because of the red sandstone formations; there are also grey stones and blue stones) VIPs can take a rest cure while gazing at a backcloth of snow-capped peaks and mountain greenery. Or they can take the waters at the spa, with its English Gothic revival (1849) and Indian imperial (1903) style buildings. Both the spas in the Caucasus and the beach resorts of the Black Sea are popular with less elevated Russians, although the accommodation and service are somewhat less exclusive.

In Russia there is no question of checking into the hotel of your choice. Factories and offices across the Soviet Union issue "houses of rest" and sanatoria, and holidaymakers say they live like kings for a few weeks compared to the drudgery of their daily lives. Most Russians expect their leaders to live well and do not seem to resent ostentatious privilege (not aloud at any rate). As they sunbathe at Sochi and Sukhumi, Soviet holidaymakers are aware that their leaders enjoy a more luxurious lifestyle behind well-guarded walls, but say there is not much they can do about it and admit they would probably do the same if they were in power.

In this sense, Mr Andropov, while satisfyingly stern and disciplinarian over public policy, is rather disappointingly austere and spartan in private life. Russians identify rather more with Brezhnev, who unashamedly enjoyed the good life. Not long before he died he invited a foreign communist leader to his Crimean *dacha* and sat with him on the vast and otherwise empty beach. Drinking cognac brought out by the *dacha* servants and listening to dissident songs on a portable gramophone, Brezhnev was observed by a Moscow intellectual who was holidaying on a VIP beach near by.

It is difficult to imagine the *Narzan*-sipping Mr Andropov either getting mellow on the beach over a bottle of cognac or allowing anyone to get close enough to watch him.

Moscow
15 August 1983

Spartan delights of the crop-spraying airline

AEROFLOT THE SOVIET airline, this week marked its sixtieth birthday with a litany of achievements but also with an admission by the Aviation Minister that there were "shortcomings" which had aroused "justified criticism". Anyone who has endured an Aeroflot flight, especially an internal one, will agree with him.

The first regular Aeroflot flight was from Moscow to Nizhny Novgorod (now Gorky) in 1923. There were six passengers on board. By the end of the year, Soviet Russia had built its first native aircraft (the five-seater AK1) and had carried 229 people. It now carries more than one hundred million passengers a year on a vast international and internal network, thus qualifying as the biggest airline in the world.

Aeroflot also carries more than three million tons of cargo and mail a year and is a vital link in the sprawling territory of the Soviet Union. Its aircraft are sometimes the only means of transport to ice-bound communities. Aeroflot is also an integral part of the defence system, and all its pilots have military training. It has been described as a "no frills" airline, and is certainly spartan and unpretentious, as I found out recently when flying on a Tupolev 154 (the airline's workhorse) to the south of Russia. Although all passengers have tickets and are checked rigorously, there is invariably a seething mass of would-be passengers at the foot of the aircraft steps, held back by hefty stewardesses. Aeroflot tends to issue more tickets than there are seats and throws passengers off if officials, VIPs and foreigners need to travel. Unexplained delays are common.

On board — where tickets are rechecked — the interior is cramped and bare, rather like a scruffy city bus. There is no question of extra leg-room. Nor does the reality much resemble the advertisements in the terminal buildings, which show a smiling blonde air hostess offering caviar and cognac to a well-spruced couple. Your neighbour is more likely to be a country dweller laden with food and string bags. Smoking and drinking are forbidden at all times, and no meals (cold chicken is the staple) are served on flights under three hours.

The priority is to get the job done, and there is no time left for the finer points of comfort. On the other hand, Aeroflot has an estimated fleet of more than 2,000 aircraft (the number is a state secret), and carries out duties from crop-spraying to monitoring fish shoals, often in harsh conditions which call for skill and dedication.

What the authorities do not like to admit is that Aeroflot's safety record is poor. Reluctance to divulge disasters — unless foreigners are involved — is partly due to traditional Russian secrecy and partly to national pride. Air crashes (the Ilyushin 62 was the aircraft most often involved in unadmitted crashes last year) are hushed up. So, too, is the fact that Soviet technology has lagged behind that of the West, though it is now catching up.

According to Aeroflot officials, there have been no aircraft designers to match the Tupolevs (father and son), and there were no supersonic airliners until the appearance of the ill-fated Tu144 "Concordski", now withdrawn from service.

This understandable sensitivity about the prestige attached to the national carrier also affects ordinary Soviet citizens. Most are not aware, for example, that Western airlines, like JAL and Air France, were not allowed to fly wide-bodied jets such as the Airbus into Moscow until the Russians had developed their own Il 86, which went into service between Moscow and Berlin last year, and now flies to Paris and Madrid as well.

As we flew back to Moscow in our Tu154 and the stewardess handed round the mineral water, my Russian companion asked politely: "Tell me, do you have jumbo jets in the West, just like us?"

Moscow
12 February 1983

Finland: friendly country where Russians explore West

THERE WAS A time when Finland was the playground of the Russian aristocracy, its lakes, forests and villas seasonally populated by high society from St Petersburg, just across the water. Nowadays Finland is still playing host to the Russians, but to the new bourgeoisie rather than the old aristocracy. At most times of the year groups of Russians from official delegations can be seen trudging round Helsinki, looking into shop windows with a mixture of fascination and glumness. They are presumably fascinated by the relative opulence of their small neighbour, and glum at the thought of the relative poverty back home.

No Russian, official or unofficial, likes to admit that "they" in the West have better goods and facilities than "we" do. Finland is popular with Russians (those few able to travel, that is) because it does not rub Soviet visitors' noses in their "otherness". It accepts them, which is a relief to Russians used to seeing the outside world as hostile and condescending.

Finland is conveniently close, and the volume of trade is such that a large number of Soviet delegations come to Helsinki every year. They are invariably accompanied by their wives, who take full advantage of the opportunity to shop for goods not available in Russia. They appear conscious of their privileged status, but with the slight insecurity of the *arriviste*. Soviet wives walking through the dining-room of the Intercontinental Hotel seem torn between gawping and pretending that they do this sort of thing every day. The Finns, diplomatic to a fault, offer the Soviet Union a useful halfway house, neutral but friendly territory where Soviet leaders can explore the West. It is "capitalist, but not hostile" in the words of one Finnish journalist.

The Russians have several properties in and around Helsinki apart from their embassy, including a splendid villa (originally built for a wealthy building contractor) in the fashionable suburb of Kuusisaari. The Kuusisaari villa is used officially by visiting Soviet leaders, but also unofficially when they prefer a low profile. "They say Andropov has never been to the West," commented a Finnish friend, "but I wouldn't bet on it. We don't always look too closely."

The arrival in power of Mr Yuri Andropov might have been expected to send shivers up Finnish spines, given his record during and after the bitter Winter War between Finland and Stalin's Russia. As an activist of the Young Communist League, Mr Andropov was sent to Karelia to help "absorb" it into the Soviet Union. The Finns lost a large chunk of territory, including the historic town of Vyborg which lies across the border in Leningrad province.

The Finns are philosophical, however, and say tactfully that they do not attribute Soviet policies to particular personalities. "Finland's security depends on its acceptance of realities," said one Finnish source. "We may get Vyborg back one day, who knows. For the moment, it's a Soviet town, and that's that". Finnish tourists visit Vyborg in busloads, to see its gabled houses and thirteenth-century fortress. Soviet guides describe the town as Finnish from 1918 to 1940, but point out that it was part of the Russian Empire in the eighteenth and nineteenth centuries.

The Finns may even turn the Andropov connection to advantage, on the grounds that the Soviet leader knows Finland and the border area well and was not responsible for what happened after the Winter War. There was even some disappointment when it was shown that Mr Andropov's wife (about whom almost nothing is known) was not from Karelia as had been suggested.

Helsinki

31 January 1983

Flying in the face of frosty Aeroflot

GETTING IN AND out of the "evil empire" has been something of a problem lately. Returning to Moscow after a brief break, I found normally pleasant Aeroflot officials distinctly frosty, their manner matching the icy rain which enveloped Sheremetyevo, Moscow's international airport.

Russians do not like being attacked for their "tyrannical" or "barbaric" behaviour, least of all by Mrs Thatcher or Mr Reagan. They like being punished for "atrocities" even less, and adopt an air of injured innocence over the Korean airliner tragedy which set it all off. "You're lucky we let you in at all," said an Aeroflot lady in a smart blue uniform, only the ghost of a smile hovering somewhere around her severely set lips.

Soviet officials are still smarting over the recent incident at Heathrow when an Ilyushin 62 landed before maintenance workers had ended their boycott of Aeroflot flights. The Soviet pilot who backed the Ilyushin out of the bay and took off with precious little fuel is regarded at Sheremetyevo as a hero — although any Western pilot who tried the same trick at Moscow would be condemned as a "provocateur". The situation is gradually returning to normal, or what passes for normal nowadays in East-West relations. It is hardly true, as Tass claimed, that President Reagan's call for further sanctions is being "drowned by the roar of airliners landing at Moscow". There are not all that many Western flights to Moscow in any case (Sheremetyevo has only one 747 parking bay) and the relatively small airport is dominated by Aeroflot and East European or "fraternal" airlines from the Third World.

On the other hand, Air France, which used volunteer crews throughout the boycott (and only lost two flights), resumed normal service at the first opportunity, the moment the international airline pilots lifted the ban, and most others followed suit.

British Airways had one or two false starts, apparently because the Heathrow ban on Aeroflot lasted longer than the Western pilots' boycott of Moscow. BA gave various reasons for not resuming on time (flights were under-booked or over-booked) but the risk that a British plane might have been given the Ilyushin treatment no doubt played a part.

There have been anomalies and loopholes all along, with some countries — like Britain — taking the ban seriously, and others — like France — maintaining air links with Moscow (much to the relief of businessmen, diplomats and journalists who would otherwise have been stranded). Despite its close involvement in the Sakhalin disaster, Japan last week resumed its air service to Tokyo from London via Moscow, carrying a number of British passengers who might otherwise have flown the flag.

It was difficult to suppress a slight twinge of anxiety as the Japan Airlines 747 left the West behind, lumbered over Riga and headed inland. Getting out of Moscow in the first place had been even more of a problem. There had been one remaining direct flight to Britain, Air India from Bombay to Birmingham with a stopover in Moscow. Unfortunately for us, British ground staff spotted the anomaly hours before the Air India flight was due in, and closed the loophole. Panic ensued, with passengers milling around Moscow airline offices, and unflappable Air India officials doing their best to speed up elephantine Aeroflot procedures ("No, you may not transfer your ticket, you have paid in roubles"). Miraculously, Air France came to the rescue, and most travellers were rebooked to Paris with minutes to spare. On the plane an Indian businessman handed me a full-page newspaper advertisement praising Mrs Gandhi's non-aligned policies, and pointed silently to the headline (taken from Jefferson): "Peace, commerce and honest friendship with all nations, entangling allegiance with none." At Paris, puzzled Air France officials coped manfully with a sudden influx of unexpected arrivals from Moscow, all of whom had tickets for Birmingham and none of whom seemed to want to go there. "Tell me, monsieur, what is wrong with Birmingham?" asked one exasperated official before putting us all, with Gallic aplomb, on the last Airbus to London.

Moscow
17 October 1983

DOWN AT THE KOMSOMOL DISCO:

YOUTH AND POP MUSIC

Pavel takes gilded ladder to the top

YOUNG PAVEL WAS bright but lazy and wanted to find the quickest route to the top of Soviet society without having to work for it. So he enrolled at one of Moscow's most esteemed institutes of higher education attended by the sons and — more important — the daughters of the élite. There he met Manya, the daughter of a man who had worked his way up from humble origins to become director of a large enterprise. Pavel persuaded Manya to marry him, and they moved into a fine Moscow apartment with all the amenities of life unavailable to most ordinary citizens.

The Pavel-Manya marriage inevitably collapsed in divorce, with Pavel even having to endure a beating at the hands of his wife and mother-in-law over the division of matrimonial property. He none the less ended up much better off than he was when a student, with his own flat in the centre of Moscow.

Komsomolskaya Pravda, which has drawn the attention of its youthful readers to this story, does not regard the tale of Pavel and Manya as edifying. On the contrary, the newspaper describes their behaviour as reminiscent of the aristocracy which was supposed to have been swept away by the Russian Revolution. *Komsomolskaya Pravda* was particularly shocked by the fact that, at the institute which the couple attended, lists were circulated of well-connected girl students thought to be a good match for fortune hunters like Pavel.

The Soviet authorities are seriously concerned at the social attitudes of the younger generation, and particularly at the tendency of some young people towards materialism, good living and privilege, at the expense of hard work and the common welfare. This is especially true of Russia's gilded youth, the children of highly placed party officials, government bureaucrats and industrial bosses, who tend to dash about in fast cars and ape Western manners. Soviet newspapers complain that the virtues of commitment and diligence on which the country was built are being brushed aside by members of a generation which has not known the real hardships endured by its parents.

Komsomolskaya Pravda (the newspaper for young Communists), pointing up the moral of the tale, describes such behaviour as "infantile", and deplores the fact that a generation is growing up which apparently expects society to provide it with all the luxuries and cannot seem to achieve anything without help.

Another newspaper for young people, *Moskovsky Komsomoliets*, recently came to the same conclusion, and in a review of a new book on "philistine social behaviour" urged its readers not to concentrate on material gain and consumerism at the expense of spiritual values. "There are some people," the newspaper remarks sadly, "who regard others merely as a means to an end, and are guided only by the selfish principle of personal advantage." Unlike the majority of Soviet youth, it says, these youngsters give themselves such airs and graces that anyone would think they were descended from one of the great princely Russian families of the past.

Moscow
24 August 1982

Adult Party stamp confronts teenagers' disco beat

ROCK MUSIC, WITH its ability to generate powerful emotions and surging adrenalin, is worrying strait-laced Communist Party officials in Russia, who fear that Soviet youngsters' love of loud and raucous pop is instilling in them a spirit of anarchism and independence.

The focus of current Soviet concern is the discotheque, a phenomenon which reached the Soviet Union in the 1970s by way of the more Western-orientated Baltic republics, and has caught on in Russia proper over the last year or two. The newspaper *Sovietskaya Kultura*, which has been conducting a debate on the issue, has been inundated with letters from teenage readers saying that discotheques and rock music are an essential part of the modern scene. "When you go to your local club and suggest a disco evening," one young man wrote from Minsk, "the officials tell you to think about your future career, and not waste your free time on frivolities." In reply, *Sovietskaya Kultura* agreed that it was quite possible to be career-minded and disco-crazy at the same time.

The latest article on the subject in *Sovietskaya Kultura* indicates that Soviet cultural officials are now trying to subject the disco phenomenon to stricter Party control. The Party's administrator of cultural policies in Minsk, taking up points from the readers' letters, says that it is about time discotheques and rock concerts were regulated by specially appointed adult committees. Far too often local authorities cannot be bothered to organize such events, or do not know how to, with the result that teenagers take it upon themselves to provide their own entertainment. The result is often a disco-show "full of empty and anti-artistic ideas". It quotes the example of a disco held after hours at a textile factory which had pulsating music and a video show "of dubious content". By contrast, the official writes, properly organized functions "answer the spiritual demands of the people" and include "serious conversations on musical themes". The kind of disco which will meet Party approval in future should be modelled on a recent evening at a palace of culture in a Minsk car factory, the theme of which was "philosophical reflection on the place of man in his environment and his responsibility to the beauty of the earth".

It seems unlikely that events of this kind will attract the young people who prefer to dance the night away to the accompaniment of heavy metal and flickering strobe lights.

The authorities have been trying for some time to transform the imported idea of discos and rock concerts into a native Russian event which includes — besides music — poetry readings, slide shows and even political and social commentaries. Teenagers have tended, however, to organize alternative, more informal and less structured entertainments, often procuring the necessary equipment despite the obvious difficulties. The dilemma for the authorities is how to harness the apparently irrepressible demand among Soviet youth for Western-style pop music without allowing it to go too far.

Moscow
7 September 1982

Kremlin stifles pop music explosion

ANDREI IS YOUNG, tousle-haired, wears a leather jacket and carries a briefcase, more like a sociology lecturer than a man who manages several pop groups in Moscow and the provinces. A year ago, Andrei was riding the crest of a wave, putting on pop concerts for wildly enthusiastic audiences of Russian youngsters. Today, he is downcast, and fears for his job as a concert hall director.

The turning point was the Party's Central Committee plenum in June, at which Mr Konstantin Chernenko made a tough speech signalling a determined Kremlin crackdown on unorthodoxy in the arts.

Mr Chernenko, who is seventy-one, had been out of the limelight since losing the party leadership to Mr Yuri Andropov last November, and he used the ideological campaign as a vehicle for regaining influence. He called on party officials to enforce strict Marxist orthodoxy in the arts, and in language which recalled Stalinist socialist realism inveighed against "alien" Western influences.

Some musicians, artists and writers had hoped the Kremlin would be content with tough words, but the plenum has been followed by tough action. Pop music, lambasted by Mr Chernenko, is an obvious target, since in the authorities' eyes it undermines their attempt to mould Soviet youth. A number of popular rock groups have been disbanded or barred from performing, including Time Machine and Cruise.

Russian pop music is sophisticated, with styles ranging from "heavy metal" to jazz-rock. But the Kremlin's wrath has even fallen on more innocuous, middle-of-the-road bands such as *Vesyolye Rebyata* (the Happy Kids), who used to have a zany pop show on Soviet Television. Senior cultural officials recently wrote in the newspaper *Sovietskaya Kultura* that the group had performed songs of "dubious ideological content". The officials — who included the Deputy Minister of Culture — warned a number of groups that they would be broken up by 1 October if they had not repented of the "lack of discipline" in their work and replaced it with "an adequately high ideological and artistic level". Rock groups were damaging the moral and aesthetic education of working people, especially the young, the paper added. "It's a disaster," Andrei said as we walked to a concert by one of his remaining rock groups. On the wall of a building near by a fading poster flapped in the breeze, advertising a concert earlier this year by a group called — appropriately enough — Last

Chance. "It takes years for a group to form an identity, and for different types of modern music to develop. Now they want to turn the clock back."

Some rock groups, such as Magnetic Band from Estonia, or Moscow's Dialogue, continue to function sporadically, and many of their young fans believe the current cultural chill will pass.

"Our leaders are trying to defend the fortress against us," one student said, "but it is too late, we are already inside." Moscow intellectuals agree that the process has gone too far, and that the authorities are fighting a losing battle against Western influences. "The younger generation has been formed by influences — including rock music — which men of Mr Chernenko's generation cannot begin to understand," another commented.

The rearguard action is none the less being fought with all the resources of the state apparatus. A number of discotheques have been closed in Moscow, and dancing has been banned in some of the capital's more popular clubs. The conservative weekly magazine *Ogonyok* recently complained that clubs and discos were "sleazy dives" where the music was Western and the signs were all in English. "It is time the Komsomol did something about it," the magazine demanded.

Outside the concert hall, someone had scrawled in large, defiant letters "Dark side of the Moon", the title of an album by the British rock group Pink Floyd. Inside, the youngsters were listening restlessly to a middle-of-the-road singer, and calling for the main attraction — a rock group. "I may be wrong," Andrei said, "but as far as pop music goes I think we'll be looking at the dark side of the moon for some time."

Moscow
9 August 1983

Sergei's safety-pins needle Moscow

SERGEI IS AGED seventeen and wears safety-pins on his clothes. He sports a narrow black tie and has a bell attached to his left knee-cap which tinkles as he walks. He is, of course, a punk. The style is not that common in the Soviet Union, but when it does turn up, its power to *épater le bourgeois* is far greater than in the West. Officially, classes do not exist, but the professional and bureaucratic establishment does adhere to a somewhat Victorian, strait-laced orthodoxy, enforced by a dim sense of proletarian decency.

The older generation, brought up on wartime austerity and suffering, wears its Sunday best and, by and large, takes the Party's calls for discipline and social cohesion seriously. The younger generation, especially the sons and daughters of the élite, wear Western jeans and T-shirts, attend the smarter colleges and talk about Western films and pop music. This father and son conflict has almost become an accepted part of the Soviet scene. Punk, on the other hand, challenges both the establishment and its slick, fashion-conscious offspring. Sergei, with his safety-pins and tinkling bell, caused something of a stir when he appeared recently at the offices of the *Literary Gazette*, which had asked young people with problems to call. It emerged he had been a punk for two years. His parents were working class, and he had entered a vocational training institute (or technical college) rather than university (a socially divisive trend which worries Soviet sociologists).

The *Literary Gazette*, which discussed the case of Sergei with its readers, took the enlightened view that the punk style was not only a "youthful whim", but should be taken seriously, since it challenged some of the less attractive features of Soviet culture. Unlike some other young people, punks were not concerned with consumerism and trivialities, or even with themselves.

For many thinking Russians the problem is how to persuade the young to come to terms with the system at a time when the privations of revolution and war are a distant memory and the slogans and exhortations of Communism have become largely meaningless. As the *Literary Gazette* put it, the younger generation is undergoing "trial by peace and prosperity" rather than trial by war and austerity. The West seems desirable because of its abundance of goods and technological toys.

For many party *apparatchiks*, on the other hand, punk is much like any other imitation of Western lifestyles — and just as harmful. Since Mr Chernenko came to power in February, the Kremlin's campaign against foreign influences has gathered pace. It culminated this month in a session of the Central Committee of the Komsomol, or Communist Youth League, which called on young people to spend more time studying the works of Marx and Lenin.

The Komsomol is led by officials in their forties or even fifties, but is supposed to instil in teenagers a sense of Communist duty and Soviet patriotism. In July, the Kremlin issued a decree taking the Komsomol to task for failing to combat Western ideas and religious influences. In a passage not seen since Stalinist times it also ordered the Komsomol to instil in young people "a feeling of love for the motherland and hatred towards its enemies, as well as high political and class vigilance."

The Komsomol leader, Mr Viktor Mishin, a man in his early forties, responded by vowing to fight hooliganism and law-breaking among young people. Local committees would see to it that their meetings became "more politically active and interesting" and that Russian youngsters studied Marxism-Leninism "creatively".

As in the West, the majority of Soviet teenagers do not rebel but study, have fun and make orthodox careers. But officials are worried by the long-term problem of cynicism about the system. When *Komsomolskaya Pravda* discussed the phenomenon of teenage games recently, a young reader wrote from Leningrad to say that at his local Komsomol meetings "you all sit down, someone reads a report, the same people who have already discussed it hold a debate, everybody mechanically votes 'for' and then leaves. That is not likely to give us a sense of purpose or direction."

Moscow
28 August 1984

Jackson cult is giving Kremlin the blues

Michael Jackson, the black pop superstar, is a swindle, according to the Moscow cultural paper *Sovietskaya Kultura*. The singing and dancing phenomenon, who has sold more than thirty-five million copies of the album, *Thriller*, has been foisted on pop music fans the world over by brilliant marketing techniques and the genius of Quincy Jones, Jackson's manager and arranger. Both the album and the video-tape of *Thriller* amount to "great show-business swindles", *Sovietskaya Kultura* said. It added that Jackson had once performed original black rock music but had sold his soul to a white audience. "He is apolitical in the extreme, a vegetarian, sentimental and a religious believer," the paper declared, damning the pop star for ever in the eyes of all good Soviet citizens. "He wanted to be a hundred per cent white so much that he underwent plastic surgery."

The Kremlin is increasingly worried that what a Ukrainian paper recently called "empty and senseless Western Music" is crowding out "glorious, inspiring, Soviet songs".

Along with Western pop songs come what Soviet youngsters imagine to be Western fashions and attitudes, exemplified in T-shirts adorned with the American eagle or the stars and stripes. "We must not let the stars and stripes into our life at this time," one paper said, referring to the new cold war.

Most Russian pop fans know all about Michael Jackson, including the fact that he suffered second degree burns when his hair caught fire during the making of a Pepsi Cola commercial. Aware that both Jackson and Pepsi seem glamorous to Russian youngsters, *Sovietskaya Kultura* ridiculed the way in which the hair-burning incident had overshadowed riots in Miami and violence in Lebanon in the American media.

In Moscow's discos and night clubs the fans remained unconvinced. At one night spot the resident pop singer gave impeccable renditions of two bouncy numbers from *Thriller* to great acclaim before revealing that he had heard them on Western radio and copied them.

Moscow
18 June 1984

Can this girl ever love Russia?

THE ANNOUNCEMENT CAME at the very end of the news bulletin, just before the sport and weather. There was only one innocent-sounding sentence: the Supreme Soviet had decided to restore Soviet citizenship to Svetlana Iosifovna Alliluyeva, and to grant it to her daughter, Olga. The effect on those Russians of the middle and older generations who knew the name "Alliluyeva" was electrifying. "Stalin's daughter," exclaimed one. "Why has she come back, after all these years? How can they give her back her citizenship after what she did?" And then: "Who is Olga — was she born over there?" Those in the know explained that Olga, now thirteen, was the child of Svetlana's brief and unsuccessful marriage to William Peters, an American architect. "Difficult," came the reply. "Svetlana is one of ours. But for the girl — difficult."

Even for Svetlana, the adjustment after seventeen years will not be exactly easy. She has returned convinced that there is little to choose between East and West, drawn by a longing to see her children and grandchildren, and perhaps by the eternal Russian attachment to the Motherland. In his memoirs Khrushchev wrote presciently that Svetlana might one day return and said she should be given another chance. She should recall the poignant lines by the Russian poet Nekrassov, Khrushchev said: "The sight of the clearing brings tears to her eyes, she remembers the birch trees that once flourished there."

Some aspects of Moscow have changed, making it seem to Svetlana's eyes a different place to the one she left in 1966 for New Delhi and America. Russia has moved on, and Moscow is more up to date, with new hotels and Pepsi Cola kiosks on street corners. But in other, more basic respects, the drab and authoritarian system which led her to denounce Russia as a land of pain and trauma is essentially the same.

Many of the leading figures Svetlana knew from her father's intimate circle are dead, or nearly so, but the system shaped by Stalin, Molotov, Mikoyan and Malenkov is still more or less intact, with the same cumbersome and inefficient centralized economy, the same gap between privileged and masses, the same shortages, the same lack of colour, variety and initiative, and the same stifled intellectual life.

For Olga, the shock of adjusting to this world will be rather like stepping from a space shuttle on to the surface of the moon, as those who have gone through a similar experience can testify. Now and again in Russia one comes across people who carry a faded memory of "over there". Some were brought to the Soviet Union at an age when they were not old enough to decide for themselves, some married Russians, were divorced and stranded, or somehow found themselves Soviet citizens after the chaos of war. They have had to adjust to a world where teenagers join the

Komsomol — and where all citizens embrace Soviet patriotism and the Kremlin's one-dimensional view of the world. For Olga, as for any other Soviet teenager, it will become obligatory to recite that Lenin was a genius and the creator of a new world, that Marxism-Leninism is the only valid philosophy, that Russia desires peace and the United States is an aggressive imperialist power with blood on its hands.

Ahead, provided she proves politically reliable, or with a little help in high places if she is not, lies entry to a prestigious institute and a state-provided job.

From the material point of view, perhaps, life will not be too bad for either Svetlana or for Olga. Svetlana will presumably resume her place among the privileged of Soviet society, with access to goods and food unavailable to ordinary working Russians. The family will enjoy a comfortable flat and a *dacha* in the woods outside Moscow, with cars and probably a driver.

But even the world of the élite is, at least for the young, a world in which videos, pop records, makeup and even T-shirts are desirable and highly prized possessions from "over there", and to be suddenly unable to take the props of teenage life for granted will be hard indeed. As Svetlana herself has remarked, Olga at thirteen is as "American as apple pie". But as one American here said: "There is no apple pie in Russia — and no hamburgers either."

Technically, both Olga and her mother are still American citizens. On the other hand they are both now Soviet citizens too, and like any other Soviet citizen must apply for a passport and exit visa if they wish to leave the country. Whether Olga is allowed to go back and forth to the West therefore rests with the Soviet authorities, and her mother. "In a way you can see why Svetlana, especially with her problematic background, might finally find the West distasteful," said one observer with experience of those who try to straddle the two incompatible worlds. "Many émigrés find they cannot cope with Western freedom of choice and individual responsibility. But Olga was born to it."

Olga must have absorbed some "Russianness" from her mother. But will her reaction to Nekrassov's lines about the birch trees, or to the birch trees themselves, be the same as that of a native-born Russian who loves this country with all its absurdities and drawbacks? Even the children of Soviet diplomats abroad tend to come back with their heads full of the Rolling Stones, American films and advertisements rather than Lenin, or even Tolstoy and Tchaikovsky. Soviet officials will be hoping that for Olga such "trivialities" and "distractions" will give way to a more sober and mature view of the Soviet Union as the society which, unlike the West, is based on social and economic justice and is therefore destined to surpass the doomed capitalist system and lead mankind towards a brighter future.

Moscow
6 November 1984

WAR AND PEACE:

HISTORY

Some corner of a foreign field

"VALKOT?" SAID THE doorman at the Metropole Hotel. "Valkot? never heard of him. Is he from the Baltic?" No, we said, he was an Englishman. His name was Walcott, and he designed the Metropole in 1899. The doorman regarded us sceptically. "I don't know anything about that," he said suspiciously. "This is a Russian hotel."

There are times in Moscow when foreign influences leap to the eye and ear. But usually it is only to foreign eyes and ears. The Metropole Hotel, only a stone's throw from Red Square (or indeed from KGB headquarters, were anyone foolhardy enough to throw stones at it) is a familiar part of the Moscow landscape, a solidly Russian building, now throroughly Sovietized into the bargain. It is a local masterpiece of *art nouveau* architecture, known in Russian as "*style moderne*". Very little is known about Walcott beyond the fact that his name was William and that his father married a Russian. Most Muscovites do not know about him, or assume that — like the equally elusive Vladimir Sherwood, who built the history museum — Walcott was a Russian of distant English origin. Most non-Russians who have contributed to Russian architecture, science or the arts, or even the Russian language (*vokzal*, railway station, comes from "Vauxhall") are swiftly assimilated. Their names acquire a Russian flavour, and their origins are obscured.

This is possibly a hangover from the days of Stalin, when there was a preposterous campaign to prove that all modern inventions were first thought of and put into practice by Russians. This Orwellian decree was apparently retroactive, since in Leningrad guides habitually refer to the architects who built St Petersburg in the eighteenth century as if they were natives, even though their names were Rastrelli, Quarenghi and Rossi.

The fact remains that Westerners — and particularly Western Europeans — have been drawn to Russia by its oriental, alien and mystical aspects for centuries. Although the Soviet authorities emphasize that Russia is as much a European as an Asian power, its customs and ways of thought often appear Asiatic to foreigners, and some of the more European elements have been grafted on by assimilated Westerners.

One of the mysterious Mr Walcott's distinguished predecessors was an itinerant English actor and showman called Maddox, who founded what is now the Bolshoi Theatre, just across the square from the Metropole Hotel. The Kremlin itself was very largely designed by architects brought in from Italy, where the art of construction of walls and towers was in a more advanced state. Yet another itinerant Briton by the name of Galloway also had a hand in designing the Kremlin, building the original clock for the Saviour tower and a pump for the walls (neither still extant, unfortunately).

My own favourite example of British influence is the Muir and Merrilees department store next to the Bolshoi Theatre, known nowadays by the unlovely acronym "Tsum", or *Tsentralni Univermag* (Central Department Store). Muir and Merrilees was built by a well-known Moscow architect, Roman Klein, but was clearly modelled on British equivalents.

For most Muscovites, even after the founding of Anglo-Soviet relations, Britain remains a distant and dimly perceived mixture of lawns, tea rooms, industrial gloom, political tolerance, elegance and unemployment. Although it often serves the Kremlin as a convenient whipping boy for the United States, Britain is regarded benignly by most Russians, who remain blithely unaware either that Englishmen founded the Bolshoi and designed the Kremlin clock or that television, the jet engine and underground railways (all thought of as Soviet inventions) were pioneered in Britain. It is poignant to reflect that if history had taken a different course in 1917, Russia and Britain might be better informed about each other than they are. Trust House Forte might be running Mr Walcott's hotel and Mr Muir and Mr Merrilees might still be tempting shoppers to pop in to make a purchase before going to the Bolshoi.

Moscow
25 January 1984

Moscow blessing on the Tsarist past

WITH SILENT HOMAGE to the shade of William Howard Russell we crossed the river Alma at a place called Pleasant Meeting. This is not, it turns out, an ironic reference to bloody clashes between British and Russian troops in the Crimean war of 1854–1856 but relates to a much earlier encounter between Catherine the Great, the Russian empress, and her chief minister, the attentive Count Potemkin.

It was at this spot on the Alma that Potemkin erected his celebrated fake village, all façade and no substance, so that Catherine could get the impression that all was well in the empire, including the mountainous peninsula so recently conquered from the Crimean khans.

Potemkin also hired a movable flock of sheep to pose by the façades to indicate economic prosperity. As we passed through Pleasant Meeting a flock of sheep, possibly the same one, obligingly appeared, although the peasant houses behind them seemed solid enough. The modern equivalent of a Potemkin village is possibly the model collective farm, although Soviet officials insist that the latter springs from a desire to show Russia at its best (which is no doubt what Potemkin said).

Catherine was on her way to the fabled city of Bakhchisarai, headquarters of the Crimean khanate. In the Tatar language Bakhchisarai literally means "Palace of gardens", and the ancient seat of the khans lives up to the name, with tall minarets, quiet, fragrant courtyards and marble fountains. The most famous of these, the Fountain of Tears, inspired the poet Pushkin, who wrote one of his most popular poems after staying at Bakhchisarai for just one night. The fountain's tears are those of an otherwise heartless and cruel khan who mourned the loss of a young bride. Pushkin left two roses on the fountain, one red and one yellow, a practice perpetuated by today's Russians, familiar with both the poem and the Bolshoi ballet based on it.

The Crimea was annexed by Russia during Catherine's reign, in 1783, and although it is now technically part of the Ukraine it is essentially Russian. There are occasional reminders of the peninsular wars with Turkey and Britain, such as the English cemetery at Sebastopol (closed, alas, to foreigners, although Churchill visited it after the Yalta conference of 1945). But there are few traces left of the Muslim khans or the Islamic inheritance. Bakhchisarai is a museum, wistfully visited by Muslims from Tashkent and Alma Ata. There is a working mosque at nearby Simferopol, but it is poorly attended. This is not due to the imperial conquest, although the Tsars did not encourage the Crimean Tatars to stay. The last khan was "invited" to settle well away from the Crimea in the provincial gloom of Tambov, in European Russia. He stood it for three months before decamping to Turkey, where he was executed for having given the Crimea away to Russia. But the Tatars survived in large numbers until 1945, when some 250,000 were deported by Stalin on suspicion of collaboration with the Nazis during the German occupation. The Tatars were formally "rehabilitated" in 1967. The Kremlin has still not acknowledged that an injustice was done or allowed the Tatars to resettle in the Crimea. Soviet officials simply say that the Tatars "now live in Central Asia".

But there is still Bakhchisarai, which preserves stonework and stained glass, much of it made by Italian craftsmen on their way to Moscow and St Petersburg. And the khan's private mosque and personal Koran stir profound historical and spiritual echoes, provided you can ignore the banal observation by Marx stuck on the wall, to the effect that the Koran provided the basis for social legislation under Islam.

For the Russians the Islamic culture of the Tatars has been rightly overtaken by Soviet Russian achievements, an attitude exemplified by an oil painting depicting Count Sheremetyev, blond and blue-eyed emissary of the tsars, bravely defying the torture of a mean and swarthy khan.

It is not an image that the Tatars themselves would necessarily accept, but it illustrates the point that the Soviet regime, which in other respects rejects the tsarist heritage, regards the imperial Russian annexation of the Caucasus, the Crimea and Central Asia as legitimate.

Moscow
8 September 1984

More red flags in the sunset

RED BELLS is the Soviet answer to Warren Beatty's *Reds* — or rather a reverse image of it. Both films are based on John Reed's *Ten Days that Shook the World*, the vivid eyewitness account of the Bolshevik Revolution by a committed radical American journalist. But whereas in *Reds* the Revolution is almost incidental to the life (and love life) of Reed, played by Beatty, in *Red Bells* the upheaval in Petrograd occupies centre stage. Reed, rather woodenly acted by Franco Nero (it is a Soviet-Italian co-production) is a cipher who observes "the birth of a new world", the sub-title of Sergei Bondarchuk's version (his film is in two parts) — the first, sub-titled "Mexico Ablaze", deals with Reed's experiences in the Mexican Revolution).

At a preview of *Red Bells* in Moscow, Bondarchuk said he had made "the people, the masses" the hero of his film. In Russia, where the sixtieth anniversary of the founding of the Soviet state is being marked with much self-congratulatory looking back, history is dynamite. Bondarchuk handles it with care. *Red Bells* has all the orthodox scenes — uncannily close to the old newsreels — of Lenin urging on the proletariat, red flags filling the screen as he gesticulates. There are more red flags than Lenin (or Reed) ever saw, but then, as Bondarchuk observes, "The artist is entitled to exaggerate in pursuit of the truth". The end is foreseen at the beginning, the muscular proletariat sweeps away the dithering provisional government, and the Bolshevik victory is inevitable and just.

The real hero, for all that, is Petrograd, unreal city on the Neva, its every stone lovingly captured by the camera. The place bustles with excitement and dislocation, crowds of soldiers and sailors pouring across the bridges against a stark night sky, searchlights stabbing across the water through air thick with the black smoke of ships' funnels and the whiter smoke of explosions. Equally remarkable, this electrically charged Petrograd is peopled with real political figures, each trying to carve his own way through the chaos. Lenin, bent intensely over his latest diatribe, is convincing, but so are Trotsky and Kerensky (all Bondarchuk's actors are unknowns). Bondarchuk has perpetuated some of the cinematically effective myths of Eisenstein's *October*, such as the heroic storming of the Winter Palace (which in fact fell to haphazard infiltration by the Red Guards). But Kerensky, pacing up and down in the near-deserted palace, emerges as a patriot, a weak and misguided man hamstrung by a disastrous war and what he describes to the Duma with tears in his eyes as a "threat to our free and democratic Russia" (an episode in fact witnessed by Reed). At the end Kerensky is driven off in the American Ambassador's car, but Bondarchuk resists the temptation to make him a figure of fun.

The glimpses of Trotsky are even more intriguing. The firebrand orator of the Revolution dominates Reed's book, which was consequently banned under Stalin (and is still not available). Reed — accurately — made Lenin and Trotsky the moving forces, and only mentioned Stalin in passing. Bondarchuk's Trotsky remains marginal, but is not a dyed-in-the-wool villain. He is aloof, too clever by half, but none the less a Bolshevik, and at the centre of events. So is Stalin, baleful, stolid, forceful, but also flanking Lenin, on the edges of the Bolshevik centre.

For the Kremlin, the revision of history is not an academic exercise. There are ideas and traditions within the history of the Party which may one day be drawn on and rehabilitated as the Communist leadership grapples with Russia's economic and political problems. But it has to be done carefully, in order not to undermine the legitimacy conveyed by the Bolshevik ideal.

For the present generation of leaders, it has also to be done under the shadow of Stalin. The latest one-volume edition of the Soviet Encyclopedia omits all mention of the purges, as if Khrushchev (himself now a non-person) had never made his 1956 revelations. In *Red Bells*, the extraordinary figure of Antonov-Ovseenko, looking (as Professor Adam Ulam of Harvard once put it) like a cross between an artist and a second-hand clothes dealer, roars around Petrograd on a motorbike before arresting the provisional government in the Winter Palace.

Soviet historians still cannot record, however, that Antonov-Ovseenko was a supporter of Trotsky, and perished in the terror. "We cannot forever live as a nation without coming to terms with our history," said one Moscow historian with a smile. "In my lifetime perhaps, but not forever."

Moscow
11 December 1982

The political art of naming streets

ANY VISITOR TO Moscow must get the impression that the most popular Russian folk heroes are Lenin, Pushkin and Gorky — not because of their undoubted merits as politician, poet and writer respectively, but because everything in town seems to be named after them. Naming streets, towns, ships and factories after modern Soviet figures is a tricky business, since the man praised today as Russia's gift to the world can all too easily be cast tomorrow into what Trotsky (who should have known) used to call "the dustbin of history".

So far both Leonid Brezhnev and Yuri Andropov have survived history's remorseless dustpan and brush and are both commemorated in the names of towns (one each), districts, schools, army units, and — in the case of Brezhnev — an ice-breaker. Nikita Khrushchev, however, still languishes in oblivion, since he had the misfortune to be ousted from power by Brezhnev rather than die in office. In fact, the key to immortality in the Soviet system is either to die at the height of your power or to die before you can be disgraced, defeated and denounced. Yakov Sverdlov, one of the first Bolshevik leaders, is now remembered by the city of Sverdlovsk, formerly Yekaterinburg, in the Urals, as well as in the name of one of Moscow's main squares. He died in 1919, so there is no knowing whether he would have become caught up in the power struggle which followed Lenin's death in 1924, or whether he would have fallen foul of Stalin as Trotsky, Bukharin and other "non-persons" in Party history did.

Ironically, a number of those who crossed Stalin at the height of his megalomania in the 1930s were immortalized after their deaths from mysterious causes, possibly because they were not strictly speaking victims of the purges. They include Kuibyshev, who died in 1935 (the city of Samara was named after him in that year); Ordzhonikidze, who died in 1937 of an alleged heart attack, though Khrushchev later claimed he had been shot (the town of Vladikavkaz was called Ordzhonikidze from 1931 to 1945, and again from 1955 to the present day); and Sergei Kirov. For most people Kirov means the famed Kirov Ballet from Leningrad, formerly the Mariinsky Ballet in imperial times. In the early 1930s, Kirov, the young, able and handsome Leningrad Party boss, was Stalin's chief rival in the Politburo, and when he was assassinated in 1934 many thought Stalin was implicated. None the less, he entered the official pantheon since Stalin claimed to be grief-stricken and avenged Kirov's death by launching a bloody purge.

Strangely, those who survived the Stalin era by serving him loyally were not so rewarded. There is no town of Molotov. The naming of Gorky Street, Moscow's main shopping centre, formerly Tver Street, followed Gorky's death in 1936 — again, according to whispers, at Stalin's orders (he was rumoured to have been poisoned). Pushkin, the venerated founder of Russian literature in the nineteenth century and the product of an earlier age of intrigue (he died in a duel at the age of thirty-eight), is commemorated in numerous institutions, including — rather incongruously — Moscow's principal fine arts museum, which could have been named after any number of great Russian artists and art historians. Stalin has no memorials except in his native Georgia, and except for the battle of Stalingrad, renamed Volgograd in 1961, but originally called Tsaritsyn.

"What's in a name?" the shade of Mr Andropov might groan, especially since he was during his lifetime a modest man with an aversion to self-aggrandizement. After his death the town of Rybinsk on the Volga was renamed "Andropov". It was an appropriate choice considering that he began his political career there, but perhaps less fortunate for the local citizens, who have already suffered several name changes. It seems likely, however, that in an era when leaders are being given a place in history by their successors, rather than obliterated, Rybinsk will remain Andropov and Nabereznie Chelny — to the relief of those who could never get their tongue round it — will remain Brezhnev.

Moscow
4 April 1984

A different war altogether

"We will never forget," a lady in a blue headscarf carrying a nylon shopping-bag said. "Never." Tears welled up in her eyes. We were standing by the local railway station, in front of a large placard saying "Forty years of victory". Next to it was a big reproduction of a wartime poster depicting Mother Russia, gaunt but indomitable, finger pointing Kitchener-style, "The Motherland needs you". Memories seem to be becoming more powerful rather than the reverse as the war itself recedes. The words *Sorokoletie* (fortieth anniversary) and *Pobieda* (victory) have by repetition taken on the symbolic force of "revolution," or "great patriotic war", the myths by which the Soviet regime lives and which justify its power. All Russians say this year's gigantic official celebrations and outpouring of patriotic emotion far exceed anything witnessed during the thirtieth or twentieth anniversaries of Hitler's defeat. The celebrations have amounted to a sustained assault on the senses for months rather than just the past week, with victory and armed might the main themes (no talk of post-war reconciliation here). The kind of war films shown in Britain this week are shown in Russia almost every day, year in, year out. The war is always with us, Russians say. Like today's Red Square march past, the posters, speeches and endless films portray the war as a Russian rather than a worldwide event.

The statistics tell a story most Westerners cannot grasp: 20 million dead, 25 million homeless, nearly two thousand towns ruined, some 100,000 farms, 30,000 factories. According to Soviet textbooks, the Nazis threw more than 600 divisions at Russia, losing three-quarters of their forces on the Eastern front, including 10 million men, and 56,000 tanks. You can still feel the impact at haunting cemeteries at Volgograd (Stalingrad) or Leningrad. Yet memories are selective. Richard Sorge, the wartime spy, is being commemorated — but not the fact that Stalin ignored his warnings of Nazi attack, or that Stalin murdered millions of Russians. Few Russians had much to say about Stalin at all yesterday, preferring instead to recall their own sufferings and pride, or folk heroes such as Marshal Zhukov. Nor did they seem aware of other fronts, other battles in which the

Western Allies bore the brunt, although Marshal Petrov, the Deputy Defence Minister, gave a rare acknowledgement of them this week.

Down by the Kremlin wall, the British, American and other Nato ambassadors laid wreaths. They seemed to be commemorating a different war altogether, and a different post-war world.

Moscow
9 May 1985

Traumatic memory set in granite

IT LOOKS, JUDGING by the artist's impression, like a vast furled-up flag swirling into the sky. Set in parkland on a hill above one of Moscow's main arterial roads, the red granite "Victory Monument" will dominate a memorial complex containing a "Museum of the Great Patriotic War", white marble pillars with the names of heroes etched in gold, military busts and "three-dimensional battle scenes".

When it is finished (work has already started), millions of visitors will come in coachloads from factories and schools to listen to guides and look at the exhibitions. Yet apart from the dwindling numbers of ex-soldiers and airmen, very few of the visitors will remember what the monument project commemorates — the Second World War. Foreigners in Moscow are often struck by the way the war is still recalled as if it happened yesterday. Westerners, especially those under forty, tend to regard the war as ancient history, the subject matter of grainy newsreels and dusty tomes. It belongs to another age. For Russians it is a living memory.

Wartime memories are kept alive artificially by the regime: they dominate Soviet films and books, and you cannot seem to turn on the television without seeing a group of bemedalled veterans reliving their battles. The war provides the Kremlin with a convenient theme for reinforcing national unity and the need for strong defences at the expense of living standards. It also justifies the suppression of deviant views as traitorous or unpatriotic. On the other hand, for many Russians the war against Hitler, which claimed 20 million Soviet lives (a figure much repeated), is a trauma which needs no artificial respiration to keep it alive. The Young Pioneers who stand guard by the eternal flame in cities all over Russia are left in no doubt that their parents or grandparents endured terrible suffering which must not be repeated.

There are some Muscovites, though, who can be heard to mutter that the Victory Monument is a colossal waste of meagre public resources, and that the victims of Fascism are already commemorated elsewhere in simpler but no less striking monuments. One of the most telling is the series of huge, rust-coloured crossed metal bars — like gigantic anti-tank barricades — by the side of the Moscow to Leningrad highway, not far from Moscow airport. They mark the furthest point reached by Nazi tanks in 1941, proving that Hitler's troops came so close to entering Moscow they could have caught a bus into town, had there been any buses running.

Still, literary-minded Russians point out that Tolstoy erected his monument to the 1812 war against Napoleon half a century after the war had ended, yet nobody thought *War and Peace* old hat. The comparison is apt, since the new Victory Monument is to rise on a hill above Kutuzovsky Prospekt, where there are already several reminders of the earlier Russian struggle against foreign invaders. Known, ironically, as "Welcome Hill", it guards the approach to Moscow from Smolensk, Minsk and ultimately central Europe. It was on this hill that Napoleon stood and waited in vain for the Moscow city fathers to come to and greet him as a conquering hero. Down below, the great triumphal arch, moved here from the Leningrad highway, straddles Kutuzovsky Prospekt, while General Kutuzov, the Russian hero of 1812, is commemorated in an equestrian statue and the circular panorama painting of the Battle of Borodino.

The coach parties will no doubt pause at these memorials to the patriotic war of 1812 before going up the hill to consider the Great Patriotic War of 1941 and the new Victory Monument. The Moscow city authorities recently announced that 31 million roubles had been raised during voluntary work on a Saturday — the tradition known as a Communist *subotnik* — and that the money would be spent on constructing the new memorial park complex. The official announcement said the capital's workers had "decided" to donate the money to the Victory Monument, and though very few seem to have been consulted there were no voices raised in dissent.

Moscow
8 December 1983

Kremlin mobilizes wartime memories

A RATHER GRUBBY typewritten notice was tacked up the other day on the main door of the Russian block of flats next to ours, not far from the centre of Moscow. It was signed by the "*domkom*" (the "house committee" or "residents' committee"), which keeps an eye on communal behaviour and enforces collective orthodoxy. "All those citizens who possess medals won in the Great Patriotic War", the notice read, "are to hand them in for checking by 1 January 1985, in preparation for the victory parades."

The Soviet Union, like tsarist Russia before it, is a very status-conscious society, and almost everybody boasts a number of wartime decorations and orders. Memories of the "heroic struggle against the fascist aggressors" are kept alive deliberately by the constant reminders of the threat from without. Even now, when Moscow is gearing up for a rapprochement with the United States after President Reagan's re-election, American generals and politicians are depicted in terms almost indistinguishable from those used to describe the Nazis. The message is clear: We defeated Hitler's Germany yesterday, and if necessary we will defeat Reagan's America tomorrow. All over Russia, foreigners falling into conversation with local citizens are likely to find themselves rounded on with the heartfelt cry, "Why do you want to make war on us? We only want peace." The response, "But we don't want war either," tends to be brushed aside, since by harping day in and day out on the aggressive threat from America and Nato, the Kremlin has succeeded in terrifying most of the Soviet population into believing that nuclear war is imminent and that only passionate Soviet calls for peace prevent Mr Reagan from pressing the button.

"This Reagan hates us, he wants to destroy us," a middle-aged lady said recently to a Western diplomat visiting a provincial Russian town. "But I am not American," the diplomat protested. "You are all the same," the woman spat back. Any attempt to discuss Soviet weaponry compared to American weaponry is swept aside with the simple formula: You want war. We want peace.

The campaign will reach a crescendo in May, when Russia celebrates the fortieth anniversary of "the victory over fascism". Already a huge, grandiose World War Two "victory" monument is rising on a hill on the road to Borodino, site of an earlier battle against Napoleon, and a spate of articles is appearing glorifying Soviet feats of arms and ridiculing the suggestion that the Western powers aided Russia through the wartime Lend-Lease. Already the medals are being polished up. "I think I shall leave town next spring", one West German diplomat remarked, reflecting a widespread feeling that this barrage of overwhelming propaganda is producing a wave of anti-German (rather than anti-Nazi) sentiment.

There are drawbacks to the campaign, including the uncomfortable fact that Russia's wartime leader was Josef Stalin, now all but unmentionable because of his crimes (or "errors"). Some of those handing in medals have been told that the face of the great dictator which adorns one side must be erased and replaced. A no less serious drawback for Russia's present leader, President Chernenko, arises from the embarrassing fact that he lacks a wartime record to match that of the millions who will be marching in the victory parades. Mr Chernenko spent the war as a Party official in his native Krasnoyarsk, deep in Siberia. To compensate, the Soviet press has been building up Mr Chernenko's image as a man of courage, who experienced combat as a border guard in Kazakhstan in the 1930s. A film of these exploits, called *Frontier Post Youth*, has been made. The film was reported to have been released in Moscow, although it has not so far been advertised on any posters. One reason could be that comparisons are bound to arise with the books and films of Brezhnev's wartime exploits under fire, still fresh in people's memories. For that matter, the main film now showing in Moscow cinemas is *Marshal Zhukov*, a biography of the man whose brilliant generalship during the war made him a genuine folk hero.

Moscow
14 September 1984

Yalta: still waiting for the thaw

RONALD REAGAN'S LITTLE joke about bombing the Russians is still reverberating in Yalta, as elsewhere in the Soviet Union. But his remarks about the 1945 Yalta conference and not accepting the "permanent subjugation of Eastern Europe" also arouse powerful echoes, especially at a time when Moscow is at loggerheads with two of its East European allies, Romania and East Germany. "You see," said one Yalta resident, standing on the path outside the Livadia Palace where the 1945 conference took place, "it just goes to show what Reagan is after — he wants to destroy the Soviet system and bring down the entire socialist community as well."

The white palace at Livadia, just along the coast from Yalta on the Black Sea, is certainly a good place to reflect on the course of history since the conference there. In the space of one week, the "Big Three" sealed the fate of post-war Europe as the end of the Nazi Reich approached and Soviet troops reached the gates of Berlin. An oil painting inside the palace captures the scene: Stalin in his marshal's uniform, cigarette in hand; Churchill, opposite, grasping the arm of his chair to glare round, bulky and bulldoggish; and Roosevelt in the middle, emaciated and bespectacled, not far from death. At their elbows Molotov, Eden, Stettinius — and standing up, a piece of paper in his hand, the tall and youthful figure of Andrei Gromyko.

More than 2,000 attended the conference, if you include aides, journalists and observers. But the shape of the post-war world was decided by three men, in the long, airy conference room (formerly used for balls) and in the courtyard outside. Stalin agreed to help in the war against Japan, and to join in establishing the United Nations. But the heart of the matter was Eastern Europe, and especially Poland.

The boundaries were drawn at the Curzon Line in the East and The Oder-Neisse Line in the West. A "declaration on liberated Europe" (the three scrawled signatures can be seen at Livadia) affirmed the need for "democratic institutions" in territories formerly under Nazi occupation, and Stalin agreed to "free elections" in Poland.

Forty years on, with Solidarity still a fresh and worrying memory for the Russians in Poland, and with Erich Honecker, the East German leader, about to make a trip to West Germany against Soviet wishes, Yalta is again headline news rather than the stuff of faded documents. President Reagan stirred controversy this month by saying at a White House lunch commemorating the fortieth anniversary of the Warsaw uprising that the United States "rejects any interpretation of the Yalta agreement which suggests American consent for the division of Europe into spheres of influence". There was no reason to "absolve" the Soviet Union from its commitment at Yalta to independence and democracy in Eastern Europe.

This approach, subsequently echoed by George Shultz, the Secretary of State, has been seen by some as a vindication of President Roosevelt, who in the years following Yalta was accused of having brought Russia into the Far East and "sold out" Eastern Europe to Stalin. The Reagan interpretation, by contrast, would seem to be that Roosevelt and Churchill rightly bound Stalin to the idea of free elections, but that Soviet duplicity and the presence of the Red Army in Eastern Europe led to the betrayal of Yalta and the division of Europe into spheres of influence, with the resulting borders sanctified at the Helsinki conference of 1975.

The corollary of that is that as the captive populations of Eastern Europe grow restive, the question of Yalta is still open. Few Russians, most of whom regard the Communist monopoly of power, the Warsaw Pact and Comecon as eternal and immutable, would take this seriously for a moment. The Soviet press none the less constantly harps on the alleged desire of both Bonn and Washington to "alter the agreed post-war frontiers" (known in the case of West Germany as revanchism) and undermine Communism in the Eastern bloc. The Kremlin view, reiterated by Soviet historians and commentators, is that the current revival of the 1950s' policy of "rolling back Communism" began with a speech in Vienna by US Vice-President George Bush after his visits to Hungary and Romania. Bush, one *Izvestiya* columnist said, had questioned post-war "realities", and was obviously nostalgic for Eastern Europe's pre-war "bourgeois regimes". He and Reagan obviously regretted that, for example, Soviet rather than American troops had entered Prague in 1945.

At Livadia, where the 1945 conference room is being carefully redecorated to measure up to the splendour of the Tsar's study and billiard room next door, official guides underline this by claiming — without batting an eyelid — that the Soviet Union has scrupulously observed the Yalta undertaking to allow each formerly occupied nation to "choose the form of government it preferred". The guides also express regret that President Roosevelt's hope, spoken in the billiard room at the end of the conference, that allied wartime unity would continue in peacetime has been disappointed.

Down the corridor a photographic exhibition drives home the Moscow line that it was Soviet force of arms that largely dictated events, with pictures of Russian troops entering Berlin, Bucharest, Belgrade, Prague and Warsaw. For Russian visitors, the photographs are a reminder that the Soviet Union made untold sacrifices to rid Europe of Nazism, and that the peoples of Eastern Europe have cause to be grateful to Russia for liberating them and bringing them proletarian, socialist regimes rather than the "restoration of the old order" that Churchill wanted.

Yalta
1 September 1984

Russian farewell to a British traitor

DONALD MACLEAN, THE man who betrayed Britain's secrets to the Soviet Union, was cremated yesterday as an honoured Russian citizen, although his ashes are to return to the country he turned his back on thirty years ago. Maclean's funeral was organized and attended by colleagues from the foreign affairs institute where he worked. Only the discreet team of broad-shouldered KGB men mingling with mourners served as a reminder of Maclean's career as a spy.

There was no sign of H. A. R. (Kim) Philby, who, like Maclean, settled in Moscow after defecting to Russia, but who, unlike Maclean, became an important Soviet official, with a high KGB rank. The 150 mourners who crowded into the crematorium at the (de-consecrated) Donskoi Monastery were mostly from the Institute of World Economy and International Relations, where Maclean analysed British affairs from a Soviet-Marxist viewpoint.

There were no relatives present. Maclean's son, Fergus, is reportedly to take his father's ashes back to England. Fergus lives in Britain now while his other son Donald lives in the USSR. His daughter Melinda (named after his Russian wife, who deserted for Philby) lives in the United States. Even though his children left the country he had chosen, Maclean stayed on in lonely exile with his housekeeper, a curious mixture of the British diplomat he had once been and a fully assimilated Russian. In this he was different from the homosexual Guy Burgess, who fled with him to Russia in 1951 and remained a misfit.

Maclean wrote anti-British articles under a Russian pseudonym, but also used the English name "Mark Fraser". He looked the part of a scruffy Russian intellectual, slightly professorial. But there was also something of the patrician expatriate in his bearing, in his voice, and in the flat he lived in near the embankment, with its English prints and the BBC on "the wireless" until he died on Sunday, aged sixty-nine. His views (except for a twinge of sympathy for Britain over the Falklands crisis) remained solidly Marxist to the end. "He had no other way out," said a friend who saw him shortly before his death. "He made his choice, and had to stick to his beliefs." In an obituary notice, signed by a "Group of Comrades", *Izvestiya* said Maclean had been a "convinced Communist" and a man of "high moral qualities" who had served the Soviet state and worked for peace. He had been in poor health for some time, and spent two months in hospital late last year.

Out at the institute, a tall plate-glass building, colleagues filed past the red crêpe-covered coffin. Unusually, the coffin was closed, possibly because there were no relatives to stoop and kiss the dead man's face in the Russian manner. Then, also in the Russian manner, the coffin was taken in a bus to the cemetery, where it was preceded by wreaths, his portrait and his medals on red plush cushions into the "Hall of ritual" for burning. An organist, muffled against the Moscow cold, played solemn music. "Farewell, dear Donald Donaldovich", ran the message on the wreaths. A woman official told us we were burying a good Soviet citizen, and asked the mourners to respect his memory. There was one minute's silence and the coffin disappeared, lowered into a hole in the ground. Outside, with light snow falling, Maclean's friends and colleagues hurried back to their coaches, reluctant to talk about him. Had it occurred to them that in adopting one country — Russia — he had betrayed his own, and earned that most terrible of Soviet epithets, "traitor"? "I would rather not say", said a lady with tears in her eyes. "He was a fine colleague, a good Communist."

Moscow
12 March 1983

Khrushchev returns from the shadows

THE WALLED MONASTERY of Novodevichy in Moscow is a quiet and mysterious place at this time of year: the winter sun glints on the golden cupolas and spires, the lake beneath the walls is frozen and still. In the adjoining cemetery, where many of Russia's great men lie buried, snow falls with a slight sigh on to the paths and gravestones from the trees above. Along one of the icy paths is a monument to the man who aroused both admiration and enmity as ruler of the Soviet Union before he fell from power twenty years ago: Nikita Khrushchev. Some Russians still refer to him familiarly as "Nikita Sergeyevich".

Khrushchev's burial at Novodevichy as an "ordinary pensioner" in 1971 was a concession by his successor, Leonid Brezhnev. Although Khrushchev was in disgrace, and did not therefore merit commemoration in the Kremlin Wall or behind the Lenin Mausoleum, he was allowed to join numerous generals, scientists, politicians and writers in the tranquillity of the monastery garden. For a while Khrushchev's grave, surmounted by a bust designed by the sculptor Ernst Neizvestny, was an object of pilgrimage. Khrushchev's free-wheeling political style, his economic schemes and — perhaps above all — his relative liberalism in the arts had embarrassed and infuriated many officials. But the Khrushchev style also aroused affection in those who found his earthy, "peasant" image — even with its tendency towards buffoonery — both endearing and refreshing. Because of this the Brezhnev regime closed Novodevichy cemetery to the general public. Now only special visitors can see the thickset bronze head set in black and white marble.

There are some signs though that the present Soviet leadership is prepared to reconsider Khrushchev's role in history twenty years on, and that the Kremlin may make "Nikita Sergeyevich" less of a non-person. Khrushchev and his associates have rarely been mentioned since 1964. Even his death only merited a few lines in *Pravda*.

But Khrushchev's son-in-law, the once powerful Aleksei Adzhubei, recently resurfaced with a prominent article in the monthly magazine *USA*, and there have been several mentions of Khrushchev himself in the press. Mr Adzhubei, who is now nearly sixty, was editor of *Izvestiya* during Khrushchev's rule. After Khrushchev's fall Adzhubei disappeared. His article in *USA* has therefore aroused comment especially since it deals with President Kennedy, Khrushchev's adversary and negotiating partner. Khrushchev's confrontations and negotiations with Kennedy are still not fully discussed here.

But Khrushchev's role in the Second World War has been discussed, giving rise to suggestions that Mr Andropov, a widely read man with intellectual credentials, might bring his predecessor but one out of the shadows. Shortly after Mr Andropov took over, the Party's theoretical journal *Kommunist* published an article on the Battle of Stalingrad which acknowledged Khrushchev as one of the main participants. Earlier studies had mentioned only Stalin, or Brezhnev (who in fact did not take part).

There are powerful objections to the rehabilitation of Khrushchev. For one thing, if historians can deal more honestly with him, why should they not also reveal the truth about Lenin, Stalin and Brezhnev?

Moscow
6 February 1984

War and peace, the Kremlin version

THE CROWD ROUND the park bench was about thirty strong, young and old, male and female, with a sprinkling of army and militia uniforms. Everybody was listening with intense concentration to a man, shabbily dressed and with a long, straggly beard, holding up a coloured picture book with illustrations from the life of Saint Sergius in the fourteenth century. "And this", he said in slow, careful Russian, "shows St Sergius casting out devils. For devils can take human form." The audience watched his finger on the page, apparently absorbed. "Even now there are evil men in the world who want to bring us all to destruction through nuclear war. We must therefore pray for peace and the salvation of the Russian people."

The listeners nodded, familiar with the sentiment if not with the somewhat unusual presentation. The little scene in the public garden of a monastery not far from Moscow neatly combined the two themes of Soviet propaganda on disarmament, constantly reiterated on radio and television and in the press, strung across streets on banners and plastered on the sides of buildings: the Russian people want peace, and have a duty to save the world from war. Even religion has been co-opted. The head of the orthodox church, Patriarch Pimen, appeared at the United Nations special session on disarmament to support the Kremlin's position, describing President Brezhnev's undertaking not to be the first to use nuclear weapons as "deeply humanitarian".

On one level this barrage of propaganda does touch a deep chord in the Russian view of the world. As both officials and ordinary Russians will tell you, the Soviet Union lost 20 million people in the Second World War. The assumption is that the Russians will never wittingly be the cause of World War Three. All of which is convenient for the authorities, who have been cranking up the propaganda machine with two main targets in mind: the United Nations disarmament session, and the negotiations with the United States on strategic arms reduction (START) in Geneva.

The fact is, however, that no real debate on nuclear disarmament is permitted in the Soviet Union. There is an official peace committee in Moscow, which claims 80 million members. Few of those millions on the other hand probably have any clear idea of the nuclear arsenals on either side, or any grasp of the question beyond an understandable and widely shared desire to avoid annihilation.

The fact that the United States wants to station Pershing and Cruise missiles in Europe is often mentioned for example, but not the fact that the Soviet Union has some 690 SS-20 warheads, many of them aimed at the heart of West European capitals. There is no discussion of the Soviet contention that the American proposal at the START talks for a one-third cut in intercontinental ballistic missiles is lopsided, nor of the details of ground-launched versus submarine-launched strategic missiles.

There have been some attempts to show that the authorities are prepared to discuss the issues. Three American doctors, members of a group called "international physicians for the prevention of nuclear war", exchanged views on television with three Soviet doctors. Both sides agreed that the medical effects of nuclear conflict would be horrifying, and that money spent on the arms race would be better spent on social and medical resources. For the Soviet public a Russian-American round-table discussion of this kind is a welcome innovation.

A more telling test of the Kremlin's attitude to the discussion of war and peace, however, has been its suppression of the one group which has so far tried to campaign for disarmament independently of the official Soviet Peace Committee. The group, established in June 1982 with the aim of "establishing trust between the USSR and the USA", has put forward a list of "confidence-building measures". These include the suggestion that the Moscow region should be "twinned" with the district of Colombia as a "nuclear free zone". Other suggestions include a joint syllabus for the "propagation of peace" in Soviet and American schools, the banning of war games in both countries, and scientific and educational exchanges.

The response of the authorities so far has been to place the organizers — Sergei Batovrin, Vladimir Fleischgakker and Sergei Rosenoer — under house arrest, and to threaten signatories of the group's declaration with loss of career prospects unless they withdraw support. Members of the group find it difficult to calculate the number of signatures since police confiscate them as fast as they are collected, but one estimate is that nearly 170 have signed. Only one member of the group is known to have recanted so far.

Moscow
7 July 1982

Fear of war lurks beneath normality

FEAR OF WAR is in the air in Moscow. On the surface the city has never looked more peaceful. On the Moscow River pleasure boats ply up and down, with guides pointing out the ancient gold domes of the Kremlin, the Lenin Stadium, the spires of Moscow University high above on the Lenin Hills. On the embankment grass families lounge, picnic and play, enjoying a spate of glorious sunshine. Old Russia sunbathes cheek by cheek with the new: mountainous ladies in bra and pants and sunhats made out of *Pravda* watch young girls skateboard on the towpath wearing bikinis and imported Sony Walkmans and not much else. But at night the city is shaken by fierce, apocalyptic electric storms, thunderclaps rattling the windowpanes and giant sheets of lightning illuminating the gothic skyscrapers built by Stalin, a Metropolis cityscape about to meet its doom.

The innermost mood of most Russians is doom-laden, with an all-pervasive fear that relations between the super-powers will get out of control and that a crazed President Reagan will bring Cruise, Pershing and Minuteman missiles raining down on the streets of Moscow while a cosmic nuclear war is fought in outer space. This fear is stoked by the state-run media, which harp endlessly on Mr Reagan's "pathological hatred" of all things Communist and all things Russian (the two are not distinguished). He is increasingly compared to Hitler — a potent comparison in a nation that is constantly reminded of the horrors of the Second World War and told that Russia saved the world from Nazism almost single-handed.

Even down by the river the propaganda does not stop for a second. A young man cycles slowly by, the radio on his handlebars drowning out the nightingale in the trees and the chug-chug of the riverboats: "The reckless deployment of Nato missiles . . . war psychosis . . . aggressive and militarist Washington . . . preparations for a nuclear strike". Fear of war with the West took hold of the Russian consciousness when Soviet fighters shot down a South Korean airliner with the loss of 269 lives. Few Muscovites questioned Russia's right to "defend its frontiers" by blowing up civilian aircraft, and all resented Western charges that the action was barbaric. "You would have done the same," was a typical reaction. But there was an underlying sense of guilt, coupled with a fear that the Soviet Union had gone too far. Subsequent Soviet actions — withdrawal from the Geneva arms talks, withdrawal from the Olympic Games — have been accompanied by a similar barrage of self-righteous propaganda, disguising a similar fear of having overstepped the mark.

With every turn for the worse the Russian instinct has been not to appease the United States but to become ever more defiant, ever more aggressive, ever more isolationist. No less a person than President Chernenko fuelled these fears of Western retribution in a remarkable speech to Komsomol leaders in the Army and Navy. The West, he said bleakly, is preparing for war because it fears the historically inevitable victory of Communism. Like other apparently laughable Soviet arguments this has to be taken into account, since it is seriously believed in the Kremlin and at least half-believed by consumers of *Pravda* and Radio Moscow. "Foreign policy and diplomacy cannot accomplish everything," Mr Chernenko said in an oddly ominous phrase. "The deterrent might of the Soviet Army is indispensable when one is dealing with forces to which good will is alien and which are deaf to the arguments of reason."

"The truly terrifying thing", said a senior Western diplomat watching Mr Chernenko speak, "is that this is a mirror image of what the Americans say about the Russians".

The Komsomol leaders — most of them in their forties or even fifties — may have ideas for reversing the slide to war once the old men of the Kremlin have gone, but few looked this week as if they had any intention of challenging the gloomy script written by Mr Chernenko, Marshal Ustinov and other members of the old guard.

Moscow
3 May 1984

Where the West gets it wrong

GENERALIZING ABOUT NATIONAL character is always risky, but in the Soviet Union it is doubly so. To begin with, the state is made up of a multitude of nationalities, so that to speak of "the Russians", although a convenient shorthand, is technically incorrect. Moreover the Western stereotype of "the Russians" — meaning those European Russians who have traditionally ruled the state, whether Soviet or Tsarist — is politically inspired according to *Komsomolskaya Pravda*.

The image which the Russians would like to project of themselves is the one which lay behind the staging of last month's "Friendship 84" Games: an hospitable, forward-looking and peace-loving nation devoted to man's physical and spiritual well-being, as opposed to the commercial exploitation of man's baser instincts so vividly displayed (according to Moscow) at the Los Angeles Olympic Games. Yet, according to the article — written by a senior researcher at the Academy of Sciences — Western writers on Russia persist in characterizing Russians as strange Dostoyevskian creatures given to lying, informing on one another, sharp changes of mood and a malicious delight in the misfortunes of others. They are, in fact, seen as incomprehensible, difficult to deal with and probably mad. Western propagandists, *Komsomolskaya Pravda* claimed, were deliberately spreading a false picture of a nation given to profound conservatism and psychological anomalies for the purposes of "primitive anti-Communism". Why, even Boney M's celebrated song about Rasputin and the Russian Queen ended with the exasperated sigh, "Oh those Russians!"

Drawing attention to the allegedly negative Western view of the Russian character is part of a growing campaign by the Kremlin to explain the East-West impasse in terms of Western — and particularly American — Russophobia.

Most observers of the Soviet scene might draw a distinction between the Soviet system of government and control and the Russian people and traditions or at least consider the extent to which the two coincide. Soviet officials maintain however, with some justice, that the Reagan Administration makes no subtle distinctions and regards "Russia" and "Communism" as tarred with the same red brush, much as to the knights of the Jedi all citizens of the evil Galactic empire are black. To the extent that this is true it enables the Kremlin, paradoxically, to stress that the Party and the people are indeed united (a ubiquitous slogan), and that hostility towards the Communist system and hostility to Russians as such are inseparable.

A significant article in *Sovietskaya Rossiya* by Academician Tikhvinsky, a leading historian, recently attacked the West for dwelling on the alleged "innate barbarity" of Russia. In particular Professor Tikhvinsky took issue with the French popular historian Henri Troyat, for his novel *Peter the Great.* After pointing out that M. Troyat is of Russian origin (and therefore anti-Soviet by definition), the article said Peter the Great's territorial annexations had been necessary for the "security of the motherland", whereas Troyat had portrayed Peter as Tsar of a wild, aggressive and backward people. Other culprits included Sovietologists who argued that Soviet Russia had inherited "the worst traits of Tsarist Russia" and suffered from Russia's lack of contact with civilized Europe. It was true that Russian culture had been held back, Academician Tikhvinsky wrote, but only because it protected Europe from the Tartar invasion in the Middle Ages, a "heavy sacrifice" for which the West had never shown the least gratitude.

The notion that Russia is misunderstood and isolated by a hostile world touches a deep chord in the Russians themselves, and for ordinary people goes some way to explain why — as the Kremlin puts it — the West (or at least Washington) has worsened East-West relations. If Western observers have all come to much the same conclusions about Russians, Soviet officials maintain, it is not because they are right but because they have all been given the same instructions.

Moscow
20 September 1984

Memories of war colour the peace

I OWN A Soviet tank, the KN70. So, I should add, do thousands of small Russian boys, for the tank is made of plastic and runs on the kind of flat cardboard batteries you used to find in Britain at least twenty years ago. When you press a button the barrel swivels and flashes red fire. Militaristic toys abound in the Soviet Union, and all generations are indulging in a week of war nostalgia leading up to VE Day, celebrated in Russia on 9 May. The Russians seem to see no contradiction between this aggressive display of strength and Moscow's peace-loving propaganda: the argument that "our" tanks and rockets are defensive while "theirs" (meaning Nato's) are offensive is effective.

Russians are pained when told that Moscow's former wartime allies resent Soviet belittling of the British or American role in the defeat of Hitler, and retort that it is the West which fails to give adequate acknowledgement to Russian sufferings, including 20 million war dead. They rarely mention 1939–41, or the Nazi-Soviet pact. The "Great Patriotic War" began in 1941.

For the Russians, in their present nostalgic mood ("now Roosevelt was a good President, not like this Reagan"), it is all perfectly simple: 1945 was a new dawn, when East and West shook hands across the ideological chasm amid the ashes of Nazi Germany after a traumatic war.

The mood was caught by Mikhail Gorbachov — fourteen at the time of the Elbe link-up — when he called the reunion on the Elbe at Torgau a "symbol of hope and friendship". "You turned it all sour by trying to destroy socialism in post-war Europe," Soviet officials tend to say accusingly. They do not find it paradoxical that Marshal Sokolov, the Defence Minister, should in the same breath praise the wartime alliance of East and West and lambast the "present-day imperialist reactionaries" — Reagan, Thatcher and Kohl — for being just as bad as the Nazis.

A letter to *Izvestiya* by Mr Arthur Hartman, the American Ambassador, is regarded by western diplomats here as a deft and astute attempt to meet Mr Gorbachov half way while pointing out what it is the West finds unacceptable about Moscow's attitude to VE day. Mr Hartman, a young airman in 1945, said he had been moved to find a poster in a Moscow shop depicting the "bright hopes" of the link-up on the Elbe. "The fact remains that when the tanks rumble across Red Square on 9 May, it is not East-West comradeship which will be uppermost in Russian minds. Rather, the fortieth anniversary is a chance — for many, the last chance — to recapture youthful heroism and pride, with the fact, that the Red Army was initially crushed and humiliated, obliterated by its victorious entry into Berlin four years later."

There is a wave of nostalgia for Stalin, seen nightly on television in the drama series *The Strategy of Victory*, his crimes and incompetence glossed over, his wisdom emphasized.

For the Kremlin, this cathartic outpouring of deeply-felt emotion over Russia's appalling wartime suffering and its miraculous triumph over the invader offers a way of reinforcing internal discipline and unity after four post-war decades with not much to celebrate. The Soviet victory in the Second World War, in other words, lent legitimacy to a self-appointed regime which has never been given a popular mandate in nearly seventy years of rule, and it is the war which is widely seen as justifying Soviet power. Unless Mr Gorbachov provides an alternative source of legitimacy by making good his vow to prove the superiority of Communism in economic competition — which is rather unlikely — the building of new war memorials will continue long after the last of the veterans of Stalingrad and Berlin have gone, and the war will still be part of the living fabric of Soviet life when the Bitburg row is ancient history in the West.

Moscow
3 May 1985

SEX, PRIVILEGE AND AEROBICS:

SOCIAL PROBLEMS AND HEALTH

The night passion cooled in Odessa

SUMMER IS A popular time for getting married in Russia, and every Saturday you can see young couples passing through the Palace of Weddings in quick succession, with a champagne reception to follow, sometimes held at a picnic site in the open air. But the authorities are increasingly worried because, although the receptions are well organized if not sumptuous, what follows is something of a comedown. The newspaper *Sovietskaya Rossiya* criticized the "honeymoon shambles" in Russia recently. In one case, a couple from Moscow decided to go on honeymoon to the warm and fragrant southern republics, but could not find a hotel room for love or money. "We slept wherever we could lay our heads," the dejected couple told the newspaper. "We struck lucky in Odessa, and managed to find another couple to share a room with by hanging a sheet across the middle. At the crack of dawn a cleaning woman came in with a bucket, took one look and said, 'Carry on. You're not in my way.'"

In other cases, couples have had to go on organized collective tours. The newspaper remarks that, pleasant as these are at other times, they are not conducive to the consummation of marriage in an atmosphere of secluded passion. It quotes the case of a couple from Tallinn in Estonia, who found themselves hiking up the Carpathian mountains with packs on their backs in the pouring rain and took a bus home in disgust. "A honeymoon should not be a test of physical ability," *Sovietskaya Rossiya* comments.

The problem of getting a tailor-made holiday in the Soviet Union is a serious one. Even state-issued vouchers to rest homes or sanatoria are hard to come by and have to be ordered well in advance. "You only have to go down to the central tourist office to see people queueing all night for a voucher," *Sovietskaya Rossiya* says, "and there are many disappointed faces in the morning."

Why, it asks, should it be so difficult to arrange a honeymoon when wedding rings, dresses, flowers and all other accompaniments to a marriage are available? Perhaps, the newspaper suggests, Russia should have a new system under which the engaged couple would tell the registrar beforehand what kind of a holiday they would prefer, and he would then issue them with an "invitation" to the resort of their choice once the wedding ceremony was over.

Moscow
10 July 1982

End of the line for Russian marriages

Pravda HAS ADDED a new cause of marital breakup to reasons most often cited for divorce. After adultery, incompatibility, wife-beating and mental cruelty comes having to stand in queues all day. Russian women, it seems, not only get varicose veins from endless queueing for everything from clothes to foodstuffs but are also likely to find when they get home that their husbands have given up waiting for dinner and run off with another woman.

The late President Andropov used to point out that the Soviet economy would be a great deal more efficient if people stayed at their desks and factory benches instead of rushing off to the shops, string-bag in hand, when deliveries were rumoured. But, according to *Pravda*, the erratic and shortage-ridden distribution system is threatening Soviet marriages as well as the growth rate. In an article headed "The double burden", *Pravda* confirmed what all women in Russia already know: that they are expected to do a job of work and keep house as well, leading to inevitable family tensions. *Pravda* calculated that the Russian population spends a total of 37 billion hours a year standing in queues, which means about 200 hours queueing a year for the average adult. Some authorities put the figure at more than 300 hours a year.

"How many family conflicts could be avoided," wrote a reader from Lvov, "if only we could buy basic goods close to home, get a decent meal out, or have our laundry done and shoes repaired quickly."

The problem is taken seriously in a country whose divorce rate approaches 50 per cent, with about 950,000 divorces a year. The causes, *Pravda* said, were not only endemic shortages and poor services, or the lack of up-to-date household devices, but also the chauvinistic attitudes of Russian men. In the Soviet Union — a last redoubt of male chauvinist piggery — men expect their wives to do all the cooking, cleaning and shopping and take care of the children. Meanwhile, the husbands — as the weekly *Nedelya* recently documented — come home tired, get drunk and watch television.

There is little hope for the future since, according to *Pravda*, traditional sexist attitudes are being passed on to the younger generation. Very few Russian boys are taught to cook or clean, or are given any idea that they should help with household chores when they get married. Or as *Nedelya* put it, it is not enough for Russian men to give their womenfolk flowers once a year on Women's Day.

Moscow
11 June 1984

Why better-off lock up their daughters

ANYA IS AN attractive university student in Leningrad, fashion-conscious, bright and outgoing. She is also in love with Sasha, a young man who came to her aid one day when she was menaced by drunken hooligans on the Underground. An everyday Soviet love story perhaps, except that Sasha is from a working-class family and Anya is not. Anya's middle-class parents have no intention of allowing Sasha to join a family which counts a *dacha* and a car among its jealously-guarded status symbols.

Russia is not yet the classless society envisaged by Marx and Lenin. Officially, social class — whether defined by job, income, family or attitude — has been abolished in the Soviet Union. Instead, there are only "strata" of society: workers, peasants and intellectuals, and even these distinctions are supposed to disappear when full Communism is reached. But, as some sociologists acknowledge, sixty-seven years after the Bolshevik takeover, class-consciousness is creeping back. There is a large and powerful state bureaucracy founded on privilege rather than private property and the *nouveaux riches* (especially the wives) want all the trappings of class superiority, even though the party frowns on them as ideologically unsound. In the case of Anya and Sasha, her parents would not at first even consider allowing their daughter to marry a man who was of lowly origin and worked in a factory. Anya caused a "sensation" merely by going out with him, according to a letter she wrote in despair to the youth paper, *Komsomolskaya Pravda*. Her middle-class friends shunned her for "lowering herself". She reacted by rejecting her privileged background, not unlike some conscience-stricken nineteenth-century Russian noblemen.

"I became ashamed that I could have fun and throw my parents' money around on clothes when Sasha could not enter the institute, as he dreamed, and had to work in a factory to help his mother," she wrote.

Eventually, Anya's parents — or at least her father — relented and, after meeting Sasha, agreed that he was a "good, honest lad". But suspicion and hostility on the part of Sasha's family proved stronger. When he took Anya home, his mother warned him that a girl from her background would play with him and then discard him, adding: "She's not for the likes of you." Seven months later, the pair are still trying to persuade his mother that the match is suitable, even though Anya has the "lily-white hands" of the privileged and is "not from our circle".

In an editorial note, *Komsomolskaya Pravda* said it did not receive many such letters, but there must be thousands of other couples fighting social prejudice in Russia. To reinforce the point, the paper printed another letter, from a young girl of noble origin in Tadzhikistan, a Muslim region of Central Asia "where the problems stem as much from deeply-entrenched tradition as from embourgeoisement".

Like Anya, Matlyuba had fallen in love with a working-class man and her parents reacted with fury, accusing her of "sullying the family name". Matlyuba's parents went further than Anya's and locked up their daughter, disconnecting the telephone. "They never let me go out alone," she wrote to *Komsomolskaya Pravda*. "My lover swears he will kidnap me . . . how can such class feelings still exist? Surely we are building the new society?"

The re-emergence of class attitudes is a cause of serious concern to the Soviet authorities, who are particularly anxious that the better-off should not come to regard the "lower classes" as inferior or even criminal. Like class, crime persists in the Soviet Union. A recent study in three big Volga towns concluded that most crimes were committed by individuals from low-income families rather than those from more affluent or influential backgrounds. On the other hand, Soviet sociologists have also noted a growing tendency for the bored children of the powerful and well-to-do to indulge in robbery, mugging and even gang rape "for no apparent reason", with the parents often regarding their offspring's misdeeds as "mischief" rather than serious crime.

Moscow
23 March 1984

Lives of luxury in the land of Marx

ANATOLY KARPOV, THE chess star, has a car telephone in his chauffeur-driven limousine. All members of the élite in the sporting world, the arts, and above all in the Kremlin bureaucracy enjoy carefully-graded privileges to which the ordinary Soviet worker can never hope to aspire. Karpov's car telephone puts him in the superstar bracket, but even middle-ranking officials and celebrities can expect to get a Moscow flat larger than the usual cramped allocation of five or six square metres per person (the official figure is nine metres minimum), a place at the head of the long waiting list for a car, as well as access to top health care and to the best schools and colleges. They also get a government-provided country home, or *dacha*. All Russians love to retreat to a *dacha* in the beautiful countryside around Moscow, but the definition of a *dacha* can range from a dilapidated garden-shed for the lower orders to a magnificent mansion screened by discreet birch trees and security fences for the cultural and political élite.

Karpov, who is judged to have earned his privileged status by conquering the world of chess, is building an £80,000 *dacha* outside the city, and has an Audi 100 for his personal use as well as his official car. One prominent musician recently acquired a palatial country house which formerly belonged to a KGB general and which, like other élite *dachas*, is set in a closed area rarely penetrated by either foreigners or ordinary Russians.

The extraordinary aspect of all this to a Western mind is that working-class Muscovites fighting their way on to crammed buses or standing in long queues in the snow for scarce foodstuffs do not seem to resent this hidden privilege in the least. They are aware that those who govern them, from the President downwards, have access to special shops and even Western goods.

The official Marxist-Leninist ideology, hammered home every day in the press and media, professes egalitarianism and social justice. Yet most Russians seem to accept fatalistically that abuse of power and humiliation by officialdom are inevitable, possibly because this has been so since Tsarist times. The Tsar's ministers used to drive their carriages at speed down the middle of the city's avenues, scattering the *hoi polloi* to right and left, much as today's Kremlin Zils thunder down the middle lane pushing mere mortals to either side.

Although there is no overt resentment of official privilege condemnation of the abuse of such privilege does occasionally surface in the Soviet press and at Party meetings. The late Yuri Andropov's stern drive against official abuses won him widespread popular approval, and the late Konstantin Chernenko continued to attack corruption, noting that it caused "profound anger" among the masses.

One female lathe operator from Rostov-on-Don recently wrote to *Komsomolskaya Pravda* to complain that her monthly wage of 200 roubles (£200) had little purchasing power. "I understand that our society cannot yet afford for everyone to dress well and fashionably," she wrote. "But the point is that those who deserve them should receive the most benefits, and by that I mean the workers."

There is little sign, however, of privilege being reduced — if anything the reverse. When, at the local Soviet elections, officials and their well-dressed wives turned up to vote in chauffeur-driven Chaikas, there was not a murmur of protest from the proletariat trudging through the ice and snow to the ballot box.

The newest development, which again has aroused some public protest but is likely to go ahead anyway with full Kremlin approval, is the establishment of a series of luxury clothing stores for those with spare roubles, regardless of rank or status.

The new shops are to be for those who find the ordinary Soviet stores too drab. It seems doubtful whether Lenin or Marx would have approved.

Moscow
2 April 1984

The man who died from lethargy

Alexander Ivanovich Garayev got up early one day, shaved, splashed a little eau-de-cologne on his face, put on his suit with a nice crisp shirt his wife had ironed for him, went to work, and disappeared. He arrived at the factory where he worked as a welder in the town of Togliatti, on the Volga, the centre of the Soviet car industry. But he did not go home that night, nor did he turn up for work the following morning. He was missing for four months, and was only discovered when a woman worker felt there was something wrong about the oil tank at the back of the plant. It was dark so she called for an electrician, who shone a lamp in the tank. There, floating in oil, was the body of the missing welder.

Recounting this sorry tale a year after the event, the newspaper *Sotsialisticheskaya Industriya* disclosed that Garayev had died from a malaise not unknown in Britain's motor car industry: sleeping sickness. It seemed he had often disappeared for days at a time, and in 1980 had gone missing for a month and a half. When he turned up his normally stout frame had shrunk to skeletal proportions, and he could hardly speak. His anxious wife undressed him, gave him tea, put him to bed and asked what had happened. "I've been asleep," he had whispered hoarsely. Despite the signs of serious illness, nothing was done to help him.

Garayev was a good worker, and had been awarded a medal of Communist labour. Yet his sleeping fits were attributed to laziness or drunkenness, though he drank little compared to his workmates. Doctors and psychiatrists examined him, but only gave him treatment for his periodic headaches and advised him not to work night shifts. One local doctor had given the Garayev problem some thought, and had even sent an article to a medical magazine, diagnosing his sickness as "Lethargy". But by the time the article was due to appear, Garayev had wandered off and fallen into the oil tank.

Moscow
19 August 1982

Chernenko, walling out the West

MARINA IS A young Russian girl with a lively sense of fun and little interest in Marxism-Leninism. She said as much recently to the Moscow youth paper *Moskovskii Komsomolets*, and sparked off an extraordinary public debate on her lifestyle, which largely involves drinking in bars and meeting foreigners. Sleazy, disgraceful, profoundly un-Soviet, fumed many readers, including a twenty-year-old medical student. "People like Marina are my deadliest enemies," he wrote.

But for every sternly orthodox young Communist there are those who hanker after a Western lifestyle and find mixing with foreigners the next best thing. "I lived with my parents in England, Austria and Sweden," wrote seventeen-year-old Natalia, evidently from a diplomatic family. "I have seen the beautiful life abroad and understand that this is the only way to live." Natalia said she was going out with a West German, but was keeping it quiet in case it counted against her at school.

In similar vein Christina, aged twenty, told *Moskovskii Komsomolets* she sought out Western men in bars because Russian boy-friends could offer her nothing. "Don't try and tell me there is a more interesting life than the one I lead. People have aspired to material well-being throughout history and they always will."

The Soviet authorities have long been worried by the influence on Russian youngsters of Western lifestyles, including fashion, pop music and the anti-authoritarian attitudes that tend to go with them. But in the present chilly East-West climate, the Kremlin is clamping down with more harshness and determination than usual on contacts between Russians and foreigners, passing severe new laws in an attempt to eradicate any contact between Soviet citizens and Westerners not approved by the authorities.

The Kremlin cannot of course prevent tourists from falling into conversation with Russians in Moscow or Leningrad, or from selling jeans and consumer goods to them. But a climate is now being created in which the first is becoming as illegal as the second. The message from the Kremlin under President Chernenko is loud and clear: those Russians who had begun to lose their fear of contacts with foreigners must be brought back in line. Russia is in an aggressively isolationist mood and the drawbridge is up. "Stop Marina!" said the *Moskovskii Komsomolets* article, adding that the authorities would be severe on any foreign students who came to next year's youth festival in Moscow with the idea of "forcing the values of the so-called free world on us".

The new rulings and warnings are aimed not so much at tourists, who have official guidance and schedules, as at foreign diplomats and correspondents resident in Moscow whose job it is to know about matters ranging from dissidents to Kremlin politics. Americans are a particular target.

Foreigners have been obliged to live in guarded ghettos in Russia since the time of Ivan the Terrible. But recently new fences topped with barbed wire have gone up around foreigners' compounds in Moscow, and the police who guard the entrances have been instructed to vet Russian visitors more stringently, a move which intimidates Muscovites from entering at all.

The US embassy in Moscow is described almost daily in the Soviet press as a nest of spies and provocateurs, and the anti-American atmosphere has had an effect. Russians who used to walk their dogs on the pavement outside the embassy and pause to chat to diplomats now pass by fearfully on the other side. Leading Soviet writers due to attend a literary function at the US embassy this month were ordered not to go and were further instructed not to accept invitations to travel to the United States for at least six months.

The climate of intimidation makes it more difficult for journalists and diplomats to carry out their work, especially since one of the new laws makes it a crime to pass on to foreigners "information that constitutes a professional secret". The law, Article 13 of the criminal code of the Russian Federation, gives the police very wide powers, since almost anything is a "professional secret" in Russia, from the price of meat to the number of taxis in Moscow. Another new law, about to come into effect, imposes a fine of fifty roubles on citizens who invite foreigners to stay at their homes without informing the police.

For Mr Arthur Hartman, the US Ambassador, there is only one possible response: "refusal to tolerate harassment" of Westerners and a firm threat of retaliation if Westerners are victimized for contacting Russians. Mr Hartman this month warned the Kremlin that the United States was concerned about recent incidents involving American journalists, diplomats and tourists. Western diplomats said he was referring in particular to an assault on the American Consul in Leningrad as he was leaving a restaurant after meeting a Russian, and to harassment of American correspondents, including two Associated Press journalists accused of failing to inform the authorities that one of their Russian contacts intended to defect to the West (the charge was denied). Tass said the journalists had "instigated and abetted the crime".

"What the new decrees mean", commented one diplomat, "is that Russians must not tell us anything, and if they do we must tell the authorities." In practice contacts between Russians and Westerners continue, and some Muscovites believe the current clampdown is a passing phase. The history of Russia's relations with the West certainly suggests that. But in the meantime the laws can be used to curtail legitimate political or commercial contacts as well as to stop young girls hanging around in bars. The message in both cases — as a former Soviet defector put it in a letter to *Izvestiya* at the end of May — is that Russia is better off closing the gates against the "nightmare" of life in the West. "I saw the horrors of capitalism with my own eyes," he told readers, having explained his defection as a Soviet trade official in Denmark and West Germany. "Without exception, anyone who leaves our country is headed for a poverty-stricken existence. In the West there is no future."

Moscow
28 June 1984

In search of pizza topping and pens

THERE ARE TIMES in Moscow when you are brought up short by the rough edges of Soviet society, just when you thought things were getting slightly better. Take our local pizza parlour. It is just round the corner from *The Times*, near the VIP block of flats where senior Politburo leaders live. The pizza parlour used to be called the Crystal Café, a place — despite its name — of dingy tables and even dingier food. Then last year it had a face-lift with the help of imported Italian caterers. Suddenly there were check tablecloths, candles and a passable Italian table wine. The wine is still there, but the pizzas have been reduced to one: a small, doughy object filled with cheese paste, the Russian version of *calzone*. "No mushrooms, no sausage, no tomatoes," the waiter explained with a shrug.

It is deep mid-winter, of course, and snow on snow is piled up on the memorial to Moscow's war dead visible through the steamed-up windows. But the real reason for the decline (those in the trade say) is the departure of the Italians. Under local management, the traditional Russian vices of inertia, indifference and inefficiency, which the late Yuri Andropov used to rail against, have reasserted themselves.

Visitors to Moscow are often struck by the fact that Russians are better clothed and fed than they had expected. But there are occasional sharp reminders of the huge gaps in consumer supply. A recent exhibition here on micro-computers drew vast crowds. But the massed spectators were as interested in routine office equipment such as pens and typewriter-ribbons as they were in the video games and word-processors. "It makes you think when you see a long line of people — including senior Army officers —queueing up in the hope of getting a couple of free felt-tip pens," one astonished Western exhibitor commented.

There is backwardness in heavy industry, as well as the consumer sector, as a visit to one of Moscow's leading electrical works demonstrates. The tape-recorders and door bells produced by the Kiubyshev Electrical Factory look dated, but then so do the giant transformers and reactors taking shape on the factory floor. Women in headscarves do much of the work manually. The factory is something of a showpiece, as it is part of the limited economic experiment introduced by Andropov giving managers the power to make production and investment decisions. The scheme — now being extended to encompass eighty-six Moscow plants — also links wages to output.

But the industrial system, apart from the favoured military sector, remains antiquated and burdened by over-centralization. The dilapidated Gothic red-brick structure of the Kuibyshev factory (formerly the Molotov Factory, founded in 1924) has not been renovated or re-equipped inside. The only visible computer is gathering dust in the manager's office. "We are not highly computerized," he remarks.

The Soviet leadership is constantly issuing instructions on the need to be more innovative and introduce up-to-date technologies, as well as use existing technologies, such as robotics, to full effect. The last such ukase appeared in *Pravda* on 4 January, calling for "intensification of the economy" through "quickened tempo" in the use of electronic computers and automated systems "in the period to the year 2000".

Under the school reform initiated by Mr Chernenko, Russian schoolchildren are to be taught to use micro-computers in their schools to provide the Soviet Union with a thoroughly modern new generation. But nobody has yet grasped the nettle of reform or backed the ideologically dangerous idea of a free flow of ideas to stimulate innovation.

Meanwhile an Apple or Sinclair Spectrum is a futuristic toy, felt-tip pens are prized possessions, and the pizza fast-food business is going from bad to worse.

Moscow
26 January 1985

Comrade Crank on the end of the line

THE NEWS THAT the Soviet Union is to quintuple the number of telephones by the end of the century — announced in *Pravda* the other day — strikes fear in the hearts of Western reporters here, even though the telephone is an essential tool of the news business. The country certainly needs the Politburo's new communications programme, since there are only 28 million phones for a population of just over 276 million. The Moscow telephone system was installed in 1882 by Messrs Bell and could do with an overhaul, not to mention the reintroduction of direct dialling overseas (abolished two years ago).

On the other hand, quintupling the number of phones means quintupling the number of wrong numbers and nuisance calls. At *The Times* we are asked at least once a day whether we repair televisions or sell sausages (the answer in both cases is no, regrettably). Even more peculiar to Russia than wrong numbers are the nuisance calls from patently unbalanced individuals who phone Western correspondents at all hours with rambling and incoherent tales of injustice, and sometimes accost you on the street.

Some Westerners believe such incidents are officially inspired or encouraged just to make the life of the foreign reporter more difficult. But the most common explanation is that Russian eccentrics have no one else to turn to. Like any other society, the Soviet Union has its fair share of eccentrics, but here they have no legitimate outlet.

Every utterance and activity is strictly controlled, and fringe behaviour is frowned on. Instead of phoning Moscow Radio, writing to *Pravda* or standing for some lost cause in the Supreme Soviet elections, your average Soviet nut tends to pick up the phone and dial a Western correspondent. One British reporter used to call Moscow "the fruitcake capital of the world". How the callers get hold of the numbers is a mystery, since there is no readily available telephone directory (phone numbers are a state secret).

The problem is that there are numerous genuine grievances in Russia, including human rights violations, and cases of real injustice have to be sifted from the fringe element. When the voice at the end of the telephone says, "we must meet" — meaning that the information he has to impart cannot be given over the phone or even within four walls — the reporter cannot risk assuming that the caller is unhinged. Your correspondent can recall wasting an entire afternoon walking round a park with a man who wished urgently to inform the West that there was a world conspiracy against him. On the other hand, many Russians — and not only Jewish *refuseniks* — have genuine stories of political persecution, and it is difficult to explain to such people that their grievances are not necessarily "newsworthy".

Moscow reporters, moreover, are haunted by the memory of a colleague who agreed to meet a disgruntled Soviet official from a Black Sea resort, but was not convinced by his story. In conspiratorial whispers the official revealed details of scandal and corruption which could easily have been the product of feverish fantasy. Not long afterwards it emerged in the Soviet press that the details were all true.

There is also the cautionary tale of the Western reporter who was driven to distraction by repeated phone calls from a well-known Moscow eccentric on a particularly busy day. When the telephone rang for the twentieth successive time, he hurled himself at it and in a series of Anglo-Saxon oaths told the caller what he thought of him. After a stunned silence at the other end, a hesitant, well-bred voice said mildly: "Hello, this is the British Ambassador here . . . is anything the matter?"

Moscow
22 May 1985

Russia short of rag-and-bone men

MR YURI ANDROPOV's drive for efficiency and the maximum use of resources has turned the spotlight on some unusual areas of Soviet life, including the lack of junk merchants for recycling old clothes and furniture. Until a few years ago the Russian equivalent of Steptoe and Son was a familiar sight on Moscow streets. Soviet rag-and-bone men did not use horses and carts, and trudged from courtyard to courtyard with sacks on their backs. But their street cries were similar, and so was the intention — to do up old coats, chairs, pots and pans and give them a new lease of life while turning an honest kopeck. It was all strictly illegal, but the authorities turned a blind eye. Recently, however, the rag-and-bone men have disappeared, victims not only of the Kremlin's campaign to stamp out the "black economy" but also of rising living standards.

According to two Moscow newspapers, the evening daily *Vechernaya Moskva* and the youth paper *Komsomolskaya Pravda*, expectations have risen to the point where the average citizen turns his nose up at secondhand cast-offs, however well reconditioned, and demands something new and fashionable. Even the official secondhand stores, known as *Kommissiony*, will no longer take old-fashioned household articles and clothing, according to irate readers of the two papers.

A Mr Morozov of Moscow wrote that he had found some perfectly serviceable shoes on a town dump, and for a few kopecks had provided them with new soles and shoelaces. Yet he could not persuade the *Kommissiony* to buy them. Since the shoes were too small for him, Mr Morozov told *Vechernaya Moskva*, they were of no use to him personally, yet brightly polished and reconditioned as they were he could not pass them on legally to a fellow citizen who might be glad of them.

There are a few shops in Moscow, called *Eureka*, where you can take rubbish which is beyond recycling. But several readers, many of them old age pensioners, complained that these shops were few and far between, with long queues and cupboards stuffed to overflowing with junk.

Discussing the problem with the due seriousness it deserves, *Komsomolskaya Pravda* called on the relevant ministries to take "appropriate measures" — for example, by increasing the number of secondhand stores, reorganizing the pricing system and arranging for goods to be valued at home.

After all, the paper said, when the Central Committee met after electing Mr Andropov leader it had rightly enjoined all ministries to bear in mind at all times "the need to satisfy constantly growing social expectations".

Moscow
25 January 1983

Soviet health care in need of a cure

RUSSIANS HAVE BEEN repeatedly reminded recently that the Soviet health system is second to none, and is one of the main benefits of Soviet power. Soviet citizens interviewed on television after Constitution Day earlier this month dutifully thanked the Kremlin for providing free and universal health care as well as free education and cheap housing and transport. But some Western visitors to Russian hospitals have been surprised to find them crowded, old-fashioned, poorly equipped and even dirty, and the Soviet press has been increasingly exposing the same defects. Soviet medicine is renowned in certain areas, such as eye surgery. But even *Izvestiya* has disclosed that ordinary Russians seeking routine health care face long queues, indifferent medical staff and shoddy facilities. *Izvestiya* visited one hospital near Makhachala on the Caspian Sea and found that the chief surgeon had resigned in disgust. It was not hard to see why. "I was amazed by the shabbiness of the place, the small and uncomfortable rooms," *Izvestiya*'s reporter said, "I saw orderlies washing bed linen in a trough, and the toilets and baths were out of order because there was no running water."

Boris Mozhaev, a Soviet author, gave an equally remarkable

account in the *Literary Gazette* of what happened when he broke his arm ski-ing. The arm was set in plaster rather than put in a splint for reasons of "administrative convenience": the doctors could sign him out after five days instead of having to keep him in hospital for several weeks. Mozhaev was in agony, and when the plaster was removed his arm had swollen alarmingly and there was blood dripping from his armpit. The doctors refused him proper bandages because they were economizing, and his arm became twisted as the bones set wrongly. Mozhaev appealed to another doctor for help, but was told to put up with it. "What's the matter? You don't want to be a ballet dancer, do you?" the doctor asked coldly. "Can't you write with a twisted arm?" Finally Mozhaev went in desperation to a famous clinic at Tallinn in Estonia, where his bones were set properly. But even in Tallinn he was horrified to see that the corridors were used for eating, sleeping and even treatment and consultation.

Part of the problem is that medicine is not a highly regarded profession in Russia and doctors, the majority women, are badly paid and poorly trained. Drugs such as antibiotics are in very short supply, and disposable syringes or even sticking plasters are almost unknown. Not surprisingly, Russians are increasingly turning to alternative medicine, folk remedies and occult healers, rather than run the gauntlet of a state system which involves bribing doctors to jump the queue and gain access to scarce drugs. Some medical experts approve of the unofficial healers, but others such as Academician Uglov of Leningrad favour reform of the state medical service. In an article in *Izvestiya* entitled "Thoughts on the profession of doctor", he praised the pre-revolutionary medical profession, a rare admission that health care existed under Tsarism, for serving the nation selflessly by treating patients in remote country areas.

Soviet medicine has scored notable success in recent times. For example the Kurgan Institute of Experimental Traumatology has developed new methods of healing bone fractures. One of the most celebrated Kurgan surgeons, Dr Yakov Vytebsky, has developed a new method of diagnosing stomach cancer by analysing gastric juices, and has pioneered stomach operations.

But there is criticism of the medical authorities for not applying such discoveries to the system as a whole, and for allowing specialists to flourish while health care for the average citizen deteriorates. "What will our grandchildren be like?" the *Literary Gazette* asked recently, criticizing the state of health of Soviet teenagers, which it said did not meet the requirements of either modern industry or the armed forces. "It is time we changed our attitude to health," the paper said. "Health is not one's private property, it belongs to the state."

Moscow
29 October 1984

Keeping afloat on a sea of vodka

IT WAS DAWN at Syktyvkar, in the Komi autonomous republic, and the morning shift was about to clock on at the local sawmill and timber works. But as the sky lightened no workers appeared, and the saws stayed silent. Finally the shift showed up and lurched through the gates, only to be confronted by the Andropov-style "peoples inspectors" that Mr Gorbachov has revived as part of his discipline campaign. The workers offered befuddled excuses: they had forgotten their keys, or taken their children to school. But one blurted out the truth: "been having a beer or two," he confessed. The People's Inspector found a bar just round the corner with a sign saying: "No beer today". "There was," the barmaid said, "but they drank 600 litres in an hour and a half."

The issue of *Sovietskaya Rossiya* which carried this cautionary tale on its front page recently was almost entirely devoted to the evils of drink. It was part of a determined anti-alcoholism campaign mounted by the Kremlin in the official media, to prepare the ground for new draconian measures. The main target of the campaign and the new measures is not beer, which is relatively weak, but vodka, and *samogon*, a lethal homemade moonshine. The relationship between a Russian and a bottle of vodka is almost mystical. The press campaign pulled no punches, with even drunkenness in the armed forces — including the strategic nuclear missile forces — being exposed to public gaze. No area of Soviet life has been sacrosanct, except the hallowed corridors of the Kremlin itself, where sobriety is presumed to reign.

Komsomolskaya Pravda turned the spotlight on sport and found that Pakhtakor Tashkent's disastrous relegation to the second division last season was due to heavy drinking by top players, some of whom had missed days of training in order to get blind drunk.

The scale of the problem is certainly staggering, and has a deleterious effect on industrial production. Mr Gorbachov, who called for a determined fight against alcoholism at the first Politburo meeting after he took power, sees it as an obstacle to his economic reform plans. The average Soviet citizen consumes over eight litres of spirits (mostly vodka) a year, one of the highest levels in the world. *Pravda* cites a range of resulting social ills: divorce, a growth in birth defects and retarded children, and a fall in male life expectancy from over 65 in the 1960s to about 62 today. The fairly brutal "sobering up stations" increasingly cater for children and teenagers.

Suggested remedies canvassed in the press varied from the pious hope — increased soft drink production, and collective teetotal groups with tea, biscuits and morally uplifting lectures — to the lash. The only answer was a sharp shock, a senior Soviet economist from the Ukraine said in *Pravda*, and not necessarily a short one either.

Alcoholism was a crime like any other, he wrote, and drunks should be punished by imprisonment "for the protection and prolongation of their lives". Addicts had to be isolated from drink "for as long as it takes to cure them".

The problem, as the Tsarist regime also discovered after it introduced the "dry law" in 1914, is that vodka sales are a valuable source of state revenue. At Ulyanovsk — Lenin's birthplace —workers' wages are being paid into savings schemes in an experiment designed to stop Russians taking their cash straight to the vodka shop, not least on public holidays.

But paradoxically vodka taxes, unlike private savings, keep the national treasury afloat. In any case, drink is a centuries-old Russian remedy for counteracting the cold, the government and general misery by seeking oblivion in "a hundred grammes". As a reader's letter in *Pravda* noted, anti-alcohol propaganda was a waste of time "because drunks never even notice it".

Moscow
17 May 1985

Aerobics get the ideological nod

JANE FONDA MAY not like this, but she is better known in the Soviet Union for her leotard than for her radical politics. The Soviet authorities find Miss Fonda's brand of leftism puzzling: on the one hand they were happy to show *The China Syndrome* in Soviet cinemas, since it showed the folly of Western nuclear policies, but on the other hand Miss Fonda slipped into Russia recently to give aid and support to a Jewish dissident. Much easier, then, to give approval to the non-political Jane Fonda work-out and produce a home-grown Soviet version.

The Russians tend to react initially to Western fads and fashions as capitalist gimmicks which have no place in Soviet society, in which all activities are government-controlled (except one or two). Eventually, however, Western innovations tend to trickle through by mysterious means, and the authorities decide (as with video) to take over the latest vogue and give it a Soviet twist, for all the world as if Moscow had invented it.

In the case of aerobics, the Soviet élite has for some time been watching Miss Fonda go through her paces on expensive and often illegally imported video machines. Soviet officialdom was sceptical at first, arguing that there was nothing wrong with the good old-fashioned physical jerks on radio and television, which somehow retain the flavour of earnest and muscular proletarian fitness.

The demand that exercise should be fun finally won, however, and the Kremlin decreed that aerobics was ideologically acceptable, in spite of the fact that it involves pulsating disco music, frequently attacked in the Soviet press as a pernicious Western influence designed to undermine Communism.

A Jane Fonda equivalent now runs a regular work-out programme on Moscow television, and the unfit can enrol in aerobics classes at the giant stadium in Luzhniki Park. As *Sovietskaya Rossiya* noted, aerobics has caught on in Russia faster than yoga, dieting or vegetarianism, thanks to the attraction of "beautiful music, beautiful outfits and beautiful bodies". Classes at Luzhniki and other sports stadiums were booked solid. There are drawbacks, not the least of which is that the state has to provide the obligatory leg-warmers and head-bands in bright colours, there being no private enterprise to cash in on the fad, and so far the state has failed to do so.

Even leotards are difficult to find in the shops. The state sportswear manufacturer, Glavsportprom, says it hopes to have aerobics gear on sale "in a couple of years' time". Private enterprise has sprung up to meet the demand for aerobics classes, on the other hand, and there are a growing number of unofficial instructors (mostly physical education teachers) holding illegal work-outs in their relatively cramped flats. The cost, according to *Sovietskaya Rossiya*, which tracked down one underground aerobics class, is five roubles (nearly £5) per person per hour. Since official instructors are paid only one rouble an hour, the profits of private aerobics are considerable. You can, of course, simply put on your track-suit and jog for nothing, and Russians — most of whom seem to be dismally unfit, in contrast to the Soviet propaganda image — are constantly being urged to do so.

One health magazine recently told male readers that jogging could revive their flagging libidos and help them to face up to new, lithe-limbed Soviet woman in her hard-won leotard. Jogging, the magazine asserted, stimulated the male prostate gland, and was therefore to be recommended for those suffering from impotency. Jogging had a calming effect on the nerves, thus reducing stress, and was good for the overweight. It was also beneficial for men obliged to abstain from sexual activity, the magazine said, since jogging provided a channel for pent-up energy.

Moscow
27 August 1984

CRIME AND PUNISHMENT:

SCANDAL AND CRIME

Fiddlers on the Socialist bus

THE RUSSIANS ARE an honest and scrupulously law-abiding people — in theory. According to Marxist-Leninist ideology, crime is the product of bourgeois society and the internal contradictions of capitalism. Yet examples of violent, criminal or merely anti-social behaviour keep recurring and in some cases are on the increase, much to the distress of the authorities, who are turning to sociologists to explain why a "hangover from the past" is still clinging on rather than obediently withering away. Take the question of bus fares. When you board a Moscow bus you do not pay the driver, or a conductor (there are none). Instead you force your way through the crush to a machine, pop a five kopeck piece in, turn a handle and tear off a ticket from the roll. Trolleybuses and trams are cheaper at four and three kopecks respectively, but the same "honesty system" applies. It worked well enough in the beginning, but in today's more lax atmosphere an increasing number of Soviet citizens either cannot be bothered to fight their way to the ticket machine or forget to pay the fare accidentally on purpose. Older people tend to pass coins down the bus, from hand to hand — a custom said to be derived from the communal passing of candles towards the altar in an Orthodox church. But even this is becoming less frequent, and youngsters especially take a cynical view of fare paying — not least because the ticket machines are poorly maintained and the ticket rolls often run out and are not replaced.

All of which might seem fairly trivial, except that according to Moscow transport officials the city loses about 14 million roubles a year — over £12 million — in unpaid fares. Moscow is better off than other Soviet cities — it is supposed to be Russia's showcase to the world, and for that matter to visitors from the provinces — but it cannot afford to lose revenue. One official said in *Komsomolskaya Pravda* that unpaid fares last year could have provided 300 new buses (most are imported from Hungary) to replace the efficient but antiquated bone-shakers which at present ferry Muscovites about at hugely subsidized costs. But fare avoidance is also worrying because it suggests a steep decline in civic consciousness and an equally sharp rise in "irresponsible" attitudes to public property and the state, especially among the young.

It is still safe to walk the streets at night alone, and Moscow is a model of sobriety (and dullness) compared to Western cities. Both petty and serious crime are at a low level. But there has been an erosion of the civic duty and good works mentality which is supposed to underpin socialist society, and a corresponding growth of cynicism.

Muscovites still turn out to provide a day's free labour on a *subotnik* — a Saturday devoted to voluntary labour for the community — and another *subotnik* is due next month. But in many cases all it amounts to is a few hours leaning on a broom and chatting to the neighbours while cleaning up a local street. One socially useful custom which persists is the collection of waste-paper for recycling, with the reward of a set of books as the incentive. At the moment, sixty kilograms of paper (called *makulatura* in Russian) buys you a four-volume edition of works by Jack London, mistakenly thought by Russians to be one of the most wildly popular Western authors of all time (for his socialist novels rather than his tales of man and nature in Alaska).

Even *makulatura* is open to abuse, however, as the paper *Rural Life* recently revealed. It described how a thirty-year-old rowing coach in Saratov — the kind of fine young man who ought to be a shining example of socialist morality — had taken to stealing newspapers and magazines systematically from mail boxes in the lobbies of blocks of flats. He got away with it because he was well-dressed and respectable, and accumulated quite a collection of highly prized books (many of them unavailable in the shops) before being caught red-handed.

As far as fiddles on the buses are concerned, the fine for non-payment is to rise from one rouble to three.

As for serious crime, such as mugging or rape, sociologists say it is committed mostly by those from low income groups.

Moscow
27 March 1984

Scandals a touchy subject in Moscow

RUSSIANS PRIVATELY ENJOY a scandal as much as anyone, so it is surprising how little impact the Parkinson affair has had in Moscow. *Pravda* made its first comment yesterday on the Conservative Party conference, but despite a promising headline — "The celebration that never was" — most of the shafts were aimed at Mrs Thatcher and Mr Tebbit, with no mention of Mr Parkinson or Miss Keays. Tass did refer in a report on Mrs Thatcher's reshuffle to a "scandal connected with Mr Parkinson's immoral behaviour" but that was all.

The affair would seem tailor-made to fit Marxist theories about the decline of late Capitalism, and further homilies are no doubt in the works. Soviet reticence, in the meantime, may have something to do with the fact that *Pravda* has quietly reported a number of home-grown scandals and disasters recently, without any need for foreign imports.

Corruption in high places has been given carefully controlled exposure since Mr Andropov came to power, the object being to reinforce the Soviet leader's austere campaign for discipline and efficiency while discrediting his predecessor. Ministers who served Mr Brezhnev loyally over many years suddenly stand revealed as scoundrels, though their misdeeds are mostly financial rather than sexual. One minister who fell from grace was rumoured to have a private sauna next to his office. Most seem to have been fatally tempted by goods and money rather than women, however.

The most recent example is the Russian Minister for Light Industry, whose downfall was associated with that of the Minister for Fruit and Vegetables. Both were accused of "rampant fraud and embezzlement". Transport officials have similarly been upbraided. The deputy head of the musical agency, Rosskonsert, was last week sentenced to ten years in prison for demanding money and gifts from performers. Among his ill-gotten loot, the court was told, were jewelry, after-shave, an ice bucket, western pullovers and a folding umbrella.

Sensationalism is unknown in the Soviet press, and items of gossip or scandal are tucked away in small, soberly-worded articles. They are only released when it suits the Kremlin politically, or to encourage "responsible" behaviour by Soviet citizens.

It would be a pity if the Politburo's latest injunction to the press to step up "ideological propaganda" was to eliminate these occasional oblique glimpses into human mystery and misdeeds altogether. Russians enjoyed a particular frisson of excitement last week over the strange disappearance in Venice of Mr Oleg Bitov, a correspondent for the *Literary Gazette*. Defection or murder?

The paper, in a black-edged article, plumped for murder by the CIA, on the grounds that Mr Bitov had been investigating an aspect of the assassination attempt on the Pope in 1981. Many readers, however, seemed to favour kidnapping or death at the hands of the Mafia or the Red Brigades.

Moscow
18 October 1983

Salting away a Soviet fortune

THE ATTRACTIVE, MIDDLE-AGED woman arrived at Moscow's international airport to catch the Paris flight, loaded with luggage. Most unusually, she had no trouble finding a porter, who took her bags straight to a Customs inspector. The inspector — again most unusually — failed to examine a single piece of luggage, but "our *chekisti* (security police) were not asleep", as *Izvestiya* proudly remarked. The gimlet-eyed men of the KGB had spotted something amiss, and pounced. Out of the bulging cases poured icons, gold, jewelry and precious coins worth 30,000 roubles (about £15,000), not to mention $2,000 (about £1,150) in cash and several five-kilogram jars of black caviar.

The Soviet police had uncovered a complex smuggling ring, and *Izvestiya* had been giving its readers a two-part account of dark goings-on involving crooked officials, Georgian racketeers, foreigners (the French connection) and even sex. The *femme fatale* of the story was Albina, a vivacious forty-five-year-old Russian who in the 1960s married, then divorced an Arab, retaining only his name and a foreign passport. It was not long before Mrs Stokou was using her status to smuggle icons and jewelry between Paris and Moscow. Even beautiful smugglers with Arab passports need accomplices, however. And at this point a "charming and extravagant" Georgian by the name of Tristan enters the story. Tristan, according to *Izvestiya*, had a "conjurer's talent for turning Soviet money into dollars and dollars into icons and jewelry". The two made a natural pair, and "Tristan and Albina" soon had a number of officials at Moscow airport in their pocket. The idyll ended with the arrest of the crooked Customs officials, and hence of Tristan and Albina, who got twelve years in a labour camp. The story is told more in the style of a romantic thriller than is usual in the sedate *Izvestiya*. There is even an illustration in the best James Bond tradition, complete with pretty, long-haired girl, mysterious attaché case and wads of cash. But the object of the exercise is not so much to entertain Russians with a spicy scandal as to warn of the dangers of making money illicitly in the Soviet Union.

Not surprisingly, few Russians take the risk. But there are enough enterprising and daring souls to worry the authorities. A drive against corruption is under way, spearheaded by the KGB, and fresh impetus has been given by the appointment of General Vitaly Fedorchuk as head of the security services. General Fedorchuk acquired a reputation for ruthlessness as head of the Ukraine KGB, and exposure of the rotten elements in Soviet society seems to be a reflection of this zeal.

Corruption is endemic in a society where goods are scarce and survival depends on the giving and receiving of favours — the system known in Russian as *blat*. But the KGB are not after small-time corruption. Their target is the kind of underground millionaire who leads a secret resistance, surfacing only when he gets caught.

Soviet millionaires tend to accrue their wealth in undetected obscurity and those who do not, meet sticky ends. Take the case of the recent scandal in which Anatoli Kolovatov was dismissed from his post as head of the Soviet Union's national circus and allegedly suffered a "heart attack". Mr Kolovatov, and an acrobat named Boris Tsigan (Gypsy), gave circus performers permission to join troupes in the West provided they handed over diamonds and foreign currency on their return. Diamonds worth more than a million dollars were found in a raid on the circus director's flat. The scandal touched even the top leadership because Boris was said to be the lover of Galina, Mr Brezhnev's daughter. Some said the anti-corruption drive was being used for political in-fighting, but this was never proved.

Senior officials are often implicated, however. Mr Vladimir Rytov, formerly deputy fisheries minister, was executed for his part in a high-level caviar scandal. Mr Rytov headed a gang of nearly 200 exporting caviar labelled smoked herring. Once abroad, the caviar was repacked and sold on the Western market at normal prices. Profits were split between the foreign firms and the Soviet officials in the racket and paid into their bank accounts abroad.

Capital punishment for "economic crimes" in the Soviet Union was introduced in 1963. Senior officials are not normally shot for misdemeanours. But there are frequent press reports of executions of less-elevated individuals for such crimes as theft of state property, misappropriation of state funds and the acceptance of bribes on a large scale. The mayor of the Black Sea resort of Sochi escaped execution but was sentenced to thirteen years for accepting bribes. He was the proud owner of an American Ford and kept a small fortune in jewelry at his house when amazed police discovered a water fountain in his living-room. Another independently minded entrepreneur, the director of the social security office for industrial enterprises in Baku, amassed two large apartments and a *dacha* with a swimming-pool, orange grove and black swans. Thirty-four kilos of gold was found in his possession on his arrest.

The problem for underground millionaires is how to spend their ill-gotten gains. Most of them seem to come from the southern republics, and it is not uncommon to see well-off Georgians entertaining lavishly in Moscow restaurants, or even — the latest status symbol — taking over an entire restaurant for the evening. But the aim of most millionaires is to avoid detection. The Georgian "mafia" are sometimes able to persuade the authorities to turn a blind eye, and staff at luxury hotels and *dachas* in the Caucasus firmly fend off unwelcome inquiries about the identities of their more flamboyant patrons.

Illegal money-making therefore seems likely to continue despite spurts of zealous campaigning against the black economy, if only because the Soviet economy is so inefficient that natural entrepreneurs find a ready outlet in the numerous gaps left in consumer demand.

There are, very occasionally, signs that the present Soviet leaders acknowledge the power of the entrepreneurial spirit, not least in agriculture, where the peasants' private plots are vital to food production. But the Soviet Union remains the guardian of ideological purity, the bastion of Marxism-Leninism. In Hungary, Mr Rubik is able to invent his cube and garner the immense proceeds. In both Hungary and Poland ordinary citizens are able to keep dollar accounts in their banks, and they are not always asked where they got them. No such aberrations are allowed in Russia.

Moscow
24 July 1982

Naked truth about Volga bath house

RUSSIAN BATH HOUSES, unlike certain kinds of sauna baths in the West, are not normally associated with sin. They are strictly segregated, and in the ladies' baths women can sweat, swat each other with birch twigs, and gossip in the knowledge that their menfolk are safely out of earshot next door. Comrade Tylkin had other ideas. As head of the baths administration in Saratov, on the Volga, he obviously thought he had the right to inspect all his establishments. Or so he had told a colleague from Moscow one day as they shared a bottle of vodka in his office. "Let's go and look at the ladies," Tylkin said thickly. Moments later the two stood swaying in the doorway of the ladies' bath house. The female attendant, thinking they had got lost, gently pushed the two men out, but they came back. "Don't you know who I am?" demanded Mr Tylkin, peering through the steam. "I am the director of the baths. . . . "

The naked ladies advanced towards him, birch twigs in hand. "Er, this is a random on-the-spot inspection," Mr Tylkin said, stepping backwards. "My colleague from Moscow. . . . " But his colleague had already retreated. One of the ladies phoned the police who threw Mr Tylkin out. Comrade Tylkin rushed next door to the men's section, where he persuaded the beer-swilling customers to testify to the police that he was not drunk, as the women had claimed. He then called for beer for himself, and hearing that there was none left ordered the attendants to confiscate it from the customers.

The last straw came a few days later when Mr Tylkin, apparently unabashed, began checking the baths for unauthorized customers who had been admitted without tickets. The baths attendants appealed to the newspaper *Trud*, which sent two reporters down to Saratov to uncover the naked truth. Men and women bathers all told *Trud* that Mr Tylkin was a tyrant, a drunkard, and a lecher, who had also run a tidy business on the side selling soap, cosmetics and towels. Comrade Tylkin's fate is being decided by the People's Control and the Ministry of Housing and Communal Services.

Moscow
31 August 1983

Pravda takes lid off party bosses' nights of sex and scandal

Pravda, NORMALLY AN organ of strict sobriety and party orthodoxy, has revealed that Russia has its own version of the Helen Smith affair, and upbraided police and Party officials for their cover-up of a case involving sex and scandal.

The newspaper described, with distinct disapproval, the goings-on at Flat 2, Number 29 Zavodsky Street in Kursk, an important industrial city south of Moscow. The flat belonged to an unnamed young woman who allowed it to be used for what *Pravda* called a *debosh*, a word which embraces not only debauchery but also drunkenness and rowdiness. One such wild party ended tragically one evening when the girl fell from a third-floor balcony. She was taken to hospital with severe head injuries. But what incensed *Pravda* even more was that the life and soul of the "*debosh*" was the deputy chief of police in Kursk, Aleksandr Ivanovich Kovyniev. When the local police were called to the scene and realized that their boss was intimately involved they turned a blind eye, *Pravda* reported. Neither the police department nor local Party organizations took any action against Mr Kovyniev, who in the course of time discreetly resigned his post and took a new and profitable job as director of a trading enterprise.

Pravda did not go so far as to say that Mr Kovyniev had pushed the girl off the balcony but it did take the firm view that incidents such as the drunken orgy at Kursk must not go unpunished. "As Comrade Chernenko has said, it is high time we put our own house in order," the article declared.

Other cases in which official misdemeanours had been covered up because the officials concerned had connections in high places were mentioned by *Pravda*. It said the Party district secretary in Kursk had broken a police official's leg during a drunken row and had been dismissed, yet only a short time later had been promoted to deputy head of agriculture for the Kursk region. Even more remarkably, given the wall of secrecy surrounding appointments and dismissals in Russia, *Pravda* complained that no reason had been given for sacking the Kursk official in the first place.

Soviet journalists will no doubt refer to the article when investigating low-level comings and goings, and can cite *Pravda*'s disapproval of the way in which Party officials often refuse all comment on the grounds that the revelation of official misdeeds which reflect badly on the Party apparatus as a whole and undermine confidence in its fitness to govern is undesirable.

Moscow
16 November 1984

Comrade Popov falls victim to a poison pen

ALEXANDER POPOV WAS about to defend his thesis at an agricultural institute, and was in a state of nervous tension. Suddenly he was summoned by the director, and told that the examination would be delayed, for reasons which the director was reluctant to reveal. Gradually it emerged that Mr Popov, hitherto a research worker of unimpeachable probity, was suspected of plagiarizing the work of a fellow candidate and of trying to bribe the examination board into turning a blind eye.

As a result, the newspaper *Sovietskaya Rossiya* said, Mr Popov's valuable research on how to improve meat production in semi-desert areas of the Soviet Union was put back two and a half years while the accusations were investigated. Mr Popov, it turned out, had been a victim of an anonymous poison pen letter. The practice of denouncing fellow citizens for alleged crimes against the state reached its height under Stalin, and was frequently used to settle old scores when a piece of malicious gossip could send a man or woman to a labour camp.

More recently, Soviet authorities have become concerned at the damage done to individuals' reputations by the persistence of *anonimki*, as they are called in Russian, and more particularly of the waste of time in checking them.

In the case of Mr Popov, which arose in the Kalmyk autonomous region on the Caspian Sea, the trail led to a disgruntled worker by the name of Bovaldinov at an experimental station for research on sheep and goats. After lengthy procedures involving typewriter comparisons and even laboratory analysis of the saliva with which Bovaldinov had sealed the envelopes, it was finally established that over the years he had "anonymously slandered" thirty-nine people. In a number of cases the victims were examination candidates who at one time or another had crossed swords with Bovaldinov. His mistake, apart from using the same typewriter, was to use accusations of bribery and plagiarism once too often. The unfortunate Mr Popov was additionally accused of stealing wool from the research stations so that his wife could knit sweaters and sell them. According to *Sovietskaya Rossiya*, the case against Bovaldinov ran to two thousand pages of evidence. The paper comments that the authorities had obviously paid too much attention to his anonymous letters, and should have assumed that those denounced were innocent until proved guilty, a principle not frequently observed in Soviet jurisprudence. "Honest Soviet people have become the victims of dirty slander," the paper said, but added that anonymous letters were sometimes sent by citizens who were on the righ track but "lacked the civic bravery to sign them".

Moscow
2 September 1982

Pravda reveals murder at sea

WESTERN SHIPPING MAGNATES, fearful of cut-throat competition from the Soviet merchant navy, may be comforted to know that it sometimes suffers from indiscipline, drunkenness and even the occasional mutiny. According to *Pravda*, the recent murder of a merchant navy captain by his second mechanic on the Sea of Azov has lessons for the rest of the fleet. Captain Levchenko was given the command of the *Sabirabad* two years years ago. He was considered energetic, modest, friendly and communicative, except by Second Mechanic Grazhdenkin, who was "a born troublemaker". On his previous ships Grazhdenkin was constantly drunk or picking fights with fellow crew, and resented the fact that Captain Levchenko ran a tight ship. The animosity was mutual, and when the mechanic went on leave last April the captain sent a cable to the Azov shipping line asking for Grazhdenkin to be transferred. Despite Grazhdenkin's reputation the request was ignored, and when he came back he went from bad to worse, striking the second mate, attempting to jump ship and threatening the captain when rebuked.

The climax came when the *Sabirabad* docked at its home port of Zhdanov — without a captain. A search had been conducted at sea, the crew told officials, but without result. The finger of suspicion pointed at Grazhdenkin, who at first denied everything but then admitted his guilt. He was coming off watch, he said, when he spotted the captain and asked him to step on to the poop to talk things over. Tempers flared, and Grazhdenkin struck Captain Levchenko on the head several times with a pair of pliers before throwing him overboard. *Pravda* said Grazhdenkin had been sentenced to death for murder, and accused the Azov shipping line of "not paying enough attention to the selection and placing of personnel". It said there were probably many more cases of drunken and insubordinate behaviour on board ship than came to light.

Moscow
17 August 1983

BEHIND THE KREMLIN WALL:

POLITICS AND ELECTIONS

Something to talk about at last in the great Kremlin palace

A MOSCOW WIT once observed that the Supreme Soviet is to a parliament what Gorky Street is to a shopping centre — the form without the substance. It meets only twice a year, and rubber stamps decisions already made by the ruling Politburo and Central Committee of the Communist Party. "The deputy who voted against" would be a suitable subject for one of Bateman's famous cartoons on socially shocking behaviour.

The Supreme Soviet surely enjoys the most enviable site of any legislature in the world. Originally intended as Nicholas I's imperial residence in Moscow, the great Kremlin palace —where Supreme Soviet deputies assemble — is surrounded by the golden domes of the three ancient cathedrals of the Assumption, the Archangel and the Annunciation. Inside, although some richly decorated halls remain, the conference hall of the great palace is plain, with tall windows letting in the bleak November light. At the far end a modest statue of Lenin is set in a niche behind the podium. The deputies file in — the Soviet is made up of two chambers, the Council of Unions and the Council of Nationalities — and sit behind rows of what look like school desks. Here and there a splash of colour in the costumes of Caucasian and Central Asian members mingles with the sober suits of Russian deputies. They sit reading Mr Yuri Andropov's speech in *Pravda* and *Izvestiya*, a low buzz of conversation filling the long hall. For once, a Party leader has given people something to talk about, with his call for initiative and enterprise and attack on inertia. The deputies try not to look inert. At the far end, from a subterranean opening, the members of the Politburo file on to the podium: Mr Andropov, followed by Mr Tikhonov, the Prime Minister, the stocky white-haired figure of Mr Chernenko, and Mr Gromyko and Marshal Ustinov.

The Chairman proposes that Mr Andropov be made a member of the Praesidium of the Supreme Soviet, a post he seems to have overlooked in his rise to power. The 1,500 deputies raise their hands in approval. The Chairman asks if anyone is against, and declares the proposal carried unanimously without bothering to look up. The government's finance ministers then appear and make speeches about the state budget, rather as Tsarist ministers used to do in the Duma (assembly), except that deputies were then expected to make interpolations. While statistics are being reeled off, Mr Andropov and Mr Tikhonov engage in deep and serious discussion, possibly on the reform measures they seem to have in mind which — if implemented — would make much of the current five-year plan irrelevant. In the back row Mr Aliyev, the newest Politburo member, chats amiably to Mr Gorbachov, the youngest. Across the aisle Mr Dolgikh the technocrat — who was not promoted into the Politburo on Monday — discusses matters with his neighbour, making energetic chopping motions with the palm of his hand. There is a slight stir as the speeches end, and the Chairman rises. Will Mr Andropov, having become a member of the Praesidium, be elected its President, and become head of state? But the Chairman announces a break, followed by committee sessions, and the deputies file out to wait for the second and final day of voting.

Moscow
24 November 1982

Andropov tries to jump the great Russian queue

ROUNDING THE CORNER from *The Times* office the other day I came across a queue three feet deep stretching for several blocks. Lucky (and patient) customers at the head of the queue were making off with their rare booty: toilet paper. Some carried unmanageable bundles, others were festooned with it. The following day the queue was still there, shuffling forward.

"The queue — any queue — is a perfect illustration of what Andropov is up against," an economist friend remarked. "Despite all our achievements, sixty-five years after the revolution we still cannot produce basic commodities. We are always laying the basis for future abundance while spending our daily lives in an endless search for everyday goods." Queueing, together with absenteeism, is the most obvious sign of Russia's economic difficulties. The two are connected. Under a new law on labour discipline, anyone found absent from his place of work for more than three hours a day is deemed absent for a day, and anyone absent for a day without good cause forfeits a day of holiday entitlement. Since three hours in a queue is not all that unusual, many Soviet factory and office workers are trapped. If they take time off to buy shoes or sausage, they risk a stiff penalty, including having to pay compensation for loss of production at work: but if they do not take their place in the queue the family goes unfed or unshod.

Mr Andropov's answer is that if all workers stayed at their benches or desks and made more effort, the economy would grow to the point where supply would finally catch up with demand, and the queues would melt away. Many Russians are sceptical, including the Kremlin advisers who recently leaked a damaging report on the Soviet economy to the Western press (previously unheard of). All senior economists from the élite research centre at Akademgorodok in Novosibirsk, the authors came to the conclusion that the Soviet economy needed thorough overhaul if it was to be transformed from a fundamentally Stalinist system of central control into a sensitive economic mechanism attuned to workers' and consumers' needs and wishes. "Tackle the cause, not the symptoms," was the message from Novosibirsk.

This apparently common-sense recommendation was put on one side as too radical after a top-level conference in April. Instead, the Kremlin announced a "limited economic experiment" in five selected industries from next January, giving plant managers vaguely defined powers over budget and manning, and with a nod in the direction of profit and loss accounting.

The reformers and their Kremlin allies have come up against the immovable object on which all Soviet reformers sooner or later stub their toes: the entrenched bureaucracy. Mr Andropov has a sharp brain, and is slowly unfolding a long-term strategy which has been forming in his mind since he had access to the real facts of economic life as head of the KGB. But the average economic administrator is neither as sharp nor as perceptive, and is more concerned to keep his largely unnecessary job than to stimulate change and growth.

It is of course not out of the question — and there are whispers to this effect in Moscow — that the Novosibirsk radicals' allies include Mr Andropov himself. Leaks do not happen by chance, least of all in the Soviet Union. Mr Nikolai Baibakov, Russia's chief state planner as head of Gosplan for nearly twenty years, gave a press conference in which he soft-pedalled the new measures, on the grounds that the economy was too large to restructure swiftly, and sought to minimize the significance of the leaked report. Yet only two days before, in a speech to Party veterans, Mr Andropov had spoken of reforms stretching well into the next five-year plan. Using language very close to that of the document, he criticized "half-measures" which had failed to overcome "accumulated inertia". One observer of the Soviet scene remarked: "Nobody looking at Mr Baibakov could fail to think of accumulated inertia." Brezhnev-era officials point out that Mr Brezhnev also called for efficiency and labour discipline, but omit to add that Mr Andropov is doing something about it, in the face of opposition from Brezhnevites.

If Mr Andropov does succeed where others have failed, it will be because he is skilfully combining gradual reforms with a tough crackdown on indiscipline. Mr Andropov has set an example by staying at his desk through much of the summer. But how far is he able or willing to go? There have been some hints in the Soviet press that a little private enterprise here and there might not be a bad thing. One senior economic official even suggested to me that a little unemployment in the grossly overmanned socialist economy would do no harm. Such unorthodox thoughts are clearly inspired by the dismal performance of an economy with declining growth rates (the growth rate target this year is only 3.2 per cent).

The reality remains that — as an Armenian economist disclosed in the theoretical journal *Kommunist* in June — the economic bureaucracy is colossal, with sixty-four ministries and twenty-three state committees dealing with all details of planning and production. "It is high time to re-examine the organization and management of the entire industrial complex," *Kommunist* declared. "It is not possible to continue multiplying ministries."

Perhaps not. Many Muscovites in the queue must have wondered why sixty-four ministries could not between them arrange for the production of toilet paper in the right quantities at the right time. On the other hand, neither *Kommunist* nor Mr Andropov, nor the Novosibirsk reformers have yet told us how Thatcherite principles of cost-effectiveness and streamlining can be applied to Russia without either undermining the ideological purity of Marxism-Leninism (sternly guarded by Mr Andropov himself) or provoking a counter-revolution from the kind of managers who know how to talk about efficiency but not how to achieve it.

Moscow
25 August 1983

Strange new role for a furtive general

IT WAS PROBABLY the first time in history that a map showing sensitive Soviet bases in the Far East had been shown in public, and almost certainly the first time a senior Soviet general had pointed them out to foreign journalists with a long pointed stick. The map, clearly prepared by the Ministry of Defence, looked slightly tatty, with missile bases and air routes superimposed on the Sea of Okhotsk, the Kamchatka peninsula and Sakhalin island. Maps are state secrets in Russia, so possibly Marshal Ogarkov's was the only one there is. The heading said — in Russian — "Area of the actions of the intruder plane on the night of 1 September". A small boxed diagram in the corner showed the tortuous route taken by the RC135 reconnaissance aircraft.

Marshal Ogarkov lectured in impeccable military academy style, explaining in firm and patient tones the route KAL Flight 007 had taken and why Soviet radar and fighters had taken it for a spy plane. It had flown over a missile base. "You can see it on the map," he said, pointing. He seemed slightly uncertain why he should be explaining such highly sensitive matters, or what we were all doing there. Would it have made a difference if the doomed jumbo had been forced to land, as a Korean airliner was in 1978? Yes indeed, the marshal answered wistfully, we would not all be sitting in this hall.

He took both written and oral questions, speaking methodically and occasionally breaking into a controlled outburst when asked for the umpteenth time why the air defences had killed 269 people, why they could not tell a Boeing 747 from a spy plane, and whether Mr Andropov had known about it beforehand. Asked whether there was not a moral aspect as well as a military one, Marshal Ogarkov said he could not see the point of the question. "It was a spy plane," he insisted, his voice rising. "This was a planned, deliberate act."

The hall, normally thinly attended for lower-level press conferences on the role of work collectives in the socialist economy, was packed to overflowing, with a giant television screen relaying the proceedings outside. The last big Soviet news conference was in April, when Mr Andrei Gromyko, the Foreign Minister, appeared. It was his first press conference for four years.

Moscow
10 September 1983

Privacy that only death lays bare

MR KONSTANTIN CHERNENKO has a wife, according to those who claim to know about these things in the Party. He also has a daughter (and a son-in-law). He probably has a son as well, although nobody can say what he does for a living. The private lives of Soviet politicians are a closed book to all but a very few intimates, and Mr Chernenko is no exception. The Brezhnev family eventually came to the fore, partly because Brezhnev's son, Yuri, was (and indeed still is) a senior trade official, and partly because the extravagant ways of the President's daughter, Galina, became hard to keep secret.

Galina Brezhnev, according to normally reliable Moscow gossip, was involved with numerous figures from the Moscow underworld, the most colourful being a character called Boris the Gypsy, who allegedly hanged himself when the KGB closed in on his nefarious activities (smuggling and illegal financial dealings). Some say the seamier side of Brezhnev family life (not a whisper of which touched the President himself) would not have become public knowledge if Yuri Andropov, first as KGB chief and then as a contender for the leadership, had not used his anti-corruption campaign in 1982 to undermine Brezhnev's relatives and associates. Galina Brezhnev was, after all, married to a deputy interior minister, Lieutenant-General Yuri Churbanov (subsequently exiled to Murmansk). The scandals even extended (so they say) to General Semyon Tsvigun, Andropov's deputy in the KGB but also, by chance, Brezhnev's brother-in-law. General Tsvigun died early in 1982, apparently by his own hand.

So far, however, nothing has emerged about Mr Chernenko's relatives — certainly no whiff of scandal. Perhaps Andropov set the style as leader by ensuring that his own family stayed well in the background. Even his son, Igor, a prominent diplomat, said almost nothing about his father at East-West gatherings in Madrid or Stockholm.

Andropov's wife, Tatyana Fillipovna, appeared for his funeral. Before then highly placed sources had said either that she was dead or that the Andropovs were separated (her evident grief made this unlikely). It is thought that Tatyana Fillipovna was the second Mrs Andropov.

It remains a curious fact of Soviet politics that the leader's life is laid bare only after his death. Pictures of Yuri Andropov as a student in the Volga region were released when he died, but not before. Even as he lay dying officials kept up a barrage of disinformation to show that he was merely indisposed with a cold and would return shortly. In the meantime, the Kremlin said, he was fully in charge of affairs of state.

The day after Andropov died Tass issued an astonishingly detailed medical bulletin, as it always does when a leader dies. It listed his ailments, *inter alia*, as "interstitial nephritis, nephrosclerosis, secondary hypertension and diabetes complicated by chronic kidney deficiency", not to mention "cardiovascular" problems.

In other words the President was a diabetic with deteriorating heart and kidneys, which is precisely what Western correspondents reported (from unofficial sources) from last autumn onwards. At the time, however — indeed right up to 10 February, the day his death was announced — all inquiries were greeted not only with evasion but with resentment that the West should be in the least interested in the health of the leader of a superpower.

During Andropov's funeral, Dr David Owen, the Social Democrats' leader, identified one of Mr Chernenko's ailments as emphysema, which is now part of the Moscow lexicon. It involves breathing difficulties and fibrosis of the lungs, and ultimately heart problems.

Moscow
20 February 1984

The freedom of no choice

"WHAT CAN BOURGEOIS society counterpose to the fundamental values of Soviet Communism?" the Central Committee asked recently in an appeal to Soviet voters before tomorrow's Supreme Soviet elections. "Freedom of speech and well-stocked shops for one thing" might be the honest response of many a Soviet citizen. The right answer, however — supplied by the Central Committee itself — is: "national and social oppression, economic crisis and chronic unemployment, despair and moral degradation". The Communist Party, by contrast, offers "developed democracy" along with "developed socialism", which is to say equality, the right to work, low-cost housing, education and health care, and other "social, political and individual rights".

It is a curious phenomenon of Soviet politics that, although voters are not in fact invited to choose between Communism and capitalism (or anything else) in periodic elections, the Kremlin feels obliged to demonstrate that it has brought Russia incalculable benefits and deserves re-election. Elections to the 1500-seat Supreme Soviet are held every five years, and the campaign ends with a nationwide vote (always on a Sunday).

To a Western eye the election campaign is something of a parody, an eerie shadow play in which the ruling party's opponents are invisible and insubstantial. Since the Bolshevik revolution — or more accurately since 1921, when Lenin decided the time had come to "put the lid on opposition" — the Communist Party has held all seats in the Soviets, Russia's national and local government bodies. Although some "non-Party" candidates are put forward as a faint reminder of the first, multi-party Soviets, Party members are nominated in the vast majority of constituencies.

The late President Andropov was to have stood as a candidate in Moscow's Proletarsky district, and televised election meetings (with the candidate himself absent) were used to give the impression Mr Andropov was still active rather than on his deathbed. Mr Chernenko, his successor, is the candidate for another Moscow district.

Apart from providing an occasion for Kremlin leaders to make speeches across the land, the elections give citizens a limited opportunity to let off steam. Meetings at local Party offices (normally only manned by old-age pensioners with a pile of unread leaflets) can be quite lively, with voters reminding candidates of local grievances. Some are even put right before polling day.

On the other hand few voters risk voting "no" if their candidate is judged and found wanting. In a Soviet polling booth the voter does not mark the ballot paper but simply folds it in half and deposits it in the box provided. Voting "no" involves crossing the hall to a separate booth with curtains, writing on the paper or crossing out the single name on it, and placing the defaced ballot conspicuously in a different box. Not an act calculated to improve one's career prospects.

From the Kremlin's point of view, elections remain a useful device on several counts. When the new Supreme Soviet convenes, ministerial changes can be made in a government reshuffle. Above all, elections offer an opportunity to remind Soviet citizens that they are better off than they would be under the alternative they cannot choose. "We made our choice in 1917," a Soviet friend said recently when I observed that Russians had not been democratically consulted since the constituent assembly of 1918, in which the Bolsheviks were a minority. "There is no need to confirm that choice." Or, as Professor Konstantin Gutsenko, a legal expert, puts it, "A choice of candidates is only meaningful where they represent different platforms. In the Soviet Union one political party expresses the interests of the whole people."

If officials feel any qualms about the fact that the people have never been asked, they are careful not to show them.

Moscow
3 March 1984

Rumours run rife in Kremlin's vacuum

THE RUMOUR SURFACED barely an hour after President Chernenko had made the opening address at the Comecon summit on Tuesday of last week. Halfway through his speech the whisper went, the seventy-two-year-old leader had collapsed and had to be taken out of the room. It was totally untrue, and Moscow television later that evening showed Mr Chernenko looking his usual self as he walked into the conference room at the Kremlin, stiff and slow but still ruddy-faced and smiling. The rumour, it later turned out, had started with a frivolous remark by a West European journalist. Within minutes the remark had been spread, distorted, and ultimately taken so seriously that correspondents and diplomats were telephoning contacts to investigate what had really happened at the summit. Eventually the rumour reached the West, and news agencies in Moscow found themselves being asked by their editors in London and New York to "check it out".

Rumours are rife in Moscow largely because of the information vacuum created by the Kremlin. The Western tactic is to fend off inquisitive newsmen with briefings, communiqués and titbits of information, coupled at the recent London summit with quantities of food and drink.

In Moscow, by contrast, the Western press was given almost no information at all about the Comecon summit, and there were certainly no refreshments. Officials answered questions on the Tuesday, but most of the answers consisted of the phrase: "You will be informed at the appropriate time." No speeches were released until Thursday.

In recent years the authorities have adopted a more sophisticated information policy, holding press conferences on subjects from Soviet Jews to nuclear missiles. Questions are now taken from the floor, an innovation initially resisted by officials more used to written questions channelled safely through a chairman. On the other hand, information remains hard to come by on matters the Kremlin considers "sensitive", which covers subjects such as internal Kremlin debates on policy or the health of Soviet leaders. Senior officials, including Mr Leonid Zamyatin, who heads the Central Committee International Information Department, insisted right up to the day of President Andropov's death that he merely had a cold and was recovering. Similarly Mr Zamyatin and others have assured Western reporters that Dr Sakharov, the dissident physicist and human rights activist, is alive and well, or at least "all right", after his hunger strike. But they refuse to say where he is or to provide proof.

The Soviet attitude to information was defined by Lenin, who regarded the press as an instrument of state policy and propaganda. To some extent the exposure of Soviet officialdom to Western questioning has made the Kremlin more responsive to foreign press methods, with veterans such as Mr Andrei Gromyko, the Foreign Minister, and the Chief of Staff, Marshal Ogarkov, well able to deal with awkward questions. But the authorities still tend to take the view: "Those who need to know already know, and those who do not know have no business asking."

Not surprisingly rumours proliferate to fill the gap, and sometimes linger to take on the status of semi-fact even when disproved. Dr Sakharov has been reported dead, first by Italian sources and then by a London paper. Last year there were rumours of a military coup in the Kremlin when Mr Andropov failed to appear in public and Marshal Ustinov, the Defence Minister, cut short a visit to Hungary and hurried back to Moscow. Not long afterwards there was a powerful rumour, which still occasionally surfaces here, that Mr Andropov was shot in his Kremlin study, either by an unknown woman assailant or by Mrs Scholokhov, wife of the disgraced Interior Minister. The rumour gained credibility when *Izvestiya* published an article on the attempt on Lenin's life by a woman terrorist in 1918, and took off into the stratosphere when a British paper reported — from London, not Moscow — that Andropov had been shot not by an angry lady, but by Yuri Brezhnev, son of the former leader.

Western correspondents in Moscow, trying to sift the probable from the improbable and the improbable from the absurd, are not given much help by the Kremlin in countering the rumour mill.

Moscow
20 June 1984

Afghanistan: Russians at last learn the facts

A CRUEL JOKE about the war in Afghanistan is going the rounds in Moscow as the fighting drags on into its sixth year. The situation is so tough, the story goes, that when Russian recruits get on the troop train for Kabul they are offered a bottle of vodka for every Afghan rebel they kill. One young soldier suddenly lets off a rifle volley through the window, jumps on to the platform and comes back triumphant to demand three bottles. "You idiot," an officer snarls. "We're still in Tashkent."

The story underlines the very real problem posed by the Soviet Union's Muslim populations. To many European Russian soldiers, Soviet Muslims are indistinguishable from the rebels they are fighting in Afghanistan, in looks and background if not in political loyalty. It also illustrates the sense of permanency that has set in over the Afghan war, which is seen by many Russians in the context of the centuries-long struggle to subdue Muslim populations in Central Asia and the Caucasus. The word *dushmani* (enemy) used to describe the Afghan rebels recalls the Muslim mountain fighters of earlier times, as does the word *basmatchi*. Few Russians refer to "rebels" or *mujahidin*.

Afghanistan is not a Soviet Vietnam. The Russians can sustain the "limited" military operation for as long as necessary and have no intention of withdrawing until they choose to. The Soviet commitment is in reality not so limited: the 100,000 troops who went in in 1979 have risen to 120,000, according to Western estimates, and some put the figure as high as 150,000. Five years on, as recent Soviet press accounts admit, the *dushmani* hold large chunks of territory and have made many roads and passes virtually unusable by the Russians.

But Moscow argues that the rebels can maintain this degree of military effectiveness only thanks to support and supplies from the United States, Pakistan, Saudi Arabia and other countries. Soviet spokesmen stonily turn aside demands for a withdrawal — backed five times by the UN General Assembly — with the observation that Pakistan, the West and the Islamic nations are "interfering" in Afghanistan, and Russia's armour, helicopter gunships and men will leave only when the interference stops.

What emerges in the pages of *Pravda* and *Red Star* is that the Russians are learning to live with mountain warfare. One day the tide will turn in their favour — at least that is what the Kremlin wants Russians to believe. There is no protest movement in the Soviet Union, but about 10,000 troops are estimated to have died in the five-year war, and the coffins come back for families to grieve over.

The press — which in the early stages kept silent, presumably in the hope that the operation would be quick and clean — has recently stressed Soviet heroism, with hair-raising accounts of the determined (and, according to the rebels, brutal) Soviet campaign in the Panjshir Valley last spring.

Pravda gave a graphic description of a drive to Kabul through the Salang Pass, with burnt-out lorries lining the road. *Red Star* offered readers a day in the life of a helicopter gunship pilot, evacuating Afghan government troops from a desperate battle, landing blind in dust clouds and strafing unseen rebels. The general impression given is that the Afghan government soldiers are fairly useless but are having their backbone stiffened by Soviet resolve. The Russians meanwhile, according to *Red Star*, are improving their tactics, learning to manoeuvre in anti-aircraft fire, to avoid ambushes and to make joint sorties using helicopters and fighter-bombers.

In all of this the rebels are portrayed as ruthless cut-throats backed by the shadowy "imperialists". Nowhere is there any suggestion that the Russians themselves have been guilty of atrocities, or that many young recruits are ill-prepared, panic-stricken and live in primitive conditions.

Many Russians accept the official line of a limited commitment. Others, reading between the lines, cannot fail to be affected, for example, by a first-hand account in *Pravda* recently headed "A night in an armoured car". Here were descriptions of drawn-out battles — "many killed or wounded" — fought painfully over flooded fields and vineyards or around Afghan houses turned into impregnable fortresses by the rebels. "One involuntarily asks, can the positions of the counter-revolution really be this strong," the *Pravda* reporter wrote aghast.

The Russians are apparently prepared to go on bearing the brunt of the fighting until next Christmas and beyond. In the meantime, Soviet sources say, they will seek a political settlement through the UN, but without giving the timetable for withdrawal that UN negotiators want. The problem for Soviet strategists is whether to increase troop levels to 200,000 and beyond in a final bid to crush the *dushmani*. If they did so, even the most credulous Russians might begin to wonder whether the nation's "heroic fulfilment of its internationalist duty" was worth the price.

Moscow
19 December 1984

One-horse races Soviet style

Mr Mikhail Gorbachov, President Chernenko's number two and the Kremlin's young rising star, has been put forward as a candidate in our district for the forthcoming local elections. More exactly, Mr Gorbachov is the only candidate. Foreigners, alas, do not have the right to vote for either the national or the local (republic) soviets. But even if they did, it is most unlikely that the personable figure of Mr Gorbachov or one of his election committee would appear on our doorstep with a sheaf of Communist Party leaflets to canvass our support. The Communist Party candidate has no opposition: Mr Gorbachov is a shooin.

The main focus of interest is whether President Chernenko will be well enough to appear at the polling booth after an absence of a month and a half, or for that matter to make a speech as a candidate. Mr Chernenko, aged seventy-three, is standing in the Kuibyshev district of Moscow, which he nominally represents in the national soviet — the Supreme Soviet — as well.

The soviets are organs of local and national government (the word simply means "council"), and have their origins in the democratic bodies spontaneously thrown up by the 1905 and 1917 revolutions, when workers, peasants and soldiers elected their deputies in a direct vote in the barracks or on the factory floor, and had the right to recall them if necessary. But those days are a distant memory, and since the Bolshevik takeover in October 1917, the soviets have been the instrument of the Communist Party, with all opposition suppressed.

Soviet elections can sometimes throw light on local problems, with "constituents" using formal election meetings to air grievances. But for most observers the political significance of the election process lies in the way candidates are nominated, which in turn provides clues to the standing of various Politburo members. Elections, in other words, become a branch of Kremlinology.

The current pattern is for Mr Chernenko to receive most attention, followed (in accordance with protocol) by Nikolai Tikhonov, the Prime Minister. All Politburo members stand in one district or another, and are nominated at televised meetings held in factories and offices. Factory hands and office workers stand in massed ranks holding large portraits of the candidate on the end of poles while a Party official makes a speech in praise of the candidate, invariably beginning: "Our state and Party know comrade X as a true Communist and faithful servant of the Party and state". The workers listen in polite silence, applaud at intervals, and vote unanimously in favour. Significantly, Mr Gorbachov, aged fifty-three, was the third Politburo member to be featured at election meetings on television, confirming his position as the heir apparent.

Russians do not find it strange that they are not given a choice in elections — or at least if they do have reservations they keep them to themselves. The only way you can vote "No" is by crossing out the name of the candidate, and because to do this you have to cross the floor of the polling station to a special booth, in full public view, not many take this bold step.

Officially the practice of one-candidate elections is a Soviet tradition rather than law, and is defended on the grounds that a contest between several candidates is only meaningful when they represent different parties and platforms. Since in Russia there is only one party, which "expresses the interests of the whole people", only one candidate is required. Simple.

The fact that the people have never had the opportunity to vote freely and thus put to the test the Party's claim to speak for them is never mentioned. Ironically, if a free election were held in the Kiev district this month there is a good chance that the personable Mr Gorbachov would still be elected — but the Kremlin is most unlikely to put that to the test either.

Moscow
9 February 1985

Annual ritual at the Hall of Columns

THE ROUTINE OF the lying in state at the Hall of Columns and the funeral on Red Square has become so familiar that it seems like an annual ritual. There was no real sense of the opening of a new era as there was when Andropov finally succeeded Brezhnev two-and-a-half years ago. The atmosphere of the changeover from

Chernenko to Gorbachov was more like that of the transition from Andropov to Chernenko just over a year ago. As on previous occasions, the centre of the city was completely sealed off yesterday and we had to thread our way through cordons of police and KGB troops to reach the late-eighteenth-century Hall of Columns, which stands on the corner of Karl Marx Prospekt, dwarfed by the giant bulk of the Stalinist Hotel Moskva and Gosplan, the state planning committee. Once again, as if in some recurrent dream (or nightmare), a long queue of hand-picked factory and office workers bussed in for the event shuffled slowly through freęzing rain under leaden skies towards the classical green and white portico.

But security measures seemed fairly relaxed. Although there was a heavy police presence, they were not patrolling vigilantly in a big show of force or lining up citizens in side streets for document checks, as I saw happening after the death of Brezhnev in 1982. Instead, there was relief that the era of gerontocracy was coming to an end, and a young and healthy man was finally at the helm.

"At least we won't have to go through this for another twenty years," murmured one Western reporter as he puffed up the elegant staircase of the former Moscow Noblemen's Club beneath huge chandeliers draped with black crêpe towards the old ballroom where Konstantin Chernenko lay in state on a flower-covered bier, his medals at his feet. He looked in death much as he had in life, his Siberian features framed beneath the familiar shock of snow-white hair. As a full orchestra played mournful music his widow, Anna Dmitrievna, sat with their daughter and other relatives to one side. With the overpowering odour of flowers and wreaths, the hothouse atmosphere of the overheated hall and presence of the military officers keeping vigil, there was a distinct sense of *déjà vu*. "The generation that made its careers under Stalin is passing away," one observer said.

President Chernenko was not by any means the last representative of the old guard. Nikolai Tikhonov is aged seventy-nine, Andrei Gromyko, the Foreign Minister, is aged seventy-five, even Vyacheslav Molotov, Stalin's Foreign Minister, is alive and well at ninety, and was recently rehabilitated.

But the death of Chernenko seemed somehow symbolic of the change of generations, and even if there was no palpable drama, the almost indecent speed and ruthless efficiency with which Mr

Mikhail Gorbachov was installed as the new General Secretary showed that the younger generation's time had come. Gorbachov and others like him grew up in a different world where education and rising living standards and expectations were taken for granted. Their formative years were the years of the Sputnik, Khrushchev and Kennedy and the beginnings of détente. Few Russians, however, as they gazed at the portrait of Gorbachov on the front page of *Pravda* were deceived into thinking that the new leader was anything other than a Party *apparatchik* in the traditional mould, whose reformist ideas are strictly limited by the Marxist-Leninist framework he has inherited.

In his speech of acceptance, Mr Gorbachov hoped the fortieth anniversary of "the great victory over Hitler fascism" in May would be an occasion for the former wartime allies of East and West to establish good relations. Few would argue with that. But younger Russians, at least, are hoping that he will begin his administration with an eye on the future rather than the past.

Moscow
13 March 1985

BUREAUCRATS AND INTELLECTUALS

Mastermind fights a paper flood

ACADEMICIAN RUMYANTSEV, AN illustrious member of the Soviet Academy of Sciences, knows all about bureaucracy. He says he is "drowning in paper". The academician is an economist and in Russia economists and bureaucrats are mortal enemies. Usually they fight it out by sending one another endless memoranda, which of course only add to the pile of what Mr Rumyantsev calls "useless paper". He has an office on the top floor of the Institute of World Economy and International Relations, which perhaps enables him to see beyond the paperwork bedevilling every Soviet citizen's life (and foreigner's too).

The hero of much nineteenth-century Russian literature was the clerk, the *chinovnik*, a small but vital human being, who seemed to inhibit a Kafkaesque bureaucracy of endless corridors and numberless officials busy with bits of paper — writing on them, signing them, stamping them, sending them. The archetypal *chinovik* was Gogol's Akaky Akakiyevich, in his novella *The Overcoat*. But Akaky Akakiyevich is not dead, he simply got transferred from St Petersburg to Moscow.

The Soviet Union, like the Russian empire which preceded it, still operates according to elaborate procedures which have to be followed to the letter, literally. The simplest request — a travel document, an interview, a requisition for paper-clips — has to be made in writing, on headed paper with an office stamp (the larger the better) over the signature. The letter is then delivered by hand. The officials themselves are often personally charming, but the procedure can make life cumbersome.

The serious side of this obsession with paper is that it makes effective economic planning much more difficult. There has been a debate in the Soviet press on economic reforms, and Academician Rumyantsev has made a contribution by pointing out in the trade union newspaper *Trud* that creating mountains of pointless documents makes administration harder.

He estimates that local managers and administrators spend up to a third of their time passing round bits of paper 90 per cent of which are useless. Another third is spent in unnecessary meetings. It has been estimated that the bureaucracy produces 800 billion documents a year, and most of them have to be discussed.

No less important, Academician Rumyantsev writes, factories and offices are hampered by the number of commissions that come to inspect them. In one case, a machine-tool factory was inspected 145 times in a single year, representing 615 working days for the inspectors.

Echoing the view of Mr Yuri Andropov, the Soviet leader, on the virtues of hard work, Academician Rumyantsev said people would do better to get behind factory benches and produce goods rather than watch other people doing so. He quoted an early Bolshevik Minister of Trade who had complained: "We shout about the evils of bureaucratization but ignore the proliferation of offices and their employees."

The flow of paper may lessen, especially if Mr Andropov's economic mastermind at the Central Committee, Mr Nikolai Ryzhkov, succeeds in streamlining the economic bureaucracy. There are already signs of improvement: it has become *de rigueur* for some offices to ask for requests and notifications by telex rather than by letter. If the day ever arrives when Russian offices are equipped with visual display units and all the other paraphernalia of the electronic age, the reformers may have a chance against the *chinovniks*. On the other hand, it is a fair bet that the man who hires out rowing boats on the Moscow river on sunny weekends will still demand to see your documents and write out the receipt painstakingly in pencil, in triplicate.

Moscow
10 June 1983

Post haste in Tolstoy's day

RUSSIANS, LIKE EVERYONE else, constantly complain that things are not what they used to be. The fact is that whether under Stalin or under the Tsars, things were on the whole a great deal worse and the official view that things are getting better all the time is not unfounded, given the abysmal starting point. None the less, Russians still talk as if there was a golden age in which eggs tasted of eggs and ice-cream of ice-cream, the trains ran on time and letters arrived the day after you posted them.

The newspaper *Literaturnaya Gazeta* has just proved them right, at least on the last point. It has published the results of a survey on postal deliveries which prove beyond all shadow of doubt that the service has markedly deteriorated since the time of Tolstoy, at the turn of the century. The much-maligned Tsarist system, it appears, managed regularly to get a letter from Moscow to St Petersburg (now Leningrad) in two days. Tolstoy used to write to the Petersburg public library from his Moscow home and in 1900 could count on a swift delivery and response.

Literaturnaya Gazeta conducted an experiment which showed that a similar letter sent today takes at least four days to get to Leningrad. Ah, the Leningrad post office said when confronted with this discrepancy, but Tolstoy was a famous writer, and a count to boot. He must have used special channels. Not so, the paper said, and numerous readers wrote in to say that their family archives proved that the Tsarist postal system had been just as efficient in the case of ordinary citizens.

The paper published a list of deadlines issued by the Soviet Ministry of Communications and said that most of them were not met. Letters posted to another address in the same town or city are supposed to reach the addressee the following morning, but rarely do. Letters between towns in European Russian should take three days to reach their destination, but the paper said even this generous provision was not observed. Almost all letters were delayed, the report said, in some cases for a week or more. The Soviet post office did not on the whole lose letters, and that mail was conscientiously and cheerfully delivered, eventually. When it wrote to the head of the postal service at the Ministry of Communications to ask for an explanation of the delays, however, it received no reply.

It turned out that the letter had been lost in the post. Either that, the paper commented, or the official concerned prefers not to talk about it publicly and finds it easier to blame his own deteriorating service for "mislaying" an unwelcome piece of mail.

Moscow
4 April 1983

New delights of press briefings

"We are getting a little worried about these briefings for the bourgeois press," the Soviet official confided. "If these distortions go on, we might have to stop the briefings altogether." Kremlin briefings are something new in Moscow, and the Russians are still discovering the pitfalls. In the West the relationship between the press and those in power is a complex one. The Soviet regime is used to a much simpler relationship: the press prints Kremlin speeches in full, and fervently supports whatever the current line happens to be. The Soviet authorities are none the less gradually coming to terms with the fact that Western newspapers and television are not — like their Soviet counterparts — official mouthpieces, and have to be dealt with more subtly if the Kremlin is to get its message across to world opinion in a credible and convincing way. One sign of this was President Chernenko's interview with the Moscow correspondent of the *Washington Post* — the first time any recent Soviet leader had spoken directly at length to a locally based reporter.

The Politburo began during the Andropov era to issue an account of its regular weekly meetings, a practice which Mr Chernenko has continued. This is a far cry from the days when leaders such as Khrushchev used to mingle with reporters at receptions, and the official Politburo accounts tend to be anodyne, with key decisions hidden under "other matters of foreign and domestic policy". But they do throw some light on who spoke, and about what.

Above all, the new Soviet practice of holding regular briefings has raised hopes of a more sophisticated Kremlin attitude towards information policy. The Russians began to hold large-scale set-piece press conferences about two years ago, and virtuoso performances by Mr Andrei Gromyko, the Foreign Minister, and Marshal Ogarkov, the then Chief of Staff, are still remembered. At first only written questions were accepted, but Soviet officials have now gained enough confidence to deal with questions from the floor. In the latest development, press conferences have given way to more intimate briefings (the same word is used in Russian) given by Mr Vladimir Lomeiko, whose long, thin face and dry, professorial manner have suddenly become the Kremlin's public persona. Since he began to hold briefings, Mr Lomeiko has been promoted to head the Foreign Ministry Press Department, a promotion which reflects his deft and sometimes humorous handling of the Western media, as well as his personal links with Mr Gromyko (Mr Lomeiko has written a book on foreign affairs with Mr Gromyko's son, Anatoly).

The Gromyko circle and the Foreign Ministry appear to be in the ascendant over the party's international information department, headed by Mr Leonid Zamyatin, who always used to dominate the Kremlin press conferences but is now rarely seen.

The briefings reflect new Soviet thinking on how best to counteract Nato and American statements and actions. The Russians have realized that a briefing by Mr Lomeiko is likely to get them more media coverage than a bald announcement by Tass. On the other hand, the Russians acknowledge they are still novices when it comes to public relations. Mr Lomeiko now insists on conducting his briefings in Russian only, with translation into English given reluctantly, if at all, on the grounds that Russian is "an international language". When asked recently whether this might not give rise to misunderstandings on East-West issues, Mr Lomeiko responded testily: "Even when we did provide a translation, the Western press distorted what I said." The recent press conference by Stalin's daughter, Svetlana, after her dramatic return to Moscow appeared to be a reversion to old-style Kremlin news management, with only a handful of reporters admitted and almost no questioning allowed.

It remains to be seen whether this heralds a return to the previous practice of excluding the Western media from the Kremlin corridors of power wherever possible, or whether the attempt to reach a *modus vivendi* with "the bourgeois press" will continue.

Moscow
11 December 1984

Orwell recruited to the Soviet cause

THE START OF 1984 highlighted a Soviet practice even Orwell did not think of — the use for propaganda purposes of a book which officially does not exist. Russians are not allowed to read *1984* —

it has never been published in the Soviet Union, and foreign editions are confiscated by Customs — yet the Soviet press is now discussing the book in an attempt to turn the tables on the West. To most Westerners it seems fairly obvious that *1984* is at least partly based on the Soviet Union. It is true that *1984* is 1948 inverted, and that Orwell's nightmare vision to some extent reflects the darker side of wartime Britain. It is also true that his warning applies to today's Western world, with computer memory banks and lie detectors. But it was Stalin's Russia, where the secret police ruled through fear and citizens recited official slogans they knew to be nonsense, which provided the force and imagery of *1984*. The book draws heavily, as Orwell acknowledged, on the work of the Russian writer Yevgeny Zamyatin, whose futurist fantasy, *We*, was published in the 1920s. Goldstein, Orwell's Enemy Number One, who provides Big Brother with the excuse for rigid internal discipline, is unmistakably Trotsky, whose real name was Bronstein. Regimented rallies, sexual repression, Newspeak and monolithic conformity are all instantly recognizable to those few Russians who manage to get hold of the book.

Hints that the Soviet authorities were planning to meet the dilemma posed by *1984* head on came last year, when *Literary Gazette* published an article suggesting the novel was really applicable to the West. Discussion of banned books poses problems for Soviet newspapers and journals: for one thing the writer has to give readers some idea of the content, which in turn carries the risk that the reader might draw his own conclusions. It is also possible that readers, instead of simply swallowing the propaganda line wholesale, will become fascinated by the vicarious taste of forbidden fruit.

The latest publication to take the bull by the horns is *Novoye Vremya* (New Times), which in its most recent issue told readers that Orwell's "sensational" novel was really a prediction of a militaristic Western world ruled by a megalomaniac, called Ronald Reagan. "For B.B. (Big Brother) read R.R. (Ronald Reagan)", the weekly suggests.

"Politologists" and "Orwellologists" have been poring over globes ever since *1984* was published, the journal adds, and have been "jabbing fingers at our country, asking: is the great chiromancist's prediction being fulfilled in Russia or not?" But readers of *1984* have been "jabbing at the wrong spot" all this time. Orwell, it seems, saw through the "falsehoods of bourgeois democracy", and anti-Communists have been vainly trying for years to "fit the tight suit of totalitarianism cut by Orwell on to the body of real socialism, when in fact it is exactly the right size for capitalism". Poor Orwell apparently only had "the vaguest notion" of Communism (so much for *Animal Farm* and four volumes of collected journalism), and therefore failed to become a convinced adherent of the Soviet system, *Novoye Vremya* said. But he rightly saw that capitalism "vaporized the individual", extinguishes thought, demands continuous war and suppresses knowledge of other philosophies. "Big Brother had a super-aim: to hold back the march of history," it commented. "Reagan has a grander aim: to stop history altogether by pressing a button."

The Soviet interpretation has spread to Eastern Europe, where an East German professor last week said that despite his "petty-bourgeois limitations" Orwell had correctly diagnosed the ills of imperialism.

In the Soviet bloc at least it looks as if discussion of *1984* will last beyond this year, even at the risk that Soviet-bloc citizens might recognize a system in which individuals are routinely humiliated by officialdom, love for the national leader is obligatory, indigestible jargon is endlessly repeated and heretical ideas are ruthlessly suppressed.

Moscow
11 January 1984

Door closes on the last dissident

WHENEVER ROY MEDVEDEV leaves his Moscow flat these days he has to negotiate his way past three hefty policemen sitting bottom to bottom on the cold stone staircase outside his door. He greets them affably, and they usually reply in kind. There is no need to follow him down the stairs, since his every movement is watched from a special observation post in the block of flats opposite. Medvedev is even aware of how the KGB describe him as he leaves the building, since he and his family can pick up the police radio transmissions. "The subject is wearing blue trousers and carrying a briefcase and a plastic bag," the disembodied voice says before Medvedev climbs into a car or heads for the bus and Metro, shadowed by his faithful minders.

Until February this year, Medvedev was almost certainly the most visited Soviet dissident in Moscow. A self-professed Marxist historian of calm, sober and well-informed views, he was able to offer valuable insights into the workings of the Soviet system, using his detailed knowledge of Party history to evaluate what is now going on in the Politburo, and what might happen next. Sceptics said he was protected by Yuri Andropov and was fed disinformation by the KGB who knew perfectly well that he was regarded as an oracle by many foreigners desperate for information in a system of paranoid secrecy. Journalists and senior diplomats still beat a path to his door, making the journey out to the distant suburb on the Leningrad highway, to take Medvedev to a restaurant — observed from the next table — or to one of the foreigners' compounds, which are guarded by police.

Thanks to telephone bugging and surveillance, the KGB is perfectly aware of whom he sees, where he goes and what he says. The object of the KGB exercise, it seems, is to prevent visitors seeing Medvedev in his flat, not to prevent him from leaving it. That, after all, would be house arrest, which would arouse an international outcry.

The Kremlin has used similar tactics against Elena Bonner, the wife of the dissident physicist Dr Andrei Sakharov, who is cut off from foreign correspondents by police whenever she visits Moscow from their place of exile in Gorky, several hundred miles away. The authorities have evidently decided they can afford to risk appearing repressive, or simply silly, in the eyes of world opinion by restricting visitors to the few remaining senior dissidents.

Medvedev lives in a tall, uninspiring block of flats in a nondescript housing estate on the outskirts of Moscow, rather than in one of the older, more elegant blocks in the city centre where officially approved intellectuals can expect to be housed (and indeed where even Dr Sakharov still has a flat, thanks to his status as an academician, although he cannot use it). Some of the greatly diminished band of Moscow dissidents regard Medvedev with suspicion, and in the past have suggested that he works directly or indirectly for the KGB. But like most enclosed worlds, Moscow dissident circles are notorious for their bitchiness, and Medvedev certainly enjoys none of the privileges that a Kremlin stooge might expect.

Now nearly sixty, Roy Alexandrovich is the twin brother of Zhores Medvedev, the dissident scientist who lives in London and works at the National Institute for Medical Research at Mill Hill. The brothers work closely together even when separated, and Roy has either contributed to, or jointly written, their books on Khrushchev, Andropov and Soviet science.

But Roy enjoys a reputation in his own right as the author of several well-balanced, perceptive and well-researched books on Soviet history, including his monumental study of Stalinism *Let History Judge* and other seminal works such as *On Socialist Democracy* and *An End to Silence*. He writes them in a cramped study in his tower block, a room with barely enough space for his typewriter, the glass-fronted bookcases containing his own works, and a couch for visitors.

He has lived by publication abroad since he was sacked from his job as senior researcher and head of department at the Soviet Academy of Pedagogical Sciences in the early 1970s. He has been harassed, persecuted and warned, but not — so far — arrested, tried or exiled — the fate most of his fellow dissidents suffered in the late 1970s, when Andropov, then head of the KGB, launched his remarkably successful campaign to neutralize and disperse the dissident movement.

Roy Medvedev is the sole surviving member of the band of leading dissidents that dominated the Moscow scene in the late 1960s and '70s. He wryly recalls that when President Nixon came to Moscow the KGB sealed off the homes of Alexander Solzhenitsyn, Dr Andrei Sakharov and Roy Medvedev, in case of unspecified trouble. "Solzhenitsyn is in Vermont, Sakharov is in Gorky, and most of the others are in prison or are silent. There is only me," Medvedev says.

His troubles really started in January 1983, when Andropov — supposedly his protector — was still alive. Out of the blue Medvedev received a summons to the Moscow prosecutor's office, where, in the presence of KGB officers, he was warned to stop publishing "anti-Soviet" articles and books abroad. He asked his interrogators to specify anything he had written or said which could be construed as anti-Soviet. When they failed to do so he said he would carry on writing and researching as before.

(His most recent publication in Britain was a biography of Nikita Khrushchev, who is now a non-person in the Soviet Union, but whose fascinating career Medvedev has done more to illuminate than any other Russian scholar, either inside or outside the Soviet Union.) The prosecutor also warned him to stop seeing foreign diplomats and journalists since some of them were "dubious characters and spies". Medvedev replied that he would receive anyone who asked to see him, and that it was the job of the authorities, not his, to decide who should be allowed into Russia and who should be kept out because of "dubious" activities.

The warning was something of a puzzle, since it was not followed up at the time by any further action. Possibly the authorities wanted to gauge Western reaction to a deliberate act of harassment against a man who enjoys a high reputation in the West, not least in left-wing circles. Many of his articles appear in Western socialist publications.

Barely a week after Andropov had died and Chernenko succeeded him as Party leader, the police suddenly materialized on Medvedev's doorstep.

There was no warning, no official announcement, and no explanation of why this action had been taken, or how long it was likely to last. At first, his uninvited guests were plain-clothes agents from the KGB, but fairly soon — possibly when the KGB became bored with their rather fruitless vigil — they were replaced by ordinary policemen, few of whom had the faintest idea who it was they were guarding. "They knew I was a writer," Medvedev says with a gentle smile, "but that was about all. After a while some of them started asking my neighbours about me, and one of the policemen somehow got the idea that I was a writer of detective fiction. In fact, he asked me if I could lend him a detective novel to read while he was sitting on my staircase doing night duty. I lent him one from my collection, and he returned it politely the next day without a word. He has not asked again."

Medvedev's neighbours are on the whole bewildered by the latest turn of events and are not sure what to make of it. They have of course always been aware that there were "strange goings-on" in the writer's flat at the top of the building, but some were not sure why a man who sat typing all day should have a constant stream of visitors in expensive foreign cars. The appearance of the police guards and the KGB observation post have increased the neighbourhood's bewilderment. Is Medvedev perhaps a dangerous criminal? Possibly: but on the other hand he seems to be able to come and go at will, so perhaps he is in fact a most important person who has been granted government protection. On the whole, Medvedev says, the neighbours keep their distance, but are friendly and even sympathetic.

Perhaps the most irritating aspect of the situation to Medvedev is that the policemen on the stairs block the way not only to foreigners but also to the pool of young Russian translators and research assistants on whom he relies for his work. Technically, of course, preventing one Soviet citizen from visiting another is an offence even under Soviet law, and both Medvedev and his assistants could lodge a complaint. But that, he thinks, is precisely what the authorities want. Once he starts complaining he can be publicly branded as a "troublemaker". He prefers to carry on working as best he can, in the hope that the police — or whoever put them there — will eventually tire of their pointless assignment. "It really is rather absurd, don't you think?" he says quietly, looking across the table for confirmation. "Three grown men sitting reading detective novels outside my flat while I work inside from 8 am to 11 pm. I really think they ought to do something useful as well."

There are lighter moments, or at least incidents which amuse Medvedev himself. At one point, walking down a Moscow street, he stopped short, turned on his heel and confronted the agent he knew was following him. "Look," he said, "I am rather tired and I've had enough of this. Why don't we go home?" "I am at home," the man mumbled, and walked away pretending he had nothing to do with Medvedev at all.

But, despite his gentle irony, self-deprecation and defiant optimism, the strain of being Russia's only surviving important dissident is beginning to show in his crumpled face and his rather slow, stooping walk. He will not give in, "because if I said: All right, I will not meet foreigners, I will not write articles, I will just sit at home and write books which will never be published, they would consider that a total victory. There is no concept of dialogue or compromise in our country. Either you make no concessions of any kind, or you give in completely. And I will not give in."

Moscow
4 May 1984

YEVTUSHENKO

Yevtushenko, the Russian Peter Pan

YEVGENY YEVTUSHENKO AT fifty is a hard man to pin down, in more ways than one. Far from sinking gently into respectable old age, reminiscing about the time when he was the firebrand voice of Russia's young generation, Yevtushenko has thrown himself into a whirlwind of activity: he is poet, novelist, photographer, film director. His current obsession is his autobiographical film, *Kindergarten*, which has now grown into a two-part epic and keeps threatening to strangle him in endless spools of expensive footage.

It is difficult to get him to pause for a moment to reflect. His film, like his poetry, is essentially about Yevtushenko himself. But who is he? Tomorrow Yevtushenko is celebrating his imminent birthday (he will turn fifty next Monday) by giving a mass poetry reading to an audience of thousands in a sports stadium in Moscow, recapturing those heady days in the Sixties when he was mobbed like a pop star—lean, taut with energy, declaiming aloud verses which expressed daring thoughts most Russians had kept to themselves. He is now an institution, of course, and together with the echo of past mass adulation will come the first part of a three-volume *Selected Works*, and medals from the state—a banner here, a red star there. Yet he is still battling with the censorship, trying to publish a bitter poem about shortages and corruption in Russia, and Russians still look on him as eternally youthful and boyish, the hero of the *Precocious Autobiography* which Yevtushenko now regards as painfully immature and superficial.

At his home outside Moscow I pinned Yevtushenko down long enough to ask him why even young Russians still thought of him as "their" poet and why the present young generation had produced no "voice" of its own. He came downstairs from his study, still lean and wiry, but drained after a day wrestling with the film studios. He had been trying to write verse, but his mind was still full of technical problems to do with lighting and slow motion. He chain-smoked and drank Georgian wine as we talked about the present "vacuum" in literature.

"The whole world has lost giant talents, and they have not been replaced," he said. "In Russia we had terrible losses—Pasternak, Akhmatova, Zabolotsky, others the West has not even heard about. Then came my generation — Voznesensky, Akhmadulina, Okudzhava, myself. After that, nothing. Do you know" — he leans forward — "five student generations have passed without producing a single poet of any stature. It's a disaster. I go round the country, and I ask young people, 'Who is your favourite poet?' And do you know what they say? Yevtushenko, or Voznesensky. Well, that's very nice for us, but we have to draw young poets out of the ground, as if with a magnet."

Perhaps the younger generation has nothing to say, I suggested. "Not exactly, not exactly. You see; all over the world, not just in Russia, pragmatism rules. That's the problem. But you need idealism, a touch of the Don Quixote."

Kindergarten is itself a quixotic attempt to grapple with a medium in which critics say he is hopelessly out of his depth, having come to it too late. Some (including officials) ask aloud whether it will ever be finished. The theme is Yevtushenko's own childhood, when he was evacuated to Siberia from Moscow in 1941.

Why suddenly choose cinema as the medium? "You know, Fellini once said cinema was the closest we came to direct competition with God, and I think there's something in that. I always admired Fellini and the Italian neo-realist directors. Of course, my poetry is still read by tens, thousands — I don't know — millions of people, and I like that. But cinema is a universal language, accessible to all. I haven't lost faith in words, but after all I have written something like 120,000 lines, and up to a point I'm tired of poetry. I should think only about thirty per cent of my verse will survive, if I'm lucky. I'm putting that thirty per cent in my collected works, and a lot of the rest is garbage. I'm still writing, of course — I won't abandon poetry as long as poetry doesn't abandon me, but you get tired of one genre only."

He grins, and drinks wine to soothe a voice hoarse from poetry readings and shouting directions to cameramen and actors. "Unfortunately I can't draw, and I can't paint, so I tried photography, and even that wasn't enough for me. So then films. I'm an old poet and a young movie director. I've written screenplays and acted in films before, so it wasn't totally new." Another grin. "You know what they say in Moscow now? They say Yevtushenko is going to compose an opera and sing in it and then choreograph a ballet and dance in it."

What if people say that *Kindergarten* is yet another vehicle for the Yevtushenko ego? "They can say what they like. The film is about simple Russian people, though I dislike the word simple. Nearly all the actors are amateurs. As for me, do you know I don't have a single photograph of myself from those days? Not one."

A sly look at me across the table. "Journalists were not interested in me at that time. The film is not about important people. It's about the way the war was carried on the fragile shoulders of children. In Russia they even worked in munitions factories."

At this point a famous film director who lives in the neighbourhood dropped in for a chat, and Yevtushenko sought his advice on slow motion, frame speeds and lighting. I asked him whether, technical complications apart, he was running into censorship problems. The film, after all, gives an uncomplimentary picture of the shambles of 1941 and is grittily realistic, with murder and rape scenes. Surely the current ideological climate demanded a "positive hero"?

"Yes, there are those who go on about stressing the positive. But real art is above positivism, negativism and all that. I have shown people as I saw them, in misery and poverty, blood and tears. I love these people, I wouldn't insult them by thinking in terms of positive and negative. That has nothing to do with art. Art is a rainbow of many colours, including black. Art without the black element is impossible."

Looking back on his first fifty years, how does Yevtushenko sum up his life so far? "Listen, when I wrote about my fortieth birthday ten years ago, one of our elder poets asked me 'Zhenya, why go on about insignificant things like age? There are only two important dates in a man's life, his birth and his death.' True, but to be honest it is very strange to be so. Sometimes I still feel like a young boy who has been punished with a heavy burden for some unknown sin.

"If you want me to 'sum up' as Somerset Maugham did, well, as I told you, seventy per cent of my verse is crap and thirty per cent is OK — 50,000 lines, perhaps. Still, that's quite a lot. I write such a lot that some of it is bound to be good. I'm thirsty for life and for poetry. Perhaps I'm going too fast, but no one can stop me. . . ."

Yevtushenko is planning a biography of Mayakovsky, a "psychological" screenplay on *The Three Musketeers*, in which he hopes to star as D'Artagnan (and which he would like Bertolucci to direct), and a book on Stalin, if he has time.

He thinks it is still too early to assess Stalin, and that Solzhenitsyn is both too close to the events and too motivated by hatred to give an accurate picture of Stalin and his times.

He showed me to the door. "Oh, one last thing, for God's sake, please don't give them all that stuff about my being an ageing *enfant terrible*. Tell them about my film." Another grin. "Tell them Yevtushenko is looking forward to the next fifty years."

Moscow
13 July 1983

Fifty-year-old rebel shows his class

HE WEARS STEEL-RIMMED spectacles now to declaim his poetry, or at least to emphasize poignant moments, stabbing them in the air or pausing to perch them inexpertly on his nose. The face is lined, the hair no longer tousled, but Yevgeny Yevtushenko can still hold an audience in the palm of his hand as he used to in the 1960s, when crowds of overwrought youngsters packed football stadiums to hear him. Yevtushenko is older now — approaching fifty-one — and the audiences are older too. They sit on the stairs in the Tchaikovsky Concert Hall, some in sweaters and others in sober suits.

"Yevtushenko reads his verse", said the starkly simple poster outside, but it was enough to bring the fans swarming in, pushing and shoving against the police auxiliaries in red armbands, a theatre-door mêlée reminiscent of the days when Yevtushenko was mobbed like a film star. He has in fact been a film actor (he took the part of a famous Russian scientist, Konstantin Tsiolkovsky) as well as poet, novelist, photographer and most recently film director. Yevtushenko's poetry reading — the first since he attempted a repetition of a Sixties-style stadium reading during the summer — came at a critical time, with the poet under fire for spreading himself too thinly and failing to conform to the Andropov regime's instructions on socialist realist orthodoxy in the arts. His new film, *Kindergarten*, is about to be released after long struggles with the censor.

Last month the literary journal *Our Contemporary (Nash Sovremennik)* mocked Yevtushenko's film career and launched a bitter attack on his novel *Wild Berries*, which contains frank passages about the scale of Stalin's terror, particularly in the countryside. Would Yevtushenko show repentance, perhaps pull his punches to placate officialdom? He strode on, taut with the old energy, but with tiredness too. The sight of a sheaf of manuscripts next to the red and white Thermos on the table beside him caused a stir: this was clearly not a burnt-out performer going through well worn routines. There were old and new favourites. But there were unpublished offerings too, wry, bitter and sardonic, barbed shafts aimed at the corrupt, the privileged, the *nouveau riche*. This was Yevtushenko in his role as defender of the little man and scourge of the powerful, his political compromises with the authorities put on one side. The audience laughed with delight and approval, enjoying the sight of a fifty-year-old rebel scornfully depicting sleek, black cars arriving at the back door of a shop in the fashionable Arbat district of Moscow while a poor working-woman queues in vain on the icy pavement outside.

There were acid pen-portraits of Soviet "producers of ugliness", and of a corrupt shop manager with his illegally acquired imported hi-fi, beer and wallpaper. "Was it for this we stormed the Winter Palace? Was it for this we suffered in the war against Hitler?" The audience erupts, acclaiming the man who voices their humiliation and despair, and brushing aside the fact that he also toes the Kremlin line when necessary. At the end Yevtushenko autographs books and posters thrust forward on to the stage by his most faithful fans: a round-faced army officer, an old, white-haired lady, a young girl in tight white jeans. Afterwards, in the dressing-room, he seems drained. People crowd in to congratulate him, but Yevtushenko seems preoccupied with his forthcoming film, fretting over how it will be received. He pours a sweet red wine from Abkhazia, the district of Georgia where he has a summer home, and takes a gulp before running out on to the stage again to respond to calls for an encore.

Moscow
16 January 1984

War . . . and a Russian's peace plea

He strides on stage in a dark suit to tumultuous applause as the lights go up in the giant Rossiya cinema. Earlier the manager had announced that Yevgeny Yevtushenko was at the funeral of a close friend in Georgia and might not be able to attend the premiere of his film *Kindergarten*. As the final credits roll some of the audience get up to leave, thinking Yevtushenko hasn't made it. But suddenly there he is, a tall, lean figure, modestly — or with apparent modesty, for his entry was well staged — pushing his amateur cast and cameramen into the limelight before taking the microphone himself and saying he "understands people want him to read some poems".

Yevtushenko, poet turned film-maker, who in both Russia and the West is alternately lionized and derided, launches energetically into a popular poem about official corruption and backdoor trading, rounding off the evening with a recital of *The White Snows are Falling*, one of his best known verses. It was, in a way, a backdoor premiere: no famous guests, no glitter and no official beanfeast, as befits a film which upset a number of high officials, and which the Kremlin is still not sure should have been released.

Afterwards, in a private reception room in the bowels of the cinema, Yevtushenko proposes toasts in his favourite Georgian wine to the camera crew who filmed with him over long months in his native Siberia, to all those who believed in *Kindergarten* despite official obstacles and mocking critics, and — this with a slight glint in his eye — to the Mosfilm officials who finally allowed Yevtushenko's profoundly autobiographical and eccentric film on to the screens of Moscow's cinemas.

Yevtushenko had recently returned from Venice, where he sat on the jury of the international film festival. With aspiring young actresses hanging on his every word, Yevtushenko talks familiarly of the cinema legends with whom he has brushed shoulders: Antonioni, Fellini, Bertolucci. "They loved it," he said. "They all loved my film. They will love *The Three Musketeers* even more."

Yevtushenko's detractors are dismayed by his inability to understand that instead of attempting to become the Soviet version of renaissance man by extending his artistic range to films, novels and photography, he should have stuck to poetry, which made him famous in the 1960s. He is now more than fifty and moves in that twilight zone between the official Soviet establishment and unorthodox or even dissident writers and artists. He is permitted to make frequent trips abroad — Venice was only the latest in a long list of outings to the West — and awarded state honours at home.

Yet his novel *Wild Berries* (recently issued in English by Macmillan) was turned down by half a dozen literary journals in Moscow at first because of objections from the censor to its freewheeling style, and its unorthodox references to such taboo subjects as Stalin's bloody collectivization of agriculture. The journal *Moskva* even had the distinction of turning *Wild Berries* down twice. When it finally appeared, the novel sold more than three million copies.

Kindergarten, which has been in his head since he was a boy but has only now been realized on film, has a number of highly controversial passages, including a sequence in which the heroine rolls naked in the snow outside a rural sauna, filmed in lingering slow motion. (This sequence was much copied by film technicians for private use.)

In another scene, a young war bride strips to the waist to make love to her new husband who is about to be sent to the front line and almost certain death. Both passages are shocking for prudish Soviet audiences, unused to displays of nudity on the screen, but both none the less survived the censor's scissors. "In a way that is a pity for Yevtushenko," one of his critics remarked maliciously. "Otherwise he could have claimed he was being suppressed and could have enhanced his reputation as a liberal in Western eyes."

The film is too long, gauche and amateurish in parts. However, it is full of powerful and deeply felt images of Russia, including opening scenes on Red Square and in front of the Bolshoi, transformed to look as they did in wartime. There are numerous other scenes in *Kindergarten* which might seem heavy-handed or sentimental to Western audiences, but which challenge Soviet convention. President Chernenko has called for yet more films about the Second World War, or the Great Patriotic War as the Russians call it. But Yevtushenko's film is not at all the kind of war movie the Politburo had in mind. It shows the panicstricken evacuation of Moscow in 1941 in graphic detail, with Muscovites smashing the train windows and bribing the conductress, played by Yevtushenko's sister, to get themselves and children to safety.

In a kaleidoscope of colour and incident Yevtushenko depicts hunger and deprivation, Jews, gypsies and Siberian criminals, and young boys standing on orange boxes to man the machines in a munitions factory. Peasant honour and human values remain alive amid chaos and poverty, but there is none of the mock heroic which normally passes for historic truth in Soviet war films.

In a classroom in Siberia, the teacher asks for a definition of the word "motherland" and when the goodie-goodie replies: "The motherland is Comrade Stalin" the teacher says, "Yes, but the motherland begins with mama and papa".

To Yevtushenko's keen disappointment *Kindergarten* was not allowed out of Russia to be shown at the Cannes Film Festival, and although it was screened at Venice last month, it could not be entered for a prize as Yevtushenko was a jury member.

In Russia the film was first released in Siberia and then in remote suburban cinemas around Moscow. Only recently did it reach cinemas in the centre. At the Rossiya it ran for one week with matinee showings only. Kremlin officials were reportedly reluctant to have the film released at all and accused Yevtushenko of pacifism and denigration of the Soviet war effort.

Reviews in the official press were mixed, as was audience reaction. At Zima Junction, where Yevtushenko was born and where much of his film was shot, some cinemagoers objected strongly to the nude scenes. On the other hand, one steelworker told Yevtushenko he had seen numerous naked women in the snow in his time but Svetlana, the film's star, was by far the most beautiful. "The scene was too short," the worker remarked. "This is not hypocrisy," Yevtushenko explained. "We have a problem with our Russian timidity or shyness. After all, we have never had books like *Tropic of Cancer* in Russia."

For Yevtushenko the most important aspect of *Kindergarten* is that it shows ordinary people. "I don't think that famous people are the most interesting ones. I am the *Paparazzo* of the common people." For the role of his grandmother, Yevtushenko picked out a ticket lady at a sports stadium. Svetlana Estratova, who plays the gangster's moll who befriends the young Zhenya, had never acted professionally.

Since the film was finished she has vanished and did not attend the premiere at the Rossiya. Her friends say she is working as a street-cleaner in Moscow. "She must be the most beautiful street-cleaner in the world," Yevtushenko remarks drily.

As for Yevtushenko's unorthodox portrayal of the war, with its famine and panic, Yevtushenko argues that he is showing what he himself remembers. "I could not make a pompous film with big battles. This was my battlefield. It is my own autobiography and at the same time the autobiography of my generation."

Kindergarten may be distributed in America. United Artists have expressed interest in it — and Yevtushenko is very keen that his portrayal of Russian life in wartime should give Americans a more humane and sympathetic image of the Russian people at a time of sharp confrontation between the superpowers. "I want to show them that there exists a third power, namely art. In any case, I do not like this expression 'superpower', because for me the only superpower is the human soul. I don't want to overrate my film. It has certain defects, but it is a very Russian film."

Yevtushenko hopes that when they see it Americans will become closer to the Russians, as they were for a time at the end of the Second World War when American and Russian soldiers embraced on the River Elbe after the defeat of the Germans.

With the battle to screen *Kindergarten* past, Yevtushenko is already working on his next film, *The Three Musketeers*, an idea which has been at the back of his mind for five years. It sometimes looks as if Yevtushenko deliberately creates this whirlwind of activity — trips abroad, movie making, novel writing — not only because he thrives on recognition and popularity, but also to disguise the fact that he is engaged in a desperate race against time, and is not sure which of his efforts will endure either in Russian or in world terms.

He still writes unorthodox poetry ("I have never felt myself to be a poet of the establishment") but talks of last year, his fiftieth birthday, as a "sad time". Why sad? "Because when you get to be as old as fifty nothing is truly joyful. Still, Pasternak wrote his most beautiful love poems when he was sixty-six, so perhaps there is hope for me yet."

And the race against time? "You know, on the palm of my hand it is written that I will live to the age of seventy-three. Until then I will try to do everything I can to express myself." An impish grin.

"Perhaps that is a kind of egoism. Perhaps it would be better to say that what I am trying to do is to express the ideas of all the people who cannot express themselves."

Moscow
2nd November 1984

WE ARE NOT ALONE:
THE OCCULT AND PARANORMAL

Yeti fails to live up to the ideals of Communism

The main subject of conversation at Russian dining tables this weekend was not the forthcoming session of the Supreme Soviet, nor the joint Soviet-Indian space shot, nor the school reform which passes into law this week. It was not even the food programme and the Five-Year Plan. None of these can compete for Soviet attention with the shocking revelation that the Abominable Snowman does not exist.

Perhaps because the Soviet daily routine is dull and the propaganda is tedious Russians in all walks of life are fascinated by the occult, the supernatural and the mysterious. The headline "Yeti Does Not Exist — Official" has caused dismay and disbelief. The authority for this heretical assertion is Mr Vadim Ranov, a leading Soviet explorer, who on Saturday cold-bloodedly stated that the numerous Russian expeditions to track down the yeti were just a lot of nonsense, and so were the theories used by Soviet scientists to justify the trips. Mr Ranov ought to know, since he is an expert on the Pamir Mountains, in Central Asia, where the yeti's giant footprints have been pursued by a succession of Russian scientists. Mr Ranov is also a member of the Geographical Society. Speaking in Dushanbe in Tadzhikistan, he reduced Russia's favourite mystery creature to a pile of crumbling hypotheses.

In the first place, Sir Edmund Hillary had proved long ago during his assault on Everest that the hairy monster's footprints in Nepal were in fact due to "the effect of the sun's rays on tracks left by other animals". Secondly, a piece of hide once produced as the furry skin of the yeti — the only tangible evidence to emerge so far — had in fact come from a Tibetan blue bear. Thirdly, no hominoid remains, whether skeleton, skull or bones, had ever been found in either the Himalayas or the Pamirs. Finally, a creature like the yeti could only exist if there were other species of the same kind around. Yet no traces of such creatures, such as remnants of food or shelters, had ever been reported.

But Mr Ranov reserved his most withering fire for fellow

explorers and scientists who had fallen for the theory that Abominable Snowmen were Neanderthal men who had somehow survived into the twentieth century. "This hypothesis is wrong," Mr Ranov said, "and is easily refuted. It is quite impossible to imagine that a group of Neanderthal men suddenly forgot how to make stone tools and returned to living in the wild, since this runs counter to the entire course of human evolution."

The yeti-hunters, in other words, are under fire because the Abominable Snowman is ideologically unacceptable. Mankind, in the Marxist-Leninist view, is progressing onward and upward towards the Communist ideal, and the yeti would be an aberration, or as Mr Ranov put it in Dushanbe: "We must remember that *homo sapiens* evolved from Neanderthal man in a process of social as well as biological evolution."

Moscow
9 April 1984

Still a market among Russians for miracles

JUST OUTSIDE MOSCOW proper, in what used to be the countryside until Khrushchev started expanding the city limits with high-rise flats, there is a miraculous spring. Nowadays it emerges from a metal pipe in a stone wall with a chipped swan in ceramic tiles on it. But the spring — called the "Swan Princess spring" — is held to be legendary, with healing properties which go back to antiquity, or at least the eighteenth century. On any weekend, whether in the depths of winter or now as the first hint of warmer weather begins to melt the snow and ice, you can see a procession of Muscovites with tin-cans and containers wending their way down the woodland path and down steep stone steps to the spring. The park was once the estate of a nineteenth-century industrialist, who built a grandiose turreted mansion in the grounds. It is now an agricultural institute (and sadly neglected) and quite obviously a Victorian folly, but there are those who swear Catherine the Great lived in it. Equally, people queueing to fill jugs and containers with the healing waters of the spring say Catherine used to bathe in it (presumably in the summer).

There is a strong streak of the credulous in most Russians, despite the official materialist philosophy and emphasis on science and reason. Many seem to have a powerful desire to believe in legends and folk remedies. As far as is known, the health-giving powers of the "Swan Princess" waters have not been put to the test. The fact is, many Russians are sceptical of modern medicine, and home remedies abound, most of them based on herbal brews which have their origins in Russia's peasant past. Russians place great faith in healers such as the lady who treated the late President Brezhnev. She spawned numerous imitators who claimed to be able to heal through the laying on of hands, and whose customers included five-star generals and top Party officials.

Another powerful trait is the persistent belief in the efficacy of eastern potions. One of the most popular remedies at the moment is a Vietnamese ointment called "Gold Star". It comes in a little red tin, has a waxy texture and is supposed to cure any ache or pain. Rather more common are mustard packs, which can be bought in chemists but are often home-made. They are widely held to be an all-purpose cure for colds, bronchitis, pneumonia, high blood pressure and all the unidentifiable aches and pains brought on by the stress of modern life. Slap on a mustard pack is every mother's answer to illness. Belief in such remedies affects both high and low in society. The Vietnamese ointment was recently offered to me not by a peasant but by a young ministerial adviser.

Vodka, of course, is another popular panacea. Taken with salt, vodka can allegedly cure most stomach complaints, or so most Russian men argue convincingly.

But it is the miracle-working power of water which has a special hold on the Russian imagination. Not long ago a Soviet newspaper exposed an old man and his son who were selling "holy water" at an exorbitant profit in a village in the Ukraine. The paper said their fame had spread far and wide and hundreds of sick people gathered every day to buy holy water (which in fact came from a tap) at five roubles a jug.

The swindlers had accumulated thousands of roubles' worth of cash and gold, and boasted eight cars. The old man's reputation for miracle-working had been so great that he had been able to earn in one hour as much as a qualified doctor could make in three months, and his patients had ranged from "simple people to intellectuals".

It was a sign of the times, the paper noted sourly, that when the two tricksters were arrested most of the people they had "treated" were angry with the authorities.

Moscow
15 April 1983

Russia prepares for a close encounter

THE KREMLIN, ONCE sceptical about the existence of flying saucers, has finally succumbed to the unshakeable Russian belief in close encounters of the third kind. The newspaper *Trud* (Labour) reported that a special commission for the investigation of unidentified flying objects (UFOs) has been set up under Pavel Popovich, the former cosmonaut. The UFO commission is a victory for *Trud* which has been at the forefront of the battle to prove that alien invaders are not a figment of the Russian imagination.

There was a time when the Kremlin used to insist, as *Pravda* put it in the 1960s, that "all objects that fly over the territory of our country are identified either by scientists or by those who stand guard over the security of our homeland". But the Russians are incorrigible believers in the occult, and were delighted last year when *Trud* carried a series of articles and letters reporting strange bright lights seen travelling across the sky above Byelorussia and Central Russia, terrifying the inhabitants below.

The incident which has finally convinced the authorities that there are more things in heaven and earth than are dreamed of in dialectical materialism occurred in Gorky in March last year. Gorky is closed to foreigners (and hence a convenient place of exile for Dr Sakharov and his wife), but is apparently not closed to visitors from outer space. According to Mr Popovich, air traffic controllers at Gorky airport spotted a light-grey steel object shaped like a cigar flying towards them on the evening of 27 March. It was about the size of a conventional airliner, and like the Korean Air Lines jumbo which strayed into Soviet airspace last September failed to respond to radio contact. However, the air defences at Gorky, unlike their colleagues at Kamchatka, did not open fire, possibly because the intruder had no wings and was flying at an altitude of 3,000 ft at a speed of up to 125 mph. The object behaved erratically, flying forty-five miles to the south east of Gorky before turning to head back towards the airport and finally vanishing twenty-five miles north of the city.

Mr Popovich said his newly formed Commission for the Investigation of Abnormal Atmospheric Phenomena was taking the flying cigar of Gorky very seriously indeed. It had been sighted by reliable and well-trained aviation experts who had given precise and scientific observations, and who had seen the mysterious object on their radar screens for a full forty minutes. *Trud* disappointed some readers by revealing that other phenomena witnessed by less well-trained observers would not be taken up by the Commission.

Moscow
30 May 1984

Soviet scoop on space beings

AS RUSSIANS BEGAN preparations in earnest over the weekend for May Day celebrations, a Soviet astronomer revealed that world peace and the "bright future" promised by Soviet Communism may be brought about not by earthly efforts but by beings from outer space, who are already trying to get in touch with us by intergalactic telephone. The news that we are not alone was broken in the newspaper *Moscow News* by Dr Boris Fesenkø, who believes that the gently pulsing and glowing nebula, known as NGC 6543, is not merely a ball of greenish gas with a white-hot core but also a signal from extra-terrestrial beings. Since the nebula is all of 1,000 light years from here it will take time for the signals to reach us, but Dr Fesenkø is firmly convinced that we will receive them. NGC 6543, he wrote, had obviously been designed by intelligent beings who, looking down on our small planet, could foresee that towards the end of the twentieth century man would enter the technological age and be in a position to receive a message from superior civilizations.

Dr Fesenkø is rather vaguer about what the "supreme intellect" is trying to tell us. The first signal we receive may not contain information at all, and may be merely a sign that "we are not alone, someone knows about us". But we can rest assured, it seems, that the beings who have watched over us for thousands of years, sharing our sorrows and rejoicing in our triumphs, have only benevolent intentions. They may even be able to "diminish the danger of a nuclear catastrophe on Earth". It is possible, Dr Fesenkø argues, that life originates "in different places at different moments in time", so that older civilizations are able to protect newer ones from self-destruction and show them the way ahead. "NGC 6543 cannot be seen by the naked eye," he wrote, "but I believe it forebodes the possibility of a brilliant future for our descendants."

Just in case anyone takes the Fesenkø theses too seriously, however, *Moscow News* printed two sceptical views by fellow Soviet astronomers. Both agreed that the position of the nebula in relation to Earth was a remarkable coincidence, placing it almost exactly at the pole of the Earth's orbit. But the sceptics concluded that although Dr Fesenkø's theory was "elegant and attractive", it was difficult to believe — not to say presumptuous to suppose — that NGC 6543 was a "beacon from a higher civilization". It was equally fallacious, one of the astronomers remarked, to suppose that older galactic civilizations wished us well. They might have acquired "gigantic reserves of nuclear fuel" over the light years and needed somewhere to dump and destroy them, choosing the Earth's pole as a handy "proving ground".

Moscow
30 April 1984

QUEUES AND CONSUMERS:

SHOPPING AND LIVING STANDARDS

Pepsi gets few Russian lips smackin'

RUSSIAN PEPSI-COLA, that once effervescent symbol of détente, is losing some of its sparkle. Pepsi began to make inroads into the Soviet soft drinks market in the 1970s, when détente was in its heyday and the Washington-Moscow relationship was awash in what came to be called the "vodka-cola" spirit. Now, however, Pepsi has fallen victim not only to the chilly relationship between the superpowers but also to Russian inefficiency. A factory built in the Ukraine five years ago to "provide people on holiday in the Crimea with more cooling drinks" has almost ground to a halt, according to the newspaper *Pravda Ukrainy*. Due to "interruptions in supplies of raw materials" and "lack of spare parts", the bottling lines at the Yevpatoria plant never reached anything like their 1977 target of 48,000 bottles of Pepsi-Cola an hour.

One problem, apparently still unsolved, was that the bottles used were too big, with the result that they got stuck, and jammed the machinery.

Local authorities, fed up with constant complaints, hit upon a "radical solution": if the bottles kept breaking, why not make more than were needed, and back this up by ordering all used bottles to be returned to the plant? As a result, the paper said, the factory yard is "piled high with unwanted bottles".

All of which goes some way to explain one of the more puzzling features of life in Moscow: the dearth of Pepsi. On many street corners there are kiosks, first erected for the Olympics, with a cube on top carrying the words Pepsi-Cola in Russian and English. When the cube is revolving, Pepsi is on sale: when it is not Pepsi is *defitsitny*, or temporarily out of stock. Disappointed would-be thirst quenchers have noted that there are an awful lot of stationary Pepsi cubes in Moscow nowadays.

Moscow
2 November 1982

Tonik and crisps join the party

THE GREEN AND white label says "Tonik" in large brown letters, with the word "bitter" in smaller letters underneath, the liquid inside fizzes satisfactorily, but has a strange metallic taste. "Tonik" is not made by Sch . . . you know who, but by Rospivoprom Minpishcherprom RSFSR, which roughly translated means the Beer and Soft Drinks Subsidiary of the Ministry of Food Production of the Russian Federated Republic.

Tonic water is at last finding its way on to the shelves of Russian shops, although so far it is more often to be found in special stores for foreigners than in the shops to which ordinary Muscovites have access. It is difficult to see what the market for "Tonik" might be, since no self-respecting member of the British community in Moscow would be seen dead pouring it into his or her "Dzhin", except when foreign varieties are *defitsitny* (out of stock). And since "Dzhin" is almost unknown in Russia it is hard to imagine Russians mixing "Tonik" with anything. When I suggested to a Moscow friend that he might try putting "Tonik" with his vodka, it took him several minutes to grasp what I meant, and then he thought I had taken leave of my senses. Vodka is not something you adulterate with anything in the Soviet Union.

Russians may, on the other hand, take to another recent innovation: crisps. Since vodka is usually drunk with snacks, such as salted herring or pickled cucumber, crisps may have a future in the Soviet Union. They will have to think of a snappier brand name though, since "Moscow crunchy potato in bits" lacks a certain something and is a bit of a mouthful as well. "Moscow crunchy potato in bits" comes to you courtesy of the Colossus factory, which turns out to be another subsidiary of the Ministry of Food Production. The crisps are not salted, but no doubt that will come. So, too, will exotic flavours, but that is looking far ahead. Meanwhile, Soviet crisps are not bad value at ten kopecks (about 8p) a packet, with "Tonik" also reasonable at sixteen kopecks. Crisps and tonic water do not herald a new era of gentility in Russia, much as the leadership would welcome such a development.

Hard drinking, as *Pravda* points out, brings factories and building sites to a halt on Fridays and Mondays, in effect reducing Russia to a permanent three-day week. On the other hand, vodka also keeps the wheels of Soviet life turning and induces a sort of glazed bonhomie which, when coupled with unexpected upturns in erratic food supplies, makes an otherwise harsh life almost tolerable.

Despite the deficiencies of the food programme which Mr Andropov inherited from Mr Brezhnev, state shops and peasant markets have become better stocked in the past few weeks, partly to create goodwill but also to help Muscovites prepare for the new year holiday and the celebrations marking sixty years of the Soviet state.

At the fruit shop in the block where both Mr Brezhnev and Mr Andropov used to live, just down the road from *The Times* flat, oranges, lemons and even mandarins and grapefruit made a miraculous appearance. Passers-by accosted you with a brusque "Where did you get those?" and hurried off to join the long and slow-moving queue. The important thing in Moscow is not only to have vitamin-rich foods, but to have what other people do not have. Whether it is mandarins or a foreign-made lavatory (the latest status symbol), it hints at influence beyond the normal. And if it is Western, from boots to plastic bags, so much the better. In which case, "our" tonic and crisps may meet the same fate, and Smith's and Sch . . . you know who may yet make inroads into the Soviet market.

Moscow
4 January 1983

Dodging the ice as spring crashes in

The fact that Russia is a superpower sometimes conveys a false image of modern efficiency to the Western mind. This thought struck me forcefully the other day as I was splashing through vast puddles of muddy water to *The Times* office. Part of the problem is that ordinary words like office or shop have connotations in the West which they do not carry in the Soviet Union. Spring in Moscow means, not lambs and daffodils, but great chunks of ice crashing from the roofs of blocks of flats as the long-awaited thaw sets in. Occasionally it means a smashed windscreen if you park too close to the building. On the streets the mounds of ice and snow swiftly become lakes of muddy water. If Moscow has a drainage system, it does not work, hence the need for Wellington boots.

In spite of the lack of drains, Russia can be formidably efficient, in some areas, notably the armed forces. Mr Gorbachov's gargantuan task is to translate some of this efficiency into everyday life, where the general level of technology resembles the British wartime spirit of "patch it up and hope it works". Russia prides itself on its social services and amenities, yet spring is also the time when Moscow's ancient plumbing becomes contaminated and the tap water, unreliable at the best of times, is unfit to drink. Foreign families are advised by Western doctors in Moscow to boil water to avoid illnesses. Contrary to widely held belief in the West, the Soviet health system is backward, unhygienic and overcrowded, and foreigners who fall ill tend to fly out to Helsinki for treatment or turn to Western embassies.

In many ways, Russia is still backward, even in the capital. Water, gas and electricity supplies are all cheap, one of the advantages of Soviet society, but the standard of service is low. Every summer, the hot-water system is turned off in every block of flats, including ours, so that the boiler and pipes can be cleaned. After a while you take this for granted, as Russians do. As for electricity, any equipment which relies on a digital timer is useless because fluctuations in the electricity supply, familiar to Third World residents, render digital clocks inaccurate. Fortunately, perhaps, electronic goods are almost unknown in any case.

Russian pleasures are simpler: a walk through the spring puddles to the peasant market, for example, to buy wooden Easter eggs — this weekend is Russia's Easter. Even here there are linguistic pitfalls: I might say that the route takes us past a stationery store, and images of W. H. Smith come to mind. But our shop has no carpet, few Moscow shops do, the concrete floors are awash in mud and slush, and instead of colourful eye-catching displays of books, pens and records there are piles of coarse paper, cheap school notebooks and string for wrapping. The prize item is toilet paper, one kind only, of the Spartan Army-issue variety. On we go by way of a beer bar, which might call to mind a pub, tables, chatter. . . . But no, in our beer bar you stand, the watery beer comes in thick, chipped glasses, and the clientèle is exclusively male and the worse for wear by mid-day.

There are however splendid parks in which to take the spring air in Moscow, in many cases former estates expropriated by the people, the mansions turned into museums and the grounds well tended. There are boat rides, the unbeatable Moscow ice-cream — and the markets. Again, not the market that the English word suggests, but a specifically Russian place where the smells are of pickles and apples, and where jolly peasant women offer the flowers they grow in their *dacha* gardens outside the city.

They also offer, sometimes from under the counter, beautifully painted wooden eggs with religious themes in colours which enrich an otherwise drab existence. Like the thaw itself, Russian Easter eggs symbolize the coming of spring after the seemingly endless dark Russian winter.

Moscow
13 April 1985

A tickle in the nose from Stalin's summer show

IT IS SNOWING again in Moscow, not real snow, of course, with daytime temperatures of around 25 degrees C., but "Stalin snow" — puffs of white down which float in clouds off the numerous poplar trees lining Moscow streets and boulevards. Called *pookh* in Russian, the stuff looks just like snow as it drifts through the air and settles on the ground. The effect is uncanny. *Pookh* coats everything in white and gets into eyes and noses. It is an annual reminder of one of Stalin's less bloodthirsty follies, his insistence on planting poplars all over the city. Presumably he thought that as legacies go, this one was perversely amusing. Every year the Moscow city authorities try to reduce the *pookh* by cutting down poplars, but every year they fail. In the kind of scorching hot weather Moscow has been having this spring, Stalin snow is a fire hazard. It also makes the air difficult to breathe when mixed with the dust which belches from factory chimneys and falls off uncovered industrial lorries in the city centre.

Most Muscovites find relief from the heat and dust whenever they can by retreating to the beaches on the Moscow river, where the poplars give way to cool pines. Normally the exodus begins about now, but this year summer took over almost before spring had begun. As in England, the weather is much discussed, especially by the old *babushkas*, the women in black who haunt courtyards throughout Moscow.

So far we have had a false winter in October, followed by a thaw, followed by an astonishingly mild real winter, followed by an unseasonably early and hot summer. The *babushkas* say it all has to do with atomic bombs (Russian and American), or perhaps with great changes at the top (the Kremlin). The topsy-turvy weather has caused endless practical problems in a country which by and large does things to order. Central heating — which cannot be adjusted in individual flats — stays on until May regardless. More puzzling, Musçovites keep their fur hats on until some hidden instruction is given. One day the streets were suddenly full of bare-headed people, as if by magic. The main sufferers are the police, who change their uniforms according to a graded system unrelated to the weather. Fur hats and greatcoats are followed by lighter hats and coats, but spring came too soon, leaving the poor police sweating. To the relief of all, especially motorists, the police have now been issued with more comfortable white tunics and peaked caps.

Relief of a kind is also to be found in Soviet ice-cream, another of Stalin's unintentional gifts to the nation. Russia is probably the last remaining bastion of real ice-cream, and the kiosks which sell it on the busy streets are usually besieged. The story goes that when Anastas Mikoyan was Stalin's Minister for Foreign Trade he visited the United States, and was greatly struck by the taste of American ice-cream. On Stalin's instructions, Mikoyan brought the original recipe back to Russia, where it has been rigidly applied ever since. Muscovites are therefore eating honest-to-goodness American ice-cream circa 1940, much of it still made in what is now called the "Mikoyan ice-cream factory" in Moscow.

"Much of our life is an illusion, like Stalin snow," a Russian friend commented as we walked through the *pookh*-filled air to an ice-cream queue. "It is all imitation. We have things which look like their counterparts in the West because we think we ought to have them too — Fiat-type cars, modern hotels, airports, shopping centres. But they never work properly, and when you get close you see it's all a façade, the form without the content. These things grow naturally out of your society, and we try and adapt them to quite different traditions." We reached the head of the queue. "Mind you, our ice-cream is better."

Moscow
27 June 1983

Two-hour wait for Moscow's fast food

FAST FOOD HAS arrived in Russia. The talk of Moscow at the moment is the new pizza parlour on Gorky Street, and any Soviet teenager worthy of his Western plimsolls and T-shirt has to be seen discussing the latest pop music over a *pizza capricciosa* or *calzone al formaggio*, two of the six dishes on offer. The tablecloths are red-and-white check, the illustrated menu (with captions in Russian and Italian) looks appetizing, and the pizzas themselves are not bad at all, a crisp dough base with mushroom, sausage and cheese toppings flavoured with native Russian herbs. A pulsating juke-box in the corner adds to the impression that the crowd outside could be on the Via del Corso rather than Gorky Street. An Italian catering firm based in the Via del Corso in Rome first had the idea of introducing Russians to the world of pizza. The Gorky Street pizza parlour (it has not so far been given a name) is housed in the "Vesna" café, meaning spring, on Moscow's main shopping street. It was launched without fanfare a month ago, but is now coping — or rather failing to cope — with the problems of success. Not only has the fame of Gorky Street pizzas been passed by word of mouth, the pizza parlour has been featured on television and in two Moscow newspapers. As a result the queue outside is never less than fifty strong, at lunchtime or in the evening. One young man in jeans, with an "I love the Beatles" button on his jacket, had been waiting for more than two hours to get in. Did he know what a pizza was? No, but they were Italian — and, like everyone else, he wanted to try one.

Moscow
14 August 1982

Russian-made "bubbly" for the working man

"WE OWE IT all to our very own Prince Golitsyn," the champagne factory manager said. We raised our glasses of clear, sparkling Soviet champagne and drank to the memory of the Prince, who in the eighteenth century had had the foresight to lay the foundations of Russian viniculture on his landed estates in the Crimea. Even through a slight champagne-induced haze, the rough-hewn and jovial factory manager did not look like a man who could claim kinship with one of Russia's oldest aristocratic families. Nor could he, as it turned out, since (like Stalin) he was the son of a poor family from Georgia. Just to be on the safe side we drank toasts to Stalin as well.

One of the most striking paradoxes of Soviet life is that champagne is the drink of the working man. Most Russian men have vodka in their veins, and they drink quantities of watery beer in rather sad and sordid dive bars. But go into any restaurant in Moscow, or even in a provincial town, and you will find tables laden with *shampanskoe*, drunk by both men and women. Where they get the money from is a mystery. At £6 a bottle in shops, and more in restaurants, Soviet champagne is not cheap (the average monthly wage is about £150).

Yet vast quantities are produced, and consumed. There has been a deliberate government policy to make it a symbol of privilege available to the masses. *Shampanskoe* is drunk at weddings, birthdays, on numerous public holidays, when friends come to visit, to mark arrivals and departures, or for no reason at all. It has a high alcohol content, and is really powerful when drunk with vodka (as it often is).

Out at the "Sixty years of the USSR champagne factory" the huge vats of champagne bubble quietly away before being bottled and labelled on an assembly-line where most of the employees are women. In the cool, tall rooms where the scientifically controlled machinery hums to itself there are no human beings at all, just computers channelling the right mix of wine basis, sugar and gas — the process known in Russia as *shampanisatsiya*.

The hermetically sealed containers produce 100 litres of

vinomaterial an hour for filtering and bottling. It emerges as dry, semi-dry, sweet or brut champagne — in reality, sparkling wine — which makes a satisfactory fountain when the (imported) plastic cork pops out.

It is tempting to draw a parallel with the sprawling factory next door which produces the Soviet version of Pepsi-Cola and Fanta (the fizzy orange drink). Like the champagne factory, the soft drinks bottling plant is set in a raw industrial estate on the outskirts of Moscow, and was completed in time to meet the extra demand generated by the Moscow Olympic Games three years ago.

The Russians are keen to claim that their champagnes are not just sparkling wines, however. "Our champagnes are known all over the world as the very best," the factory manager said proudly. "Even in France." Some of the wine used to make Soviet champagne is imported from Argentina, although the Russians deny this. They prefer to emphasize the use of good white wine from Moldavia, Georgia and the Caucasus, brought up to Moscow by the lorry- and train-load. In the southern republics, some champagne is still made by the traditional "bottle method", but the "reservoir" or vat process is gradually taking over. The giant "Sixtieth Anniversary" factory is part of this process: it produces 20 million bottles of very drinkable champagne a year, which makes it the largest champagne factory in Europe. France and West Germany have expressed an interest in buying the technology developed by the Russians for mass production of champagne.

At present Russia occupies third place behind them in the league of world champagne production, but the current Five-Year Plan target of 300m bottles a year ought to put the Soviet Union comfortably in first place within the next two years. What Prince Golitsyn would have thought of it is quite another matter.

Moscow
2 May 1983

Russia's Harrods reopens its doors

YELISEYEV'S GROCERY STORE is back to normal, and Moscow shoppers are sighing with relief. Last month, the manager, who had been languishing in jail for a year and a half, . . . was taken out and shot. A sign saying "closed for repairs" went up in Yeliseyev's windows, but the doors are now open again. There is no sign saying "under new management" possibly because the incident was a highly sensitive matter of state. Gastronom No. 1, or Yeliseyev's at No. 14 Gorky Street, just round the corner from Pushkin Square, is perhaps the Soviet equivalent of Harrods food hall or Fortnum and Mason. The managers of Harrods or Fortnums would almost certainly not regard the comparison as apt. But then they do not operate in a system of state monopolies and endemic shortages where black market speculation thrives and shopkeepers can provide hidden privileges for the powerful.

Yuri Sokolov, the wealthy and influential manager of Gastronom No. 1 — the store's official name, although everybody refers to it as Yeliseyev's after its pre-revolutionary owner — was an intimate of the Brezhnev family who fell foul of President Andropov's stern anti-corruption drive. The advent to power in February of Mr Chernenko — a Brezhnev associate for many years — brought rumours of a reprieve for Sokolov, who had been sentenced to death for grave economic crimes. But either because the Brezhnevites proved unwilling to protect him, or because Andropov's youthful followers are too powerful in the Party, the once mighty purveyor of groceries to the Kremlin and the élite went before the firing squad.

One wonders what Yeliseyev would have made of it all, were his pre-revolutionary spirit to return and haunt Gastronom No. 1. Perhaps it does: the place certainly looks and feels different from other Soviet stores, with their bare shelves and drab utilitarian interiors. Inside Yeliseyev's there is a breathtaking hall with hig vaulted ceilings, crystal chandeliers, marble counters and stained-glass windows.

In the centre of the shop, it is true, is a scene Yeliseyev would almost certainly find dismaying: a vast, seething mass of humanity gathered round a circular counter. But around the edges of the hall something of the old style is preserved, with individual counters selling jams, eggs and fruit. The goods are in tall, Edwardian wooden display cases. Yeliseyev would no doubt have turned his pre-revolutionary nose up. But then before the Revolution the majority of Russians would not have dreamt of setting foot in so select a place. The ill-fated Yuri Sokolov supplied scarce goods corruptly to the privileged in Soviet society; Yeliseyev did the same, rather more openly, to the privileged of his day.

The Russian argument is that the Soviet system of manufacture and distribution, at present so cumbersome and inadequate, will in time adjust to the demands of a mass society. Perhaps, although a Western supermarket manager or corner shopkeeper might argue that a small dose of private initiative would do the trick. But in Russia private enterprise is ideologically unacceptable, and is likely to remain so given that under President Chernenko Soviet ideology seems to be becoming more rigid and hard-line rather than the reverse.

The Kremlin's answer therefore is not to change the system but to tackle the corruption that springs from privilege and shortages, arresting, imprisoning and even executing those managers and officials who fall into temptation. Sokolov was just the tip of the iceberg, and the momentum of the late Yuri Andropov's campaign seems to be continuing.

The director of a meat-processing factory in Kirgiziya was executed recently for fraud, and there have been widespread purges elsewhere. To a Western observer this looks like tackling the symptoms of the malaise rather than the cause, but Soviet officials do not agree. The Soviet underworld, which mistakenly breathed again when Andropov died, is bracing itself for a further onslaught.

Moscow
16 August 1984

Eight hundred unsatisfied customers a day

WITH ONE OR two exceptions, shop assistants in Moscow are notoriously surly and indifferent, if not downright rude. Customers are a nuisance. Western observers put this down to the state-controlled system of manufacture and distribution and the complete lack of private enterprise or incentive. But the Ministry of Internal Trade has come up with a different solution: psychiatry.

The Moscow evening paper *Vechernaya Moskva* says it receives hundreds of letters complaining about the appalling service in

Moscow's crowded food shops and department stores. Part of the problem, the paper points out, is that Moscow (although poorly stocked by Western standards) is a Mecca for shoppers from the provinces, so that the population is swelled every day by some two million out-of-towners. They can be seen, mouth agape and string-bags in hand, on Gorky Street and Kalinin Prospekt, the city's two main shopping thoroughfares, and clogging up the aisles in Gum and Tsum, the two main department stores. *Vechernaya Moskva* discovered that any one shop assistant in this target area has to serve up to 800 customers a day, all clamouring to buy the relatively few goods on offer.

Not surprisingly, shop assistants tend to react by becoming indifferent or offensive. The rudest assistants are in the food shops, where every cashier can expect to deal with as many as 1,400 people a day. Shoppers queue to pay, and then queue again for the goods, making stores into a milling mass of angry and sweating customers and shop assistants. The Ministry of Internal Trade has tackled the problem, not by hiving off Gum and Tsum to enterprising Georgians or Armenians as private concerns, but by instructing technical colleges to establish courses in "the psychology of trade".

Here students can sit well away from the hurly-burly of Gorky Street and consider "problems of communication between sales assistants and customers". Fully-trained psychologists are to be stationed in Moscow shops to advise the retail trade.

So far, it appears, only two psychologists have been assigned, and as *Vechernaya Moskva* noted drily, there are 5,500 to go. There are no details yet on how the two pioneering psychologists have fared, but one shop assistant in a shoe shop — not far from *The Times* offices — was sceptical. "Haven't heard about it," she said with a shy smile, turning to glare at a middle-aged woman who interrupted our conversation to ask for a pair of boots from the shelf behind the counter, which is where most goods are kept in Soviet stores.

Moscow
25 September 1982

Russia's magnificent obsession with food

ONE OF THE unwiser ways to spend an idle five minutes in Moscow (a rare occurrence) is to sit down with the airmail edition of *The Times* and read the food column on the back page of Friday's issue. "English carrots are stable at 8p to 20p per pound," one reads, "but Dutch finger carrots are up by about 3p." A stifled groan: what earthly delights a Dutch finger carrot must offer. "Cape grapes are cheaper this week, as are seedless Thompson grapes from Chile." I don't think I can take much more of this. "Tesco has leg of lamb on promotion at 154p per pound." Vague memories filter through the snowbound Moscow landscape of "loss leaders" in supermarkets, a concept unknown in a country where you fight your way to the counter to queue for a ticket to queue for meat some pampered English pets would turn their noses up at. "Chinese leaves, hothouse tomatoes, sirloin steak, topside, oven-ready ducklings. . . . " After a while, the list becomes a blur and the prices become irrelevant. Most Muscovites and resident foreigners would kill to get their hands on grapes and duckling, let alone pay mere money for them.

Food can become an obsession in Moscow, largely because there is not much to go around, except in tourist hotels. In case you should start feeling sorry for us, no food parcels are necessary: Russians do eat well, if stodgily, are ingenious at tracking food down and generous in the extreme to friends. For that matter, foreigners have special hard-currency shops, called *beriozkas* (literally little birch tree, an odd choice of name), and can order consumer goods, including foodstuffs, from firms in Finland, Denmark and West Germany. The snag is that Soviet Customs officials are placing increasingly heavy duties on imports, thereby penalizing foreigners twice: in effect, diplomats, journalists and businessmen have to pay ransom to import goods the Soviet system fails to supply.

Beriozka stores, moreover, reflect in some curious way the often cumbersome and arbitrary distribution system in the Soviet world outside. The few citizens who get in gape at the abundance. None the less, whole categories of products suddenly become *defitsitny*, or out of stock, for no apparent reason.

Not long ago it was red wine (any red wine) and cigarettes (any cigarettes). At the moment, beer and tonic water are not to be had for love or money (your correspondent has tried both). The lack of tonic is a devastating blow to the small British community. Russians, however, have been used to erratic distribution and chronic shortages for decades, and from their point of view things have looked up. Muscovites are in any case cushioned by the system of "special orders" through places of employment such as factories and offices, in addition to which the 1982 food programme and the late President Andropov's reforms are beginning to have an effect.

Mr Chernenko remarked in the Kremlin that supplies of meat, milk, fruit and vegetables were still unsatisfactory, but bananas, oranges, lemons and even grapefruit do appear at state shops and street kiosks.

Down at the peasant markets, where most Muscovites go for vegetables and salad, not much is on display except cucumbers at £2.50 a kilogram (the average wage is under £200 a month). Most Russians are waiting happily for the spring, when the collective farms will deliver to the state shops, and the stalls at the peasant market will fill with gold-toothed traders from the south — Georgia, Azerbaijan, the Caucasus and Central Asia. Prices will be high — I once paid £12 for a melon — but the money will be found somehow since most Russians complain that the problem is not that their wages are low but that there is nothing to spend them on.

Meanwhile, one of the most popular Moscow shops is tucked away in a side street near Gorky Park. Every week juggernaut lorries pull up with Warsaw mud on their wheels and disgorge pile upon pile of frozen Polish strawberries, beans, peas, plums, carrots, raspberries. The shop, called *Morozka* (snow-flake), trades in roubles, not hard currency, so foreigners and Russians rub shoulders to stock up on vitamins from Poland until the thaw comes and the Russian spring arrives.

Moscow
30 March 1984

Made in Russia — best and worst

"So WHAT HAVE you got to offer us?" the man from Moscow Radio asked the astonished British businessman in an aggressive tone. The sales rep — one of a large number at the current exhibition in Moscow of British agricultural and food packaging companies — began to list his products and inventions, none of them available in the Soviet Union. "Everything in the Soviet Union is better and of higher quality," the radio man interrupted. "Everything. Why should we buy from you?" The exhibition, entitled inelegantly "Britagroprom", is in fact doing very good business, not least because the high profile visit of Mr Mikhail Gorbachov to Britain last December wakened a surge of Soviet interest in British goods. Britain's trade deficit with Russia was halved last year, and Anglo-Soviet trade rose by £400 million to £1,589 million.

Agriculture is one of Russia's notorious weak spots, and there is intense interest in British products from fertilizers to the Howard Rotavator paraplow, which ploughs sub-soil without disturbing the surface (very handy in the dust bowls of Kazakhstan).

Computers are another weak link in the Soviet economy, and the same crowds who have been gawping at the bread-packaging machines and food technology were gazing in wonder a few weeks ago at Sinclair and Acorn micro computers.

But the Soviet journalist's outburst reveals a curious psychological trait which lurks not far beneath the surface in most Russians and bursts out now and again: a combustible combination of scorn for the West and envy — perhaps even fear — of its achievements.

Most Russians simultaneously believe that the streets of London, Paris and New York are paved with gold and lined with the bodies of the poor and unemployed. Soviet television offers a nightly view of the world in which Soviet factories attain ever new heights of production (though the products never seem to appear in the shops) while the rest of the world disintegrates in demonstrations and riots.

By the time you get to the sport and weather you tend to sigh with relief at living in a country where you may have to queue for sausages and shoes, but nothing dreadful is likely to happen as you plod along Gorky Street with your string-bag, head down against the icy wind. When you go to buy milk you have to take an extra plastic bag because you know the milk container is bound to leak.

This sense of complacency is deliberately bolstered by carefully encouraged national pride. Tears come to Russian eyes when Soviet commentators recall Soviet achievements in space or the strength of the armed forces, or (endlessly) the defeat of Nazi Germany.

The stock Soviet response to criticism of the lack of free travel or emigration is that their country is so vast, so varied, that there is no need to go abroad. It is a spurious argument, but widely accepted.

The paradox is that the same Russians who wear their national pride on their sleeves can be astonishingly contemptuous about home-grown products, turning a carton of Marlboro cigarettes over to look carefully at the label, casting the pack aside if it says "Made under licence in the USSR" rather than "Made in the USA".

When a Russian acquaintance asks if you have a "magazine" to spare, you know what kind of magazine he has in mind in these lax post-Andropov days — and it does not contain dusty tracts on Party theory. Anything that is desirable, from consumer goods to machinery, from *Playboy* to packaging, comes from "over there".

"Our" products are at the same time second to none and too trashy to bother with. This mixture of pride and shame seems to lie behind many otherwise inexplicable Russian actions, and sometimes makes Russians difficult — though fortunately not impossible — to do business with.

Moscow
22 February 1985

Bread and butter issue upsets "toaster capital"

BELTSY (POP. 123,000) is the toaster capital of the Soviet Union. Moldavia is famous for other products, mostly agricultural: its wines are distributed all over Russia, and it produces a third of the Soviet Union's tobacco, as well as cherries and strawberries galore. But it is toasters that figure largely in Beltsy's exhibition of economic achievement. The Beltsy factory makes only one kind of toaster, a long, thin, stainless steel model. But nobody else in the entire country makes any toasters at all. The situation exercises local officials a great deal, and has been taken up by the national press, which has dubbed it the "toaster-roaster" problem.

"Roaster" is the Russian for a mini-grill, and Beltsy is in the forefront of the controversy over whether the Soviet Union should produce more roasters than toasters, or vice-versa. *Nedelya*, the Sunday supplement of *Izvestiya*, has pursued the question obsessively. In a recent article headed "A toaster is a good thing", the paper complained that Beltsy, a small town not far from the Romanian border, should not have to carry the toaster burden on its own. Officials replied that a factory in Moscow would soon begin to turn out both toasters and roasters, and would produce a hundred thousand by 1985. *Nedelya* was not satisfied, and confronted the Minister for Electrotechnical Industries, Mr Mikhail Zhuchkov. Was it true that roasters were being given precedence over toasters? the paper demanded. Well, yes, Mr Zhuchkov said. Roasters were universal, whereas toasters were not. Roasters could make toasted sandwiches, for example.

"Nor is that all," the Minister added. "Roasters are more technological, and easier to make."

Officials in Beltsy were as puzzled by this paradox as most *Nedelya* readers, but showed off their new model roaster with pride. It did not look particularly technological. As for toasters, a new factory in Tbilisi in Georgia will follow the one in Moscow in 1986.

But surely demand outstrips supply? I was referred to *Nedelya* and Mr Zhuchkov. "Let us be self-critical," the Minister suggested. "The fact is, we did not foresee the demand for this very handy appliance. In my opinion, every home should have one." He said his ministry had formed a special study group, and talked in visionary terms of a time when there would be 250,000 roasters and toasters on the market every year. At present the Beltsy factory has the capacity to produce up to 11,000 a year, although one official told us that it actually turned out only 800 toasters.

The serious side of toasters and roasters is that they make better use of bread, a constant theme in the Soviet press. Bread prices are deliberately kept low, although the real cost is growing due to grain imports. Yet a great deal goes to waste, with families throwing away stale loaves after a day or less.

The booklet which comes with the Beltsy toaster gives full and careful instructions to those who may not have seen a toaster before. It says you should use a sharp knife to cut the bread into slices no more than twelve millimetres thick, but without spreading butter, fat or anything else on them. You then take the slice (Figure 1) and place it in the slot (Figure 4), pressing down the knob (Figure 2). The booklet does not tell you what to do if the knob jams or will not stay down (all too frequent occurrences in our household).

Still, it does list toaster repair shops in nine Soviet cities from Donetsk to Vilnius, which suggests that the toaster habit is catching on and Beltsy is pioneering yet another advance towards the consumer society.

Moldavia
9 July 1983

Russians praise high-living British

To the sound of bodies turning in graves from Red Square to Highgate cemetery the Soviet press has revealed that the average British worker — normally depicted as the downtrodden victim of capitalism — is in fact far better off than his Russian counterpart, not least because he works harder.

"The standard of living of a skilled British worker is somewhat higher than ours," the trade union daily *Trud* reported, referring for proof to unusually detailed statistics on jeans and colour televisions rather than the theories of Lenin and Marx. The paper's former London correspondent, Mr Aleksei Burmistenko, told readers he had visited dozens of British factories, from textile plants to car works, during a four-year stint. "In general British workers in both industry and agriculture work more intensively than ours, and their productivity is higher," he observed. "I can testify that the rhythm of work is much tighter, smoking breaks are strictly limited, and absenteeism, drunkenness, or poor quality are very severely punished, usually by dismissal," Mr Burmistenko added.

Trud was responding to a letter from a girl student asking how much bread, jeans, cars, and rent cost in the West. This is of consuming interest to all Russians, because of the fact that most desirable goods come from the West even though the Kremlin says capitalism is disintegrating. *Trud* explained that the average British worker earns £600 a month, or 684 roubles at the official and grossly unrealistic exchange rate.

Compared to the average Soviet monthly wage of 150–200 roubles this seems princely. But *Trud* points out that taxation reduces it to £390, and that exorbitant housing, gas, electricity, and telephone charges reduce it further. *Trud* had been obliged to pay £800 for their correspondent to rent a three-room London flat. Council flats, Mr Burmistenko notes, are cheaper, but there is a waiting list from which foreigners are excluded. Taking mortgages and rents together, he suggests, the average family spends £100–150 a month on housing. Families on unemployment benefit and old-age pensioners find life difficult if not tragic, with the aged dying of hypothermia and the jobless unable to pay the rent.

Yet, it seems, the British system comes out on top. With the £180 a month he has left over, Fred can buy what Ivan can only dream of or sometimes queue for. *Trud* gives a working-class shopping list (at pre-Budget prices): beef at £4 a kilogram, cigarettes at £1 a packet, whisky at £7.20 a bottle, and £10–£18 for those much coveted jeans. The British worker also reads *The Times*, which costs him £62 a year. A car, equivalent to a Soviet Fiat-style Zhiguli — though mercifully there are no equivalents — sets the British worker back £4–5,000. His Russian counterpart pays at least twice that after a two-year wait, and cannot buy foreign makes.

Mr Burmistenko reminds readers that there are many unskilled workers in Britain, and over three million unemployed, but concludes that Russians will have to work a lot harder if they are to beat capitalism. They cannot join it after all, since Communism remains "the most humane system", dedicated to social and economic justice.

Moscow
17 March 1984

A bottle for a yolka or a sosna

WHICH DO YOU prefer, a *yolka* or a *sosna*?" is a qustion which throws most foreigners here at Christmas. After all, a Christmas tree is a Christmas tree—except in Russia. Strictly speaking it is a New Year tree that a Russian puts in his living-room, since Christmas is not a public holiday and in the Orthodox calendar does not occur until January. Besides, the atheist Soviet state firmly discourages observance of religious festivals.

To meet the natural demand for end-of-year rituals New Year's Day has become the focus of Soviet celebrations, complete with all the commercialized trappings familiar in the West: seasonal greetings cards, packed toy shops, excessive eating and drinking, and of course *yolkas* and *sosnas* decorated with gaily coloured baubles and lights. A *yolka*, for the record, is a fir tree, and a *sosna* is a pine. Most Russians have *yolkas*, but those whose help we enlisted in the search for a tree were under the unshakeable impression that West Europeans go in for pines. Consequently a splendid *sosna* now stands in the window of *The Times* flat above the traffic of Kutuzovsky Prospekt, a cheerful sight for pedestrians and for officials whizzing past in Zils and Volgas.

Getting hold of a tree is not all that easy, and can involve traditional Russian ingenuity and wheeler-dealing. You can buy them in markets dotted round Moscow, and at five or six roubles each (£4–£5) they are not too expensive. But as usual with desirable goods, there are often enormous queues. Some Russians risk the wrath of the authorities by venturing into the state-protected woods near the city and taking an axe to the *yolka* of their choice. But there is a stiff fine for *yolka*-lifting, and any foreigner caught in hand would no doubt find himself charged with theft of state property and on the next plane home. Westerners can order a tree officially, provided they remember to write a letter well in advance. Those who panic as Christmas approaches tree-less can turn to a fixer, one of the invaluable middlemen who keep the wheels of the Soviet system working by finding ways round red tape and discreetly making the connection between demand and supply.

One colleague slipped a Russian acquaintance two bottles of vodka (unsure of the going rate) and asked him to put in a word with a friendly forester. Back came the man the next day with two *yolkas*. "But I only asked for one," my colleague said. "Two bottles, two trees," came the reply.

There was a time when foreigners in Moscow would enter the snow-bound forests with official sanction and ride round on a Russian sleigh to select their tree. Unfortunately, so Moscow legend has it, the sleigh rides became uproarious fun and were stopped. Nowadays you can take a romantic troika ride only within the tamer confines of the Moscow Park of Economic Achievements. By and large it is now children who ride round the snow-covered city streets in tiny sledges pulled by their mothers, usually in the general direction of Moscow's huge toy shops.

In Children's World, the main such store (next to KGB headquarters, curiously enough), Father Christmas — known in Russia as Grandfather Frost — entertains young Muscovites in his familiar red robes and cotton-wool beard for an hour each day. (The plan only allows him an hour, as he has norms to fulfil elsewhere). For five roubles a Dial-a-Santa service will bring Grandfather Frost to your home, provided you supply him with toys beforehand and a nip of vodka afterwards. He is invariably accompanied by the Snow Maiden, a product of the Russian imagination with no Western counterpart. Racy thoughts about frolics in the snow should be banished, however, since the Snow Maiden in her tightly buttoned, sparkling white outfit has a chaste and frosty manner to match. The toys in Santa's sack do not include video games or Action Man, but Children's World products are remarkably good value. Some, such as tin lorries with sharp edges or cuddly bears with detachable eyes, would not pass British safety standards. But Russian children love the imaginative glove puppets and carved wooden toys, not to mention replicas of Soviet tanks and guns, swiftly snapped up by small boys apparently unaware that war toys are supposed to be ideologically unsound and only sold in the militaristic West.

Moscow
24 December 1984

Too many bottles spoil enterprising Pioneer

MOSCOW IS A clean city, on the whole. People do not throw wrappers and other rubbish on the pavement, and huge water-carts sluice down the streets every day, even when it is raining. Armies of labourers move the dust around with mops and brooms, and you can even see men up on ladders carefully wiping the traffic lights. But the lack of litter in public places is not entirely due to the city soviet (council) or to civic consciousness: some credit goes to the old men and women who walk round the parks with large sacks, gathering up the numerous bottles left lying on the grass. Bottles can be returned at twenty kopecks (about 15p) a time, so that a couple of sackfuls make a tidy addition to the state pension.

Discussing this little-known aspect of Russian individual enterprise recently, *Moskovskiy Komsomolets* revealed that the practice is by no means confined to the elderly. It recounted the story of twelve-year-old Sasha and his large black dog, Jack. Sasha, it seems, used to take Jack out for walks in the local park, and Jack used to keep finding empty bottles — vodka bottles, cognac bottles, wine bottles — and laying them at his young master's feet. Sasha's father, a Moscow scientist, was apparently struck by this bit of canine initiative, and took to sending the boy and the dog out every evening to look for empties. Jack was rewarded with a sugar lump for every bottle he turned up. Before long, the little evening strolls had turned into a full-scale family enterprise, with mother storing the bottles out on the balcony and grandfather taking them back to the shop to collect the proceeds. By the end of the first month the family and their dog had made 123 roubles, or over half the average monthly wage, and father could put his feet up while the business prospered. A hundred roubles was stashed away, and the rest was distributed to the workforce: five roubles to granddad for beer, three roubles to young Sasha for the cinema, and seven to his mother to buy tights. Jack got a kilogram of bones and a bigger bottle-bag.

But alas, instead of being seen as a way of turning an honest penny and keeping the parks clean at the same time, Sasha's expeditions with Jack were frowned on by the neighbours, who reported them to the police. Jack, the neighbours complained, did not wear a muzzle and instead of waiting for empties to appear had taken to ripping bottles out of the hands of startled drunks sitting on the park benches. *Moskovskiy Komsomolets* also reported with disapproval that Sasha had been so taken up with bottle-hunting that he had missed Pioneer camp during the summer, and seemed to prefer doing business to going to school.

Moscow
14 November 1982

Boom in Soviet car industry — and any car will do

THE SEVEN MILLIONTH Zhiguli car rolled off the assembly line not long ago, and the Soviet car industry is celebrating. Soviet officials say that the Zhiguli, modelled on the Italian Fiat, has the best qualities of a family car, namely "comfort, reliability and efficiency". Most Russians would say that while that might have been true when Fiat first set up its gigantic new plant at Togliatti on the Volga in 1970, Zhigulis have become increasingly uncomfortable, unreliable and inefficient since the Italians left for home and handed over to local management. Many are already queueing up to get on the waiting-list for the new version of the rival Moskvich family saloon, to be produced in conjunction with the French firm Renault. The present Moskvich is nearly twenty years old and the new French-styled model is due to make its long-awaited appearance on Moscow roads in 1986.

On the other hand, for many would-be car-owners any car at all would do, since production cannot keep pace with demand. As Soviet consumer expectations continue to rise, owning a car no longer seems an unattainable dream. The result is not only a huge waiting-list but also a thriving black market in second-hand cars.

A new Zhiguli costs about 10,000 roubles (£8,000), equivalent to four years' wages for an average worker. An astonishing number of Russians are able to provide the cash and willing to join the queue. But with new cars and spare parts in such short supply, private enterprise has moved in to fill the gaps in consumer demand, and the authorities are now trying, if not to stamp it out, then at least to control the black market. As usual with illegal dealing, it is the Georgians and other southerners who are in the forefront of the used car business. On patches of waste land on the outskirts of Moscow you can see hundreds of prospective buyers bargaining with the owners of second-hand vehicles, many of which would scarcely pass muster even in the most run-down London car lot.

But sporadic attempts to regulate the car trade seem unlikely to subdue what seems to be an irrepressible Russian desire to own a car despite all the obstacles and difficulties. Officials say they want to avoid the "negative consequences of uncontrolled automobilization" and have held back development of a network of repair and service stations. Certainly facilities for the motorist remain rudimentary.

There are only thirty-eight petrol stations in Moscow, twenty-one of them for foreigners and diplomats only. Car batteries are *defitsitny* — temporarily unobtainable — and so are windscreen wipers, with the result that most prudent car owners carefully remove theirs whenever they park and put them back on only when it starts to rain. Thefts of car parts have soared, and some Russians are reluctant to buy the more elaborate Zhiguli models in case they are stripped of all external gadgetry.

The huge eight-lane highways which radiate from the centre of Moscow like the spokes of a wheel have not yet become clogged up with traffic. But they are not as empty as they used to be, and the Moscow traffic system, which is based on a complex system of ring roads intersecting the boulevards, is not designed to cope with the heavy traffic of a modern city.

One improvement now being planned is the installation of automatic traffic lights. Most of Moscow's traffic lights are still manually operated, with a traffic policeman perched above the road in a glass control-box.

Even when automation arrives, however, the traffic police will stay on in strength, if only to bring traffic to a halt when some high-level official comes thundering down the middle of the road from the Kremlin in his black limousine with curtains on the windows. For the élite there are no shortages of new cars, no traffic fines, no traffic jams, and plenty of spare parts.

Moscow
23 December 1983

Business as usual in a closed shop

One of the Russian words which all foreigners in Moscow soon learn is *remont*. Literally it means repair, redecoration, or what the American Ambassador in London once memorably described to the Queen in a fit of pomposity as "refurbishment". But in Moscow, *remont* has connotations of paralysing disruption and interminable piles of paint-tins and rubble, with workmen who tend to disappear in mid-decoration. If you are lucky your *remont* may be done by teams of young women in headscarves and overalls, who work as decorators in order to get residential permits to live in the capital, and are invariably both cheerful and efficient. None the less, the mere mention of a prospective *remont* gives rise to sympathetic head-shaking and rolling of eyes towards the heavens on the part of those who have already been *remonted*. There are times indeed when half of Moscow seems to be "closed for *remont*".

There is a large souvenir shop not far from *The Times* office which has had a "closed for *remont*" sign hanging on it for at least six months. A peer through the dusty windows reveals acres of desolate floor space, with the odd trestle-table and broom, but little sign of anything being refurbished.

In Russia, time often seems to move in accordance with some hidden rhythm of life quite different from that which drives other societies. Last week a man appeared to begin repairing the shop's steps, but after laying a few slabs and giving careful thought to his next move he left. "Close for *remont*" is only one of a number of signs which to Muscovites mean that the shop, museum, library or public baths they wish to visit is temporarily out of bounds. The satirical magazine *Krokodil* recently carried a cartoon in which a group of shop assistants were depicted standing round a heap of signs and notices. "Which one shall we use today?" the manager asks, "Closed for *remont*, closed for stock-taking, or just closed?"

In fact, to put up a sign which simply says "Closed" is an admission of defeat. Any shopkeeper or museum attendant worth his salt can think up a stream of reasons for putting up the shutters at a moment's notice. "Closed for stock-taking" is a common one, especially in outlets such as street kiosks where the stock is so small it could be assessed in half an hour. Sometimes the signs are justified: "Closed for cleaning" is one, as is "Closed for restoration", which often means that some mansion or palace is being splendidly restored by the state.

Some of the signs are a tribute to Russian inventiveness, however. My own favourite is "Closed for technical reasons". As I was approaching a café in Moscow the other morning the lady behind the counter came to the door, bolted it firmly from inside and hung up a handwritten "Closed for technical reasons" sign. She then sat down at a table, in full view of the frustrated customers outside, and proceeded to have a good natter with the lady who wipes the table-tops.

Now and then the press complains that when someone sets off to visit a museum, the baths or a restaurant, having set aside time for the purpose, he is quite likely to find the door firmly locked, without warning. The reason is indifference to the concept of public service in the bureaucracy.

One Western correspondent recently applied for permission to visit Urengoi in Siberia, to look at the construction there of the East-West gas pipeline. The authorities replied that although Urengoi is not one of the areas normally closed to foreigners, the correspondent would not be allowed to see for himself how the Soviet Union was defying the pipeline sanctions imposed by the Reagan Administration. Why? "For reasons of a temporary nature," came the reply.

The correspondent has since been trying to find out what distinguishes reasons of a temporary nature from reasons of a permanent nature, so far without success. Like the café and the souvenir shop, Urengoi is closed for the foreseeable future.

Moscow
8 October 1982

Consumerism hides in the hire shop

WHERE DOES A Russian go if he wants a film projector or a pair of skates? Not to a shop, unless he is a professional skater or cinematographer. Ordinary Russians probably could find items like these, given persistence, a large amount of carefully saved or illicitly acquired cash, and willingness to stand for hours in a shuffling, bad-tempered queue. But it is a lot easier to go to your local hire shop, and for a few roubles rent a projector or a pair of skates by the month. Hire shops (in Russian, *prokat*) are one of the "hidden" aspects of Soviet life which make the lot of the average citizen easier, and account for what otherwise appears to be a baffling willingness to tolerate a system which provides few of the conveniences of the "consumer society".

Rentals are very much in the Communist and Socialist tradition, harking back as they do — at least in the Soviet context — to utopian notions of household articles shared communally. Ironically there is nowadays a certain amount of consumer resistance to the idea of hiring everyday articles. This reluctance is based partly on a widespread belief that anything rented out is bound to be of inferior quality, and partly on a desire to own permanently rather than temporarily, a desire which is growing as Soviet living standards rise.

As with most Soviet shops, the outside of the *prokat* is drab and unprepossessing, with little attempt at window display. But inside an astonishing range of useful articles is on offer, from heavy furniture to binoculars. Hirers have to show an identity document, and are liable to fines for late returns, paying twice the value of the item if it is lost or stolen.

Sporting goods are especially popular, since they are often difficult to find in ordinary sports shops. A modest sum for a pair of skates, for example, opens up a world of entertainment for many Russians, not only in the winter, when ponds are frozen and the paths of Gorky Park are flooded for skating, but even in the summer, when the magnificent stadiums built for the Olympic Games two years ago are made available to paying customers.

There was a time, soon after the Olympic Games, when the splendid sports facilities built to impress foreign visitors and sportsmen were closed to the public and used only by professional teams for training. But even the Soviet authorities have to respond to public pressure sometimes, and earlier this year *Pravda* printed a Supreme Soviet decree making Olympic stadiums available to the man in the street. The initial reaction was sceptical ("it's another paper promise") but many are now finding otherwise.

Armed with a pair of hired skates, the average amateur skater can now glide where Irina Rodnina and the Protopopovs once carved up the ice, thus fulfilling the Party's dictum that sport and recreation are the right of every working man and woman.

On the other hand, no stadium is complete without its quota of elegant young people, sons and daughters of the élite, clad in snazzy, well-fitting tracksuits which have never graced any hire shop, and self-consciously carrying Western equipment which no *prokat* outlet could ever afford to rent out. If the living standards of the man in the street are rising, those of the Soviet élite are obviously rising even faster.

Moscow
27 August 1982

Fanfare for the common man

THE SOVIET CENTRAL Statistical Board, reaching deep into its computer banks, has produced a composite portrait of Average Soviet Man, and a fine portrait it is too. Mr Alexander Kuznetsov (the most common Russian name — Kuznetsov means Smith) stands just over five feet seven inches in his stockinged feet, and weighs eleven stone two pounds. According to Tass, which released the statisticians' results, the Russian Mr Smith is married, lives in a city rather than the country, and is employed in industry. So far perhaps not so different from Mr Smith in Britain or America, or for that matter Herr Schmidt and M. Lefevre. From now on, however, Mr Kuznetsov takes on a more obviously Soviet tinge. Thanks to "a progressing scientific and technical revolution" in Russia, our man is probably not an "ordinary practical worker" but a researcher, "a man with a creative attitude to production". He has a working week of thirty-nine point four hours, and spends his holiday (twenty-two working days, paid) at a sanatorium or health resort at subsidized prices rather than on the Costa Brava. He reads at least twenty-one books a year and several newspapers a day in a "well-equipped two-room flat" for which he pays three per cent of his income in rent. Being an intellectually curious sort of chap, Mr Kuznetsov studies in the evenings to add an advanced education to his (free) secondary education, and only has time to watch television or listen to the radio for ninety minutes a day.

Asked if thcy recognized themselves, Russian men judged the picture to be accurate in many respects. Although housing is often cramped, rents are indeed low. Literacy is high. But a spot survey of female opinion produces a slightly different gloss. Presented with Alexander Kuznetsov, most women said the portrait greatly underestimated the amount of time their husbands spent slumped in front of the television rather than improving themselves, and failed to mention their statistically significant drinking habits. "I wish my husband had a creative attitude to production," said one lady. All agreed that living standards had risen, but said the portrait overestimated Mr Average's efficiency, diligence and workmanship. It had also neglected the fact that although Mr Kuznetsov's real income has gone up forty-five per cent in the past ten years, his monthly wage is still in the region of £150. Extra cash for the Kuznetsovs' improving lifestyle is likely to be derived from the black economy, a phenomenon which is worrying the authorities, but does not appear in official statistics.

Moscow
14 September 1982

A UNION OF EQUAL REPUBLICS

Georgia's mountain men reach the top

JUST OUTSIDE TBILISI, on the famous Georgian military highway to the Caucasus, stands a gigantic memorial in the form of a knot symbolizing Russian-Georgian friendship. The 200th anniversary of the treaty of Georgievsk between the two nations fell in 1983, and although a few Georgian nationalists were arrested for protesting against the treaty, most accepted it. A fiery, black-eyed mountain race, the Georgians prefer not to speak Russian if they can avoid it, but like the Armenians have concluded over the centuries that the Russians are preferable to the Turks or Persians.

"The remarkable thing", one local resident said, "is that we have made the Soviet system work for us". The 5 million Georgians would no doubt be delighted if Moscow adopted the Chinese principle of "one country, two systems", but since the introduction of Hong Kong-style enclaves is unlikely, to say the least, the Georgians have settled for a system in which private enterprise flourishes both legally and illegally.

Mr Edward Shevardnadze, brought in as Georgian Party leader twelve years ago to clean up the republic, is still struggling with deeply ingrained corruption. Last month several officials in charge of fruit and vegetable production were sacked for large-scale embezzlement. Georgia produces much of the Soviet Union's fruit, vegetables and wine, but some of it falls off the back of state lorries and ends up in the hands of private traders, who sell it for high prices in Moscow, where such goods are scarce. Mr Shevardnadze has also called for a drive against the growing use of drugs in Georgia, mainly hashish and opium.

But the Georgians have been remarkably adept at taking advantage of politically acceptable economic experiments as well as underground corruption. The experiments which President Andropov brought into the forefront of economic policy had their origins at Abasha, in western Georgia. It was here that factory managers were first told that while still constricted by the overall framework of the Five Year Plan, they could have a degree of local autonomy, plough back or distribute profits, offer material incentives to their workers and even make their own production and operational decisions without constant reference to Moscow. The scheme has been extended to other Georgian towns, most notably the port of Poti on the Black Sea, and Georgian officials speak of its success with pride.

In agriculture Georgia has pioneered the idea of Rapos, an acronym which stands for regional agrarian-industrial complex. Behind the ungainly vocabulary is an imaginative scheme which — as in industry — decentralizes decision-making by grouping together local farms with related food-processing industries and giving the resulting amalgamation extensive local powers. Private plots have also been increased.

The result of the experiment — consciously based on Hungarian reforms — is that declining growth rates have been reversed, and so too has rural migration, an especially difficult problem in Georgia, where eighty-seven per cent of the land is mountainous and difficult to cultivate. There has been a return to "abandoned hearths", was how one Tbilisi official put it.

The results are also reflected in living standards, which are higher than in Moscow. Cars throng the roads, the shops are relatively well stocked with some good window displays (almost unknown in Russia itself).

Fruit is expensive (I paid £9 for four and a half pounds of pears and a bar of chocolate), but available, even in winter. The wine does not compare with European vintages, but there are some robust varieties of red, including *kindsmarauli*, a semi-sweet reputed to have been Stalin's favourite.

Tbilisi itself is a dusty, rust-coloured town, with factory chimneys belching smoke near the centre. There are pockets of distinctive charm, including the sixth-century churches with their round towers and conical metallic roofs.

Somehow the Georgians manage to rise above Soviet inefficiencies and absurdities. They have a national self-confidence which stretches back to the twelfth century and the reign of Queen Tanara, Georgia's golden age; and guides at the Art Museum argue seriously that Asia Minor enjoyed its renaissance long before Western Europe, whereas Russia never had a renaissance at all and remained backward.

At a restaurant at Mtskheta, the ancient Georgian capital and still its leading religious centre, the manager revealed that the enterprise has its own livestock, can distribute profits, has a turnover of 3,000 roubles a day and pays its staff twice the average industrial wage.

Tbilisi, Georgia
10 January 1985

Home town reveres its favourite son

IT BEGINS IN Tbilisi, where Stalin stares out stonily from a frieze high on the Party History Institute on Rustaveli Avenue, and gazes in full generalissimo's uniform from an oil painting in the savings bank next door. There is a Stalin Embankment, a Stalin Bridge, even a Stalin Park, an appropriately joyless place set high above the town and reached by a rickety funicular railway. Every Georgian lorry-driver's cab, every shop, has its photograph of Georgia's most famous son, revered in his homeland as he is reviled elsewhere. The Stalin cult reaches a crescendo in Gori, two hours' drive away. Here Stalin stands outside the town hall on the main square, in the place normally reserved for Lenin. The one-roomed hut in which Stalin — then Josif Dhugashvili — was born is preserved as a shrine, its sparseness emphasizing the humble origins of the shoemaker's son who rose to become dictator.

Nearby is the grandiose Stalin Museum, founded in two modest rooms in 1939 but expanded in 1958 in defiance of Khrushchev's destalinization campaign. Inside, light pours through blue and yellow glass on to white marble statues of Stalin as a young revolutionary and as a war leader, and room after room of photographs depict his career in sanitized terms. Guides speak reverently of a man who proclaimed his modesty to Tbilisi workers at a 1926 meeting, who later remarked: "As for me, I am only Lenin's pupil," and who in 1938 ordered a book about his childhood to be burned because it was "too grovelling". There is no mention of the fact that in the 1930s Stalin also ordered the deaths of millions of people in the purges and enforced collectivization of agriculture. Trotsky, Bukharin and other prominent victims have literally been erased from the photographs as they were extinguished in life.

The museum emphasizes Stalin's genius as a wartime commander, and all visitors over fifty react with emotion to the sound of Stalin's disembodied voice delivering his 1941 rallying call to the nation. In the tomb-like chill of the final room Stalin's death mask lies on a marble plinth sunk in the floor, surrounded by white columns. A painting of his lying-in-state hangs on the wall.

Not all Georgians admire Stalin, whose terror struck down the Georgian intelligentsia as well. "He was capricious and cruel," one Tbilisi resident said. "But he led us against Hitler, and left the Soviet Union more powerful than ever."

The forthcoming fortieth anniversary of the end of the Second World War has given impetus to a campaign all over the Soviet Union to rehabilitate Stalin, at least partially. All Russians have mixed feelings about him, and very few would go along with the view presented at Gori. On the other hand, the museum is expecting huge numbers from all over the country to come to Gori to mark Stalin's 105th birthday today; not perhaps the 45,000 who came for the centenary, but enough to confirm the new interest in a man who for years has been almost unmentionable.

In recent months Stalin has been increasingly discussed or mentioned in the Soviet media. Television has shown him in his white marshal's uniform at Yalta and Potsdam, and addressing the nation at the outbreak of war, when he spoke of "brothers and sisters" instead of "comrades", and appealed to history and religion rather than Marx and Lenin.

The new film, *Marshal Zhukov*, depicts a Stalin who was often indecisive or arbitrary, but who was also often firm, intelligent and wise. Even Stalin's role in the revolution is under discussion, with a re-emergence of the (false) suggestion that Stalin was prominent in 1917 and always backed Lenin.

The Gori museum intends to expand still further for next May's Victory Day celebrations, with sections on Stalin and his generals (avoiding his slaughter of Red Army officers), and one on Stalin's family, including his son, Yakov, who died a German captive in 1943. The news that Svetlana, Stalin's errant daughter, might live in Tbilisi rather than Moscow stirred local pride.

At a wine cellar in Tbilisi, the moustachioed shopkeeper pulled back a curtain to reveal a private collection of Stalin photos and mementoes. "I shall be drinking his health on Friday," he said with a broad smile, raising an earthenware bowl of Kakhetian wine. "Here's to a true son of Georgia."

Gori, Georgia
21 December 1984

A life lost in Odessa

COSMOPOLITAN ODESSA, COLOURFUL Black Sea city of crime, dockside whores, salty sailors and Jewish shopkeepers and humorists. Not any more. Ladies of the night do haunt the hard-currency bars, and Soviet thrillers about the KGB still tend to depict corrupt underworld villains living in luxury in Odessa. But there is no sign of the Bohemian café frequented once by the celebrated comic writing duo, ILF and Petrov. The café name has been retained, but the premises have moved, and the place is a run-of-the-mill Soviet cafeteria.

No streets are named after Babel, creator of the archetypal Odessa gangster Benya Krik, or after ILF and Petrov, inventors of the roguish con-man Ostap Bender. All the places seem to be named after Taras Shevchenko, a Soviet-approved founder of Ukrainian culture [Odessa is now part of the Ukraine, largely an administrative convenience].

No doubt the old Odessa had its drawbacks. The Soviet authorities are certainly taking some steps to resurrect the best of the past, such as the loving *restoration* of eighteenth- and nineteenth-century limestone buildings, including the London Hotel overlooking the sea. There is more street life than in most Soviet cities, with shoppers strolling along airy streets, and pausing at stalls or ice-cream kiosks. Fruit seems plentiful. There are good beaches at Arcadia, Odessa's contribution to the concept of the working-class sanatorium belt (*Et in Arcadia ego* suddenly takes on new meaning as a Marxist-Leninist slogan), and at the resort of Luzanovka, also known rather disconcertingly as Kemping [camping].

The port bustles, with a thriving new cargo terminal at Yuzhni nearby, constructed with Western help. The combined cargo turnover is 20 million tons a year, including grain, fertilizers and petrochemicals. The main passenger harbour was rebuilt in 1936, the only drawback being the loss of one or two of the bottom-most Potemkin steps, the legendary flight of 192 steps on which the blood of Russian revolutionaries was spilled in 1905, but which are now cut off from the water by the terminal.

The Odessa Stock Exchange, once the beating heart of the city's commerce, is now used for pop concerts. The latest attraction this summer was a group called Bim Bom. Across the road is the delightfully baroque stucco exterior of the Krasnaya or Red Hotel, a name which predates the Communist era.

There is also the music school which gave us Emil Gilels and David Oistrakh, and the magnificent Opera House, modelled on the Vienna Opera House and saved by Partisans from Nazi destruction during wartime occupation. The Communists, indeed, have restored a great deal of the Odessa the Nazis tore down.

What the Soviet authorities have not been able to restore is the vibrant Jewish life which once made Odessa a byword for Jewish humour and acumen. Thousands of Jews perished under the Nazis, but there is a significant Jewish community left. They have one synagogue, but as I found when I set out by tram and on foot to track it down one hot and dusty afternoon, the synagogue is "closed for repairs". Its windows are cracked and boarded up. It is, in any case, in a semi-industrial area, next to a railway line, a forlorn sight. The official view is that Odessa's Jews, Armenians, Greeks, Ukrainians and Russians have all intermarried and are assimilated.

In the sense that all Odessans seem to have a Jewish sense of humour and love of wisecracks, this is true. But the Jewish community which once produced the great Isaac Babel is none the less left without a focus for Jewish spiritual life.

Odessa
7 September 1984

An island of religion in a sea of Communism

"AND THIS", THE young, bearded priest said, "is the spear that pierced Christ's side". Westerners and Russians in the group both peer closely at the dark metallic shape set in gold, with the same mixture of awe and scepticism. It is the sharp, triangular tip of a spear, but then you can't expect the shaft to have survived as well. "And this", moving on to the next case, "is a fragment of wood from Noah's Ark". We are in the museum attached to the cathedral at Echmiadzin, headquarters of the Armenian Church, in the small and mountainous Armenian Soviet Republic. The cathedral was founded in AD 304, three years after Christianity had become the state religion. The Church has thus been firmly identified with the nation for centuries, and has survived a succession of foreign occupations. Our guide is a tall, black-robed man with the air of one who has inherited a tradition rather older than that of the Communist state outside. He throws open a window and points towards the distant snow-capped peaks of Mount Ararat, dimly visible through the haze. "Ararat is our national symbol," he says.

The fragment of Noah's Ark in the museum was brought back from an expedition by Echmiadzin monks to the slopes of Mount Ararat in the fourth century. The Holy Spear was carried to Armenia by St Bartholomew. Symbols are extremely important to Armenians, and most have to do with national identity, Christianity, or both. The distant peaks of Ararat are now in Turkey, under a treaty signed in 1921. Turkey is the focus of much Armenian nationalism, much to the relief of the Russians, who appear postively benign in contrast.

All Armenians, both Christian and Communist (and a large number in Soviet Armenia manage to combine the two), refer constantly to "the genocide", the massacre (denied by Turkey) of one and a half million Armenians by the Turks in 1915 during Russo-Turkish hostilities.

Armenian Christianity has long defined itself not only in contrast to the Islamic world which surrounds it, but also as distinct from both Eastern Orthodoxy (Byzantium) and Western Christendom (Rome). The Armenian Christians rejected the Concilium of AD 451, between Rome and the Eastern Church over Christ's embodiment of man and the deity, and went their own way.

Among the 3 million Armenians of the present-day Soviet republic, which proudly promotes Armenian national identity, the Church enjoys great spiritual authority, thanks to its richness of tradition. It is also well off in worldly terms, since the 3 million Armenians who live abroad — in the Middle East, Europe and America — support it generously. The treasures of Echmiadzin include the ancient Armenian alphabet, fashioned in gold, and a priceless gold cross, both paid for by a wealthy French Armenian family.

Catholicos Vazgen, the head of the Church, has presided over this island of religious self-sufficiency for nearly thirty years, and continues to tread a careful path of co-operation with the Communist authorities, who tolerate the Church's independence and international contacts in return for a discreet silence on political matters.

A small man with a white beard, the Cathilocos, who is seventy-four, tells visitors that the church confines itself to spiritual care, adding with a twinkle: "Of course, all Armenians are free to attend our services."

The Church is not without problems. There are only fifty-two functioning churches in the republic, and permission to reconsecrate any of the thousands of churches which have become state architectural monuments is not easy to obtain. But Church and state rub along together, both well aware that in the perspective of 1,600 years — more if you count the pagan temple under the cathedral — sixty years of Communism do not loom all that large. The Party, too, has its symbols, although none which quite compares with the spear which pierced Christ's side.

Armenia
11 January 1983

Letter from Baku

IT IS NOT the smell of oil and gas you notice first — that comes later, and then you cannot get it out of your nostrils. The first impression of Baku is visual, a forest of oil derricks and "nodding donkey" oil drills extending to infinity on arid soil, and the orange flame spouting from the chimney at the Baku Oil Refinery as it burns off waste gases. The flame recalls the fires nineteenth-century travellers used to see as they approached Baku, on the shores of the Caspian Sea, and the Zoroastrian fire-worshippers' temple on the outskirts, where the flame still burns. The ground around Baku is soaked with oil and naphtha springs. You feel you risk self-immolation every time you light up a cigarette.

Baku has other claims to fame. The Azerbaijanis, a quick-witted Shia Muslim people, have produced two leading Soviet personalities: Garry Kasparov, the chess grandmaster, and Geidar Aliyev, brought from Baku to Moscow three years ago to be Deputy Prime Minister. It is said that Aliyev, fired by Azerbaijani patriotism, personally persuaded Kasparov (who was originally called Weinstein) to change his name, "Kasparov" being reminiscent of "Caspian". Alas, no one in Baku could (or would) confirm the story.

Azerbaijan also boasts marvellous carpets, wrongly known in the West as "Persian". Tabriz, they tell you in Baku, is in "Southern Azerbaijan", not Iran. There are 13 million Azeris over the border, twice as many as in Azerbaijan itself. There is a well-restored old town, with the fifteenth-century palace of Shirvan Shah. There is also the more recent monument to the twenty-six Baku commissars, the martyrs of the early Soviet regime, shot during the anti-Bolshevik Transcaucasian Muslim government of 1918–20, which was supported by Britain. British troops were in Baku and Ashkhabad, and allegedly condoned (but did not carry out) the shootings. The monument refers only to "agents of imperialism", and I found no residual anti-British feeling. 1918 seems as distant as Shirvan Shah. "England?" said the taxi-driver, grinning. "Very good." There was wailing Turkish pop music on his radio, interspersed with Michael Jackson.

There is no conspicuous oil prosperity in Baku — the 13 million tonnes Azerbaijan extracts annually, both on land and offshore, is swallowed up by the Soviet economy as a whole. But the streets are clean and tree-lined, and although the nearest usable beach is 50 miles away ("We have no pollution problem," officials say implausibly), the promenade, by the Caspian, that giant inland sea, is alive with cafés, music, table-tennis and (Kasparov's inspiration?) chess. Out to sea a jetty runs for 300 kilometres, servicing the offshore derricks first put down in 1952 and still going strong, complemented now by modern oil rigs. "Glory to the oil workers of Baku!" say the slogans. Local pride is strong, and if there are more portraits of Lenin in Baku than elsewhere (odd how his features become more oriental as you move east), this is because Marxism-Leninism sits more lightly on the Muslim south than on Moscow.

Azerbaijanis point out that the first oil derrick was invented here in 1848, a full eleven years before America, forgetting that the pre-revolutionary oil industry is ideologically frowned on because it was dominated by foreign capital and oil millionaires. In Baku you can feel the kind of national self-assertion which has plagued the Russians for well over a hundred years. You also feel the tug of Iran and Turkey, and across the Caspian, beyond Turkmeniya, lies Central Asia, with the no less potent pull of China, India and Afghanistan.

Baku
August 1985

Breaking the ice in a Soviet desert

THE DAWN FLIGHT from Baku, an ageing Tupolev–134, lumbered over the Karakum Desert and headed for Bukhara by way of Samarkand. The legendary cities of Central Asia waited in their oases. But suddenly the 134 (an aircraft based on the BAC 1–11), after circling aimlessly, climbed back into the sky above the apparently lifeless sands, and headed for the Caspian again. There was no explanation, and none of the passengers — Azerbaijanis, Armenians, Uzbeks — seemed to expect one. The stout Russian stewardess came down the aisle to the two foreigners. "Fog at Samarkand," she said. It seemed unlikely, but turned out to be true: a freakish patch of fog. "We are making an unscheduled landing." Where? "At Chardzhou, in Turkmeniya. In the desert." We must have looked alarmed. "By the Amu Darya River." Her remarks, kindly meant, were directed solely at us, but others got the drift. "Fog" repeated an Azerbaijani across the aisle, in Russian. "Chardzhou." The word was passed round, until eventually the stewardess made an announcement. We landed, wheeling over sand and scrub and isolated patches of water. It was hot on the ground, and the cabin became stifling. Perhaps emboldened by the explanation — in Russia you are told the minimum, or nothing — one or two voices were raised in protest.

"What about a smoke?" called out a burly Uzbek. The Armenian steward opened the door. "Go to the edge of the desert," instructed the stewardess. "Not the terminal building."

It was difficult to see what could be worth hiding at Chardzhou, even if it was a port on the Amu Darya and not far from the Afghan border. Chardzhou, a small town, produces the finest ladies' underwear in the Soviet Union. I found this boast in a local paper. "Buy our romantic style bras," it said. Chardzhou also produces phosphates. At the airfield nothing much moved except Antonov–2 crop-spraying bi-planes, which buzzed angrily into the heat haze. Stray dogs skulked under the fuselages, and local inhabitants bicycled past like Chinese peasants. One or two soldiers — olive-skinned Azerbaijanis — lit up cigarettes under the aircraft wings. "Move away!" yelled the crew, and they moved away, setting up a cassette recorder where the tarmac ended and the Karakum began. The passengers — a living cross-section of the Soviet Union's bewildering variety of nationalities — began to dance to the wailing oriental music. The barriers began to dissolve, and the crew too became more informal. Photographs of children were exchanged, admired. Questions about England were asked. It seemed a remote and unlikely land.

"Do you grow cotton on collective farms like us?" asked an Uzbek lady in a brightly coloured dress. Her husband, a man with long black boots, a quilted coat and the profile of Tamburlaine, waited for a reply. I was still trying to think of one when the craggy, confidence-inspiring Aeroflot pilot re-appeared from the mysteriously off-limits terminal building, stragglers were rounded up, and the rattling 134 roared down the airstrip. "Respected comrade passengers," intoned the steward-ess, "our flight has been resumed". After a three-hour desert diversion, foreigners, passengers and crew resumed their allotted roles.

Chardzhou is not a closed city — it had simply not been on our schedule. Confronted by the unexpected, the unplanned for, Soviet officials tend to stick to the rule book. It is the safest course, since to bend the rules invites almost certain rebuke from superiors, who in turn fear reprimand from those more senior still.

Chardzhou
29 June 1985

Letter from Samarkand

THE ROAD TO Samarkand is bumpy nowadays rather than golden. You reach the legendary city — built by Alexander the Great, razed by Genghis Khan, built again more splendidly than ever by Tamburlaine — in an Antonov–24b, a propeller-driven copy of the old Fokker Friendship, which buzzes noisily from Bukhara and Tashkent, high above the Central Asian deserts. "Samarkandites!" says a large and ugly poster on the airport road, "Raise the level of your consciousness and organization! Prepare worthily for the Twenty-Seventh Party Congress!" Down at the Gour Emir Mausoleum, Tamburlaine (Timur the Lame), that extraordinary despot, must be turning in his nephrite-covered tomb.

But the lure and magic of the old silk routes from India and China are still there. The buildings left behind by Tamburlaine and his scholarly grandson and successor, Ulug Beg, are awesome: the massive Bibi Khanum Mosque, half-ruined by time and earthquakes; the chilling Shah Zinda street of the dead, with the mausoleums of Tamburlaine's relatives, decorated in yellow and blue majolica tiles; the tomb of Hassam Ibn Abbas, whom Muslims believe was a cousin of Mohammed the Prophet and still lives underground; the remains of the observatory of Ulug Beg; above all the Registan, the magnificent central square, bounded on three sides by the soaring façades of medressehs, or islamic seminaries (now defunct).

Samarkand, thronged with Russian and foreign sightseers, has been splendidly restored — especially the breathtaking Golden Mosque at the Registan. But the authorities, who spend over a million roubles (£1 million) a year on restoration, see Islam as an architectural rather than religious inheritance. Ulug Beg, rather absurdly, is presented as a kind of proto-Marxist for his attempts to combine Islam with science.

There is a slightly different atmosphere at Bukhara, not far away. Here the Red Army was welcomed in the 1920s, when Bukhara and Khiva became Soviet republics, partly because the ruling emir was unusually unpleasant and brutal. Under his rule the delicate and beautiful twelfth-century minaret by the Kalyan

Mosque was known as the tower of death, because the emir threw his victims from the top. Nobody found it inappropriate when Soviet power was proclaimed from the tower of death.

Whereas in Samarkand the inheritance of Tamburlaine is organized for tourism (his famous tomb is right next to the main tourist hotel), Bukhara has been left much more to itself, possibly in the hope that what was once a centre of Islamic anti-Soviet resistance would simply crumble. It has a serene, lived-in air. There are only three active mosques, and the muezzin no longer calls from the great minaret; the exquisite ninth-century Samanid Mausoleum is now surrounded incongruously by the Kirov Park of Culture and Rest. But Islamic students go about their business at the medresseh, Russia's only functioning Muslim college; wrestlers and acrobats perform at the bustling market, merchants sit under ancient stone domes at street junctions, away from the heat and dust. At quiet pools (*hausas*), now largely purified of infectious disease by the Soviets, Uzbeks in baggy trousers and turned-up shoes sit cross-legged on blue wooden platforms, drinking green tea under the mulberry trees.

It is difficult to imagine Bukhara having inflicted on it the grotesque Marxist *son et lumière* produced every evening — in Russian — at the Registan in Samarkand. Here the voice of the ancient monuments, booming from behind the illuminations, announces that the Registan has suffered for centuries under tyrants such as Genghis Khan and Tamburlaine before being liberated by the glorious birth of Soviet Communism and the Leninist Party in the victorious struggle of the Uzbek and Russian masses. The Russian tourists, mostly factory and office-workers on collective holidays in the southern sun, seemed to enjoy every minute.

Samarkand
August 1985

Feeling the heat in the Soviet deep south

HOW DO YOU survive in Ashkhabad when the temperature soars to fifty degrees centigrade and there is no chance of a drop of rain until October? You can sit at a shaded tea-house which is what most Turkomans seem to do in their shaggy Astrakhan hats; or you can retreat to leafy Lenin Park and admire the unusual pedestal of the inevitable Lenin monument, decorated in colourful mosaic to resemble Turkoman carpets (mistakenly known in the West as "Bukhara" carpets, because that is where they were traded — there are no carpets in Bukhara. The same goes for Astrakhan pelts). You can do what the small boys of Ashkhabad do and splash in the town fountains. Or you can heed the urgings of the local Communist paper and buy an air-conditioner.

The benefits of civilization are finally reaching Ashkhabad, capital of Turkmeniya (or Turkmenistan), and the southernmost point in the Soviet Union. The Red Army had a great deal of trouble subduing the Turkomans in the 1920s and 1930s, and the overpowering heat cannot have helped. There was even, from 1918 to 1920, a staunchly anti-Bolshevik local regime supported by several hundred British troops, who for a while kept the Russians at bay. Perhaps the sun eventually sapped British morale (although most of the British troops were Indian, I was told).

It is difficult at first to see why either Moscow or "the imperialists" should be remotely interested in this scorched spot on the edge of the Karakum Desert. But those mountains looming forbiddingly only forty kilometres away, the Kopet Dag, are in Iran, and not far in the other direction lies Afghanistan. Ashkhabad is a border town, the sharp edge of Russia's conflicts with both fundamentalist Islam and the West. The border-guards' hotel is even listed in local guides. Foreigners are forbidden to wander towards the Kopet Dag range, although the heat is probably enough to keep most well within the Akal Teke oasis in which Ashkhabad lies. But you can visit the Parthian ruins at Nissa, at the very foot of the Kopet Dag, provided you point your camera away from the border. And out in the desert you can inspect the Karakum Canal, a remarkable engineering feat, a thousand kilometres long. The Parthian Empire (second century BC to third century AD), like other temporary rulers of Turkmenistan, came and went, but the Tsarist army in the nineteenth century brought the benefits of modern civilization: hospitals, schools, the railway.

Last year Ashkhabad celebrated a hundred years of Russian rule, Tsarist and Soviet. Among the latest benefits of Soviet technology is the BK 1500, an air-conditioning unit produced by

Ashpromtorg, available — according to *Evening Ashkhabad* — from shop number 76 at 325 roubles (about £300). "Install an air-conditioner in your home," the paper suggested. "You won't regret it. Even in extreme heat it will create a micro-climate in your flat." Upmarket Turkomans can buy the BK 2500 at 375 roubles. The paper told readers air-conditioning had been medically proved to be beneficial to old people with heart disease and young people prone to colds. "So why not buy one today?" Alas, shop number 76 was not doing brisk business, partly perhaps because you have to risk sunstroke to get to it, but also — so I was reliably informed — nine times out of ten the BK 1500, and even the upmarket BK 2500, breaks down. Besides, £300 is twice the average monthly wage, and as they remarked down at the tea-house, two months' wages is a lot to pay just to keep cool. Sometimes, even in Ashkhabad, the old methods are the best.

Ashkhabad
18 July 1985

COMPUTERS — A DIFFERENT KIND OF REVOLUTION:

TECHNOLOGY AND EDUCATION

Videos, with love from the West

THE IMAGE ON the screen is blurred and grainy, but you can just make out Marlon Brando making somebody an offer they cannot refuse. His voice, however, and the voices of all other actors in *The Godfather*, are lost underneath a dubbed translation into Russian, read by an actor from one of Moscow's leading film studios — illegally. With the curtains drawn, and a frisson of excitement in the small audience crowded into the living-room, this might be the showing of a blue movie somewhere in a jaded Western suburb. In fact, it is the advance wave of the video revolution, which has made a limited impact on the lives of Moscow's privileged élite. Few ordinary Russians have seen a video cassette recorder. They are not available for hire, and although the Soviet Union is beginning to manufacture them, they are prohibitively expensive, up to 10,000 roubles, or four years' salary for the average worker. Most of those who can afford videos prefer to buy imported Japanese models, mostly on the black market. Customers include top Soviet officials (and their privileged offspring), and rouble-rich illegal entrepreneurs, many of them from the southern republics of Georgia and Azerbaijan, where illegal trading is practically a way of life. The main problem is getting hold of cassettes. Western films, such as *The Godfather*, *Apocalypse Now* and *A Clockwork Orange* are among the forbidden fruits, as the newspaper *Sovietskaya Rossiya* has revealed.

There is also a steady demand for pornography. Most Western films with even a mildly erotic content appear pornographic by prudish Soviet standards, but many video owners want the "real thing", which nine times out of ten turns out to be *Emmanuelle*. *Sovietskaya Rossiya* recently disclosed that Moscow police had cracked a ring of illegal traders in Western cassettes. The underground video entrepreneurs had smuggled Western video equipment into Russia, and used it to reproduce pirated copies for the flourishing black market. They had hired leading actors and translators to supply a Russian soundtrack, and had sold the results for up to 200 roubles a cassette (above the average monthly wage). The report said more than fifty people had been charged with "purveying pornography".

There is no doubt the authorities are worried by a limited video invasion. Last December General Vitaly Fedorchuk, then head of the KGB secret police and now Interior Minister, introduced a new law in the Supreme Soviet tightening up regulations on the importing of films and video, and instructed border guards and Customs officials to be extra vigilant in their search for material "harmful to the moral health of the nation".

The new regulations were so zealously applied that they affected the work of Western television companies operating in Moscow. American television networks, including CBS and NBC, were recently told that even routine material recorded in the Soviet Union would have to be examined in full by Customs officials at Moscow airport.

The United States protested that it was an imposition of censorship and a violation of the Helsinki agreements. The practice has now stopped and the Russians are turning a blind eye to their own regulations, much to the relief of American correspondents, since the careful screening of video tapes by Soviet officials takes several hours.

The main worry of the authorities is not only that the moral health of the nation will be undermined by *Emmanuelle*, but also that Western ideas, political, social and cultural, will creep insidiously into Soviet life through films, documentaries and television shows recorded on video. In the West it is called the information revolution, but in Russia information is something to be restricted and controlled, not disseminated at the push of a button.

Moscow
23 April 1983

Kremlin joins the video revolution

AFTER A YEAR or two of agonizing, the Russians have finally decided that since they can't beat the video revolution, they had better join it — provided it can be harnessed for orthodox Soviet ends rather than the "infection" of wicked Western ways. Only last spring the Soviet press was inveighing against video as yet another dark Western plot to undermine morality and the Communist system. Papers reported that the police had broken up a ring of black market dealers in video players and cassettes, seizing such subversive films as *The Godfather*, *Apocalypse Now* and *A Clockwork Orange*. Video, the press declared righteously, had become a status symbol for the privileged and corrupt. All over Moscow, video screens were flickering behind closed curtains, with grainy third-hand pirated versions of Western pornography and violence.

But while sealing Russia's borders against unwelcome imports was a necessary precaution, the attempt to stamp out "video fever" altogether may have been hasty and ill-advised, according to a recent issue of the *Literary Gazette*.

The information technology revolution which has seized the West over the past decade and transformed areas of life from commerce to entertainment poses serious problems for the Kremlin. Whereas the West assumes that proliferation of information is desirable and stimulates economic activity, in Russia, information of all kinds is kept under lock and key.

Officials acknowledge that Russia is falling further behind every day, and is a "computer illiterate" society. In an effort to get to grips with part of the problem, the *Literary Gazette* offers the heretical view that the drawbacks stem from the misuse of video in "unclean hands" rather than from video itself.

Video is no more to blame for violence or pornography than the printing press or cinema. Like them (and like computers) video is a tool which can be beneficial — in the right hands. The Soviet Union must face the fact that "the age of cassette cinema has begun", the paper said, adding that, in future, Soviet viewers might be able to watch their favourite Eisenstein or Fellini film on video, just as they can now take down a volume by Shakespeare or Dostoevsky from the shelf.

This still leaves the Kremlin with two main headaches: how to provide hardware and software on a mass scale and keep up with Western developments, and how to control illegal cassettes. There is a home-grown Soviet video recorder, but as the *Literary Gazette* frankly noted, it costs £2,000 and does not work. Those few Russians who can afford it prefer Japanese or European machines, bought on the black market for up to £6,000 each.

Foreigners cannot sell electrical equipment to Russians, and have to sign a declaration at the Soviet Customs that they will re-export all appliances or prove they have been destroyed. Nonetheless, Western goods do filter through and reach those in high places — from the Georgian underworld to the political élite.

The underground market in cassettes flourishes despite police raids and the vigilance of Customs, who confiscate even harmless recordings. The fear, as the *Literary Gazette* observed, is that passive Soviet viewers will suffer from "cultural infection".

The paper says the answer may lie in Government authorized video clubs, where enthusiasts can gather in a homely atmosphere and watch edifying documentaries and films produced by state television and state cinema organizations.

A more ingenious solution, given that some Russians might opt for Linda Lovelace rather than more films about the Second World War and documentaries on heroic steelworkers, is for Russia to mass-produce a video system which is conveniently incompatible with both VHS and Betamax, the main Western systems.

Secret talks have already begun with Grundig of West Germany for the Soviet Union to manufacture under licence the Grundig 2000, which failed commercially in the West but which the Russians could happily market in the secure knowledge that it could not be used to screen cassettes condemned by the Kremlin as unfit for public consumption.

Moscow
5 May 1984

Russia's computer fever

THERE WERE DENSE crowds at Moscow's Exhibition centre, with Russians pushing and shoving for a glimpse of goods on display with all the energy they normally reserve for shopping queues. But the sign above the stands said "Sinclair", "Quest Automation", and "Acorn", and behind the ropes holding the crowds in check were row upon row of gleaming keyboards and visual display units. "My God!" said a burly teacher from the Ukraine, up in Moscow on business. Did he have anything similar in his institute? He looked unhappy. "We have some equipment," he said, "very primitive you know. We must first grasp the idea of computers." He brightened up. "But there are plans."

The exhibition is part of the Kremlin's recently-announced concerted drive to catch up with the West in computer technology, despite the authorities' deep anxiety over the potential impact of an information explosion on a tightly controlled and isolated society. The main target is Russia's 64,000 secondary schools and the aim is to make Soviet children as computer-literate as their Western counterparts. Earlier this month a Politburo instruction laid down that the Soviet Union was to become an up-to-date technological society by the end of the century, with the stress on electronics. According to the Soviet officials who have visited the exhibition in droves, Russia is eventually to have twenty desk-top computers a classroom, with the first phase of the project coming into effect in September.

"I've never seen anything like it," said an exhausted British computer salesman as yet another deputy minister arrived, flanked by bodyguards. Britain is leading the field in the Soviet Union and Eastern Europe, with Italian, West German and Scandinavian firms also getting attention. The exhibition, which had a ten-day run, revolves round the computer as an educational aid, but officials from ministries of oil, machine tools, health and agriculture have called in for demonstrations. A good many of the crowd are in uniform, reflecting intense military interest.

Cocom, the Western organization which controls technical exports to Communist countries, last year lifted some of its restrictions, but those governing equipment with obvious military application remain in force. There are none the less grey areas. There is also a temptation — since the Russians are starting from scratch, according to Western experts — to dump outdated hardware on Russia. "They are so far behind they will never catch up," one expert confided. But Sinclair's East European marketing manager says it is wrong to regard Russia as a "second class market". "We will sell equipment as up to date as Cocom regulations allow, not inferior products," he declared.

Moscow
23 January 1985

Red tape ties up the future

IT WAS A close encounter between the futuristic world of Western high technology and the cautious, blinkered, rather Victorian world of the Soviet bureaucracy. On the one hand, the heirs of Lenin: on the other, the whizz-kid prophets of the computer age. The encounter took place at a branch of the Moscow Institute for Professional and Technical Education, a ramshackle building up a dirt road just off Leninsky Prospekt, where a British computer consortium, the Spectrum Group plc, was putting a range of electronic marvels through their paces.

The Politburo has decided to make the technological leap into the twenty-first century and the Spectrum demonstration was one of the results. Above the rows of gleaming keyboards, visual display units, video screens and software samples a forbidding portrait of Lenin looked down with apparent disapproval as enthusiastic young British salesmen explained their wares to large delegations of ponderous thick-set Soviet officials in poorly-cut East European suits and status-symbol gold watches.

The usual Soviet wallcharts had been screened off to make way for the computers but a giant quotation from Lenin still hung above the lecture platform: "The education of modern youth must consist of education in Communist morality", it said, somewhat incongruously. Next to it was a quote from Chernenko which the authorities had not had time to replace with one from Gorbachov: "There is no higher task than the instillation in young people of Marxist-Leninist ideology."

The decision to enter the computer age by buying it in from the West was made under Chernenko and was linked to his school reform. But the campaign has gained fresh impetus with the arrival in the Kremlin of Mikhail Gorbachov, whose main priority is economic modernization and reform and who is moving fast to place like-minded young technocrats in positions of power right across the Soviet Union. The head of the Academy of Sciences, Dr Anatoly Alexandrov, has compared today's computer training programme with the fight against illiteracy after the 1917 revolution.

A Politburo decree laid down a long-term policy of technological innovation to the year 2000 with the emphasis on computers. This was followed up in *Pravda* which reported that the Politburo was determined to introduce computers into every one of Russia's 64,000 secondary schools in a phased programme, to ensure "computer literacy" among staff and pupils alike.

The scale of the problem confronting the Kremlin — and the Committee for Science and Technology, which is shouldering much of the burden — is staggering. The personal computers which have flooded the Western markets are completely unknown in Soviet electronics shops. One of the drawbacks of the Kremlin campaign is that there is no back-up at home, no family use of computers and, so far, no application of computer technology in society at large.

The Soviet manufacturing and retail system is so cumbersome and backward that Western experts find the idea of computers being used, say, for stocktaking unrealistic — unless Mr Gorbachov is able to combine computerization with a radical overhaul and reform of the economy, despite objections from hardline Stalinists of the old school.

Like other aspects of the information technology revolution, computers present the Kremlin with a threat to its jealously-guarded monopoly of information, which is an instrument of social and political control. Like video, computers are only acceptable in Russia — as far as the Communist Party is concerned — if they can be kept firmly under lock and key, and are controlled at all times by politically-reliable teachers and officials unlikely to use the computers for unapproved purposes.

Soviet officials were taken aback when Western salesmen at the recent seminar used a portrait of Lenin to demonstrate the tricks of an HRX (High Resolution Graphics) computer which digitizes video signals. Seeing the revered founder of the Soviet state reduced to a postage stamp, turned upside down and surrounded by pictures of Marilyn Monroe is not quite what the Kremlin has in mind. But there is a classroom system which meets Soviet anxieties, which is called the Network and can accommodate up to 250 computers per classroom, a detail which fascinated Soviet ministers at the demonstration.

Apart from the tricky question of information and political control, the sheer mechanics of equipping a multitude of schools, offices and factories across Russia are formidable, given that the Soviet Union has only a rudimentary home-grown computer industry. British and other Western companies have to overcome restrictions on technology transfer imposed by Cocom, the Paris-based body which limits certain sales to the Eastern bloc on security grounds.

There are in any case doubts in the Kremlin over whether Russia's entry ticket to the computer age should be a wholesale commitment to Western imports. For one thing, hard currency is scarce. "What if we sign a contract and the Western firm disappears?" said the director of one computer training centre I visited in Moscow. "The computer market is highly volatile." Russians are knowledgeable in the ways of capitalism.

"Then there is the problem of supply at long distance, maintenance, downtime and changes in software," the director added. "Finally, experience has shown us it is unwise to depend on the West when it may impose embargoes or trade sanctions on us for political reasons at any moment."

The obvious answer, and perhaps the one the Kremlin will adopt in the end, is for Russia to develop its own computer industry, perhaps in combination with Western imports. But the only Soviet micro computer so far is the Agat, a copy of the Apple Two, which even officials at the Academy of Sciences admit is a failure. They say the Agat is regarded as an experimental model from which future Soviet computers will develop but the record is not encouraging and it seems doubtful whether the slow-moving, bureaucratic world of Soviet science and industry can keep pace with the lightning-fast advances of the computer world.

It seems likely, judging by Soviet reactions to Western exhibitions and sales pitches so far, that the Russians will move cautiously, picking and choosing the systems which suit them. At the training centre I visited not far from the Academy of Sciences, pupils drawn from nearby schools sit at computer terminals linked to a heavy main-frame Soviet computer, learning "fortran", the computer language, in English. But there were only twenty pupils at a time, and the system was already out of date.

The director, a sheaf of Western computer magazines under his arm, had a Radio Shack computer with a JVC screen in his office but it was, he explained, a rarity and not for general use. With his Western-style computer jargón and his enthusiasm for new technology, the training centre director typified the kind of new-generation technocrat Mr Gorbachov sees as Russia's hope. Whether the new technocrats can blow the dust off Russia's antiquated technology without also opening up the restrictive and authoritarian Communist system is another matter.

Moscow
16 April 1985

Third World studies in a cold climate

"LET'S GET ONE thing straight," the Rector of Lumumba University, Dr Vladimir Stanis, said heatedly. "We do not produce terrorists. We produce doctors, scientists and engineers for the poor and oppressed countries of the Third World." He leapt up from behind his desk and strode over to a glass cabinet, pausing by a large tom-tom in the shape of an African mask. "This is from Mozambique," he said, giving it a resounding thump. He moved on to an ornamental silver plaque with an Aztec design, mounted on wood. "Mexico. And this is a giant carved grasshopper from Guinea Bissau, a present from the foreign minister." The Rector returned to his desk. "No terrorists. We take students from poor, under-privileged backgrounds and educate them. There are plenty of places for bourgeois students in the West."

Lumumba — or, to give it its full title, The Patrice Lumumba People's Friendship University — has celebrated twenty-five years of existence, and the Russians are proud of its record. Founded in 1960 and named after the murdered left-wing Congolese Prime Minister, the university has turned out about 10,000 graduates over a quarter of a century. As the Rector says in his official handbook, *University of Friendship Lumumba*, graduates "are active in the economies of 110 countries. . . . They are a vivid example of the practical realization of Leninist internationalist policy."

But are they also expected to be grateful to the Soviet Union, and perhaps to work towards the practical realization of Soviet foreign policy? The Russians are sensitive to this charge, and even more sensitive to the suggestion that Lumumba University is a kind of guerrilla training camp, turning out KGB-trained Marxist terrorists ready to sow mayhem and subversion at Moscow's bidding.

As Dr Stanis points out, there are no squads of freedom fighters visible from his study windows, no tough young men doing Kalashnikov target practice among the grim grey tower blocks of the windswept campus on the outskirts of Moscow. If there are training camps for participants in "national liberation struggles" — and groups like the Palestine Liberation Organization have received training in Russia — the Russians keep them well hidden. Dr Stanis vehemently denies that Russia trains terrorists at all. An ebullient man who has run Lumumba for thirteen years, he raised the subject before I had a chance to consult my notes and promptly knocked it down as "gross and totally unjustified slander".

Dr Stanis is obviously used to being accused of running a centre for Third World subversives and spends much of his time on academic exchanges around the world trying to improve Lumumba's image. He wrily recalls a recent trip to New York where he watched a thriller called *Night Hawks*. The film depicts a violent and psychopathic international terrorist whose chief credential as a political gangster is that he "attended Lumumba University in Moscow". Many heads in the cinema turned to Dr Stanis when it was learned that the "terrorist chief" himself was in the audience. A stocky man with swept-back white hair and glasses, Dr Stanis professes to find the incident amusing.

But if it does not foster political terrorism, does Lumumba aim to produce Communist or Marxist Third World graduates sympathetic to Soviet aims? Dr Stanis said it would be surprising if the university had any other intention. "We have students from all backgrounds here — Buddhist monks, believers and non-believers, Communists and non-Communists."

"What I can say is that we educate them all to be friends of the Soviet Union, and of course we seek to instil in them the methodology of Marxism-Leninism." The Rector leans forward and smiles, holding his lapel badge of Lenin between thumb and forefinger. "I am a member of the Communist Party, most of my staff are Communists. This is a Soviet institution. What do you expect us to do, produce anti-Communists?"

While the aim is to make friends and influence people in the Third World, Lumumba claims that it is happy to turn deprived students into well-trained professional specialists with no particular gain to the Soviet Union. As proof of this Dr Stanis points to the example of Nepal, where the King's chief minister for many years was a Lumumba graduate, without turning the tiny mountain monarchy into a Marxist centre for destabilization on the Indo-Chinese border.

As a member of the World University Association, Lumumba teaches its students to be "both patriots of their own country and internationalist patriots as well". Would that mean proletarian internationalism, one of the central tenets of which is loyalty to Moscow? Dr Stanis replies that the main purpose of the university is to provide "countries emerging from colonialism" with specialists able to bring primitive and backward cultures into the modern world. If that makes them friendly to the cause of world Communism, so much the better. "And don't try and tell me the training of overseas students in the West is entirely disinterested," he adds.

As the then Soviet Prime Minister Aleksei Kosygin put it in the 1960s, Lumumba was founded to meet the need for higher education in countries "gaining their freedom from colonial dependence". The university, which at that time had older and more cramped premises nearer the centre of Moscow, started off with just over 500 students drawn from Africa, Asia and Latin America. It now has a sprawling new campus and about 5,000 Third World undergraduates from 105 nations. They study alongside some 2,000 Soviet students training as future advisers in Third World countries.

In the final analysis students are chosen for both aptitude and political leanings: applications (places at Lumumba are much in demand) are channelled through Soviet friendship societies or Soviet embassies. One of the most famous — or notorious — Lumumba students recruited in this way was Ilych Ramirez Sanchez, the product of a Marxist-minded Venezuelan family (though not one below the poverty line). As Carlos the Jackal Sanchez went on to give Lumumba much of its "terrorist training school" reputation, although university officials now disown him. The Jackal, they say, did not last much beyond the first introductory year of study and was expelled for his irresponsible behaviour.

There are no statistics on the drop-out rate, but officials say that those who fall at the first hurdle — a general one-year course including Russian language study — tend to be sent home. The staff-student ratio at Lumumba is generous, with 1,300 teaching staff specializing in physics, mathematics, economics, law, medicine, agriculture and engineering. (Economics, oddly enough, includes a thorough grounding in capitalism, since many Lumumba graduates go back to capitalist systems rather than centrally planned economies.)

There have been instances of racism (though the authorities deny this), and some Lumumba students are attracted by Moscow's black market. But the university tries to integrate students into Moscow life through a combination of discipline and familiarization campaigns.

Down the corridor, in the reading room of the newly-built library, students sit poring over textbooks or perusing newspapers, the majority either Soviet or African and Asian English-language dailies. The only western newspapers available appeared to be the *Morning Star* and the *Daily World*, the organ of the American Communist Party.

In the main foyer students mill about under portraits of revolutionary heroes, including Patrice Lumumba (murdered, according to the latest Soviet articles, with CIA connivance) and Che Guevara. A noticeboard announces the results of a poetry competition: the winning verse is in praise of martyred freedom fighters who fell fighting South African tyranny or American aggression in the Caribbean.

Lumumba accounts for an important part of Russia's aid to the Third World, though how much is not known. The overall figures are in any case disputed, since Moscow claims it gave $44 billion to developing countries from 1976 to 1980, whereas the Foreign Office puts the real figure at only $8 billion. But the Russians point out that the Third World is overwhelmingly in debt to the capitalist West, whereas Moscow offers developing countries economic and cultural aid designed to help them in their "struggle for decolonization". It is "selfless assistance" rendered to enable the Third World to extract itself from the capitalist, colonialist quagmire. Despite the drawbacks of a cold climate, an alien culture and economic ineptitude, quite a lot of Lumumba's 5,000 students will find the argument convincing.

Moscow
26 January 1984

ART FOR THE PEOPLE?:

TELEVISION AND THE ARTS

New life for an old master

Doctor Zhivago, PROBABLY Russia's best-known novel unpublished in its country of origin, may finally be issued in the Soviet Union — at least if the heirs of Boris Pasternak have their way. There is a chance — slim, but still a chance — that the work which won and then cost Pasternak the Nobel Prize for Literature in 1958 will be included in a new six-volume edition of his collected works.

As William Golding collected the 1983 prize at least two people cast their minds back twenty-five years to the day when Boris Pasternak should have received world recognition for his panoramic novel of the Russian Revolution. "Infinitely grateful," he said in his telegram of acceptance to Stockholm, "touched, surprised, proud, overwhelmed".

Yet, as his son Yevgeniy and his former mistress and literary assistant Olga Ivinskaya both still vividly remember, Pasternak was forced to turn down the coveted award after one of the most turbulent political and literary rows in twentieth-century Russia.

Madame Ivinskaya, now an old and frail lady living in a small, stuffy, overcrowded flat near the centre of Moscow, would be delighted to see *Doctor Zhivago* in print at long last. This is not so much because she was the model for "Lara", but because she played a key role in Pasternak's fruitless efforts to have the novel published in his homeland. She remains sceptical, and doubts whether the work will ever see the light of day, or even whether it would be wise to press the authorities too far.

Yevgeniy Pasternak, now aged sixty, has every hope that volume four of the scholarly edition he is now compiling will consist of *Doctor Zhivago*, suitably annotated. The key may lie with the preface and footnotes, since Madame Ivinskaya agrees that the novel could only appear if the original row was explained to the Russian reading public in an ideologically "correct" manner.

It seems a long time since Semichastny, then head of the Communist Youth League, and subsequently KGB chief, called Pasternak "a mangy sheep who has spat in the face of the people and befouled the place where he eats, something even a pig does not do". The question is whether the authorities are sufficiently reconciled to Pasternak and whether the inflamed passions and rivalries of 1958 are sufficiently distant for the Kremlin to take a more relaxed view.

Curiously, "Lara's Theme" from David Lean's film of *Zhivago* is familiar to Muscovites, and can often be heard in restaurants or skating rinks. But neither the book nor the film has ever been issued in Russia. The chances are that if the book was quietly included in a scholarly edition it would cause interest rather than a sensation.

Both Yevgeniy Pasternak and Olga Ivinskaya dismiss the idea that *Doctor Zhivago* is in any way "anti-Soviet". "Boris Leonidovich was never really accused of anything," Madame Ivinskaya declares when asked if Pasternak will ever be fully "rehabilitated". "What is there to be rehabilitated for? It is not a question of rehabilitating Pasternak, it is a question of restoring his poetic image. He is a poet who cannot be silenced."

The whole episode, Madame Ivinskaya now feels, was an unfortunate misunderstanding in which Pasternak made politically naïve or foolish moves, and that she herself gave him bad advice. Even Nikita Khrushchev later came to regret the banning of *Zhivago*, and remarked that he wished he had stuck to his original opinion, which was that the novel was "rather dull, with nothing much to make a noise about".

Sitting in Madame Ivinskaya's heavily furnished flat, crammed with mementoes of the Pasternak years, it is difficult to recapture that momentous week when the literary world was in uproar and Khrushchev himself was dragged into a row he later said he should have left to low-level functionaries.

Ivinskaya, then a junior editor at the literary monthly *Novy Mir* (New World) and Pasternak's mistress (he was living with his second wife, Zinaida Nikolaevna), was at the heart of the drama. Some think it was Pasternak's concern fot her safety which made him bow to Kremlin pressure and reject the prize. Ivinskaya, now ill and in her seventies, served two exhausting labour-camp sentences because of her association with the great writer, one in the early 1950s and one just after his death in 1960, which have taken their toll.

As the grey light of a bleak Moscow winter afternoon falls on the framed photographs of herself and Pasternak however, one can recapture his love of the striking Russian beauty she then was, twenty-two years younger than himself and the inspiration for his memorable love story.

Ivinskaya herself thinks the move which precipitated the onslaught — the publication of *Doctor Zhivago* in the West — was an almost absent-minded step on his part. The novel had been on the desk of Soviet publishing houses for some time, gathering dust, and Pasternak gradually became convinced that there was little or no chance of publication.

In these circumstances he was approached in the spring of 1957 by an Italian broadcaster from Moscow Radio, Sergio D'Angelo, who went out to the Pasternak *dacha* at Peredelkino, the charming writers' village not far from Moscow. D'Angelo, an Italian Communist, was acting on behalf of the millionaire left-wing publisher Giacomo Feltrinelli.

"It was a beautiful day in May", D'Angelo later recalled, "I found Pasternak working in the garden, and he welcomed me in a warm and simple fashion. When I came to the purpose of my visit he seemed taken aback. It had obviously never occurred to him before to have dealings with a foreign publisher."

D'Angelo pointed out that no Soviet official had yet formally and officially pronounced against the book. It was simply in limbo. Pasternak thought for a while, went inside and emerged with the manuscript. "As he showed me to the garden gate he said, in what seemed a joking way, 'You have invited me to take part in my own execution.'"

When the Soviet authorities learned what had happened they were furious, and ordered the Italian Communist Party to put pressure on Feltrinelli to return the manuscript. But Feltrinelli refused point blank. The novel duly appeared in November 1957, swiftly followed by a chorus of Soviet vilification directed against Pasternak.

A few lone voices in the Union of Writers defended him, saying the novel was an "impeccable work" of Russian literature. But they were in a minority, and were all but extinguished a year later when the Nobel award was announced.

When this happened, in 1958, the *Literary Gazette*, official organ of the Union of Writers, called Pasternak a "rabid literary snob" and described *Doctor Zhivago* as a paltry, worthless and vile piece of work. The union condemned Pasternak as a tool of bourgeois propaganda, and said the novel was a cry of woe on the part of an arrogant man angry that history had not taken the path he would have liked. In a strong hint of expulsion, the union said Pasternak had severed all links with his past and his country. "Let him become a real émigré", Semichastny declared. "Let him take himself off to his capitalist paradise."

Like all Russian writers, Pasternak identified himself profoundly with his homeland, and replied that he could never leave it. He refused to go to a union tribunal, saying he would never give up the Nobel Prize, although he would donate the prize money to the Soviet Peace Fund. But behind this façade of defiance he was in despair. Madame Ivinskaya recalls with a shudder that at one stage he even suggested they should make a joint suicide pact.

Hearing that Olga Ivinskaya had been sacked, and was in danger of worse retribution, Pasternak had sent a telegram to Stockholm rejecting the prize he had welcomed so gratefully a short time before. He also asked the Central Committee to have Ivinskaya reinstated. On Ivinskaya's advice Pasternak then sent letters of repentance to the Soviet authorities, including one to Khrushchev.

It was this action which Madame Ivinskaya now regards as a regrettable error of judgement on her part. She adds, however, that the circumstances were very different from those in which a later Russian Nobel Prizewinner — Alexander Solzhenitsyn — defied the Kremlin by triumphantly accepting the award. In any case, Pasternak and Solzhenitsyn were quite different in character and temperament.

Pasternak's son, Yevgeniy, also remembers the effect of this "hysterical atmosphere" on his father. When he went out to Peredelkino, he told us, he found Pasternak "a beaten man psychologically, a lost man. I could hardly recognize him. He kept asking me if I was afraid, whether they had done anything to me. I said I would share his fate whatever happened."

Pasternak's first son by his first marriage, Yevgeniy was a 35-year-old research scientist at the time. After Boris Pasternak's death in 1960 Yevgeniy abandoned physics — always considered an odd choice in so literary and artistic a family — and devoted himself full-time to his father's legacy, compiling and annotating poems, prose and translations. Thanks to the intercession of the

Academy of Sciences he holds a post at the Moscow Institute of World Literature which enables him to do this.

Like Madame Ivinskaya, Yevgeniy Pasternak and his wife live in the kind of cluttered, heavily furnished flat favoured by the Russian intelligentsia, in the centre of Moscow. On the walls are paintings by his grandfather, the distinguished artist Leonid Pasternak.

So what are the chances, as the photographs fade in their frames and memories fade with them, that the upheaval of 1958 will be forgiven and forgotten? The authorities' attitude to Pasternak remains ambiguous. His poems are published — there is even an edition of Pasternak's verse for use in schools — but the number of copies is strictly limited. In some cases the books are largely unavailable except for hard currency in special Moscow shops for foreigners, and the few which are put on sale in ordinary bookshops swiftly sell out.

A small edition of verse appeared in 1961, the year after Pasternak's death. But it was another five years before a limited volume of collected poems appeared, in the series, *The Poet's Library*, the standard Soviet edition.

Some of the poems from *Doctor Zhivago* have been published, but not the novel itself. Last year the Pasternaks issued a volume of prose under the title *Aeriel Paths.* Yevgeniy Pasternak is now putting the final touches to a two-volume collection of his father's writings — the manuscript is already in type — with the major six-volume edition to follow. He hopes that that edition, including *Doctor Zhivago*, will see the light of day in time for the celebrations marking the hundredth anniversary of Pasternak's birth in 1990.

Moscow
12 December 1983

Filmgoers see the seamy side of life

CINEMA GOING IN Moscow is a curious experience at the moment — not because of police raids on "idlers" (which have abated) but because of the films. Some conform to demand for ideological orthodoxy in the arts. Others are strikingly original and thoughtful, and show the seamy side of Soviet life. Some, miraculously, do both. Take for example *A Railway Station for Two*, directed by Eldar Ryazanov. The hero has been sentenced to labour camp for a crime — a hit and run accident — he did not commit (he covered up for his wife). The scenes in the camp, with convicts performing hard labour in swirling snow under the glare of the searchlights, send a frisson through Moscow audiences. The barbed wire and watchtowers are only usually talked about in whispers, and rarely shown on the screen. On the other hand there is no hint that people get put in labour camps for political dissent. The camp and its commandant are presented as benevolent, in line with the official view that camps are corrective institutions for those who need "re-educating" (in sub-zero temperatures).

Most of *Railway Station* concerns the affair the hero has with a station buffet waitress shortly before facing the court. These scenes arouse as much interest as the brief camp scenes, since they show petty thieving, sexual licence and peculation in a small railway town. The waitress deals in fruit brought up in suitcases by her lover, a roguish railway guard. Illegal trading brings riches, including a video recorder, a rare luxury.

Small-town corruption (and trains) figure largely in *The Train Stopped* (director Vadim Abdrashidov). Here a journalist and a detective investigate a train crash, and discover that the driver was drunk and incompetent and the train so badly maintained that it should never have left the local depot. Local officials cover up the corruption and mismanagement which led to the accident, and persuade the journalist to print a false account. The journalist explains to the shocked detective that to tell the truth helps no one, whereas the cover-up gives the town a local hero — the train driver — and a state-funded housing scheme in his honour.

Other recent films have also portrayed painfully accurate slices of Soviet life. Nikita Mikhalkov's *Relatives* concerns a fashionable Moscow girl who is ashamed of her peasant mother. Mikhalkov (who incidentally plays the guard in *Railway Station for Two*) reflects in *Relatives* the new class divisions in Soviet society. The girl learns in the end to respect honest rural values rather than passing fashion.

Ideological messages are present in most current films, and in popular thrillers and spy films for mass audiences they dominate. *Death on Take-Off*, now playing to packed houses, tells the story of a young military scientist who is seduced by a beautiful Western spy called Nora. The wily Nora photographs top secret plans for a new kind of tank armour-plating, but is finally cornered by KGB agents, who in the obligatory manner are portrayed as clean-cut, well-mannered and efficient. The message for Russians is clear, avoid contact with foreigners.

Incident in Quadrant 36–80 also shows the West in a lurid light. Here the Americans are the villains in a near-miss nuclear accident at sea. An American submarine goes haywire (due to inferior Western computers) and fires two deadly missiles at nearby Soviet warships on manoeuvres. The Soviet Navy reacts with cool professionalism, destroying the maverick missiles and saving the world from a holocaust. The Americans, by contrast, appear as gum-chewing, trigger-happy psychopaths in dark glasses.

Moscow audiences identify with the firm-jawed Russian pilots and officers — all good family men — and are fascinated by shots of Soviet jump jets on the giant aircraft-carrier *Kiev*. But they also note the assumption in the film of a superpower camaraderie.

The American admiral appeals to his Soviet counterpart on a hot line not to retaliate, while up in the air bomber crews greet each other as old friends, asking after each other's families in a cosy exchange of East-West military comradeship. In spy thrillers, as in love stories and wry social commentaries, the message is mixed.

Moscow
7 March 1983

Through a television screen darkly

LIVING IN THE Soviet Union is sometimes like living in a topsy-turvy world, in which the real world is just visible in the corner of a mirror: a distorted image which you have to focus on carefully in an effort to find the clues to what is really going on "out there", beyond the looking glass.

Take the Soviet presentation of the news. Every evening Moscow television offers a programme called *Vremya* (Time), which opens with a picture of the Kremlin and some rather unsuitably lush ballet music, as the words "Information and

News" roll along the bottom of the screen. Up pop two newscasters, much in the Western manner, except that they say "Good evening, comrades" while shuffling their papers and preparing to look the camera in the eye. Remarkably few people say "comrade" any more in the Soviet Union. But news is one area where formality prevails. News is a serious business. There is no hint of the Western dilemma over whether news should entertain, inform or educate. So far as the Soviet authorities are concerned, control of news is a means of educating the population in accordance with the precepts of Marxism-Leninism. There are cases where Russians know, either from the highly efficient grapevine or from foreign broadcasts, that an event of importance has taken place, and the television and radio news either mention it last, in sparse detail, or not at all. The authorities' view is that "the people" are probably better off being kept in ignorance of things which do not concern them.

All of which presents the news organizations with a few problems, especially as the gap widens between what people know to be true and what the authorities choose to tell them. Many of those in Tass and the Soviet newspaper world are highly sophisticated newsmen who might not share Western news values, and who deplore (perhaps rightly) the Western obsession with bad news, but who are trying to adjust to a more modern way of presenting the news. Tass, in particular, is increasingly run as if it were just another news agency, like Reuters or UPI, complete with short exciting headlines, numbered news stories, and now "world news summaries".

The trouble is that on closer inspection the news according to Tass is much the same as it ever was, only the wrapping is rather more attractive. A typical recent summary began with the news that the Supreme Soviet of the Russian Federation had discussed "questions of dwelling houses in the countryside and other structures". It went on to say that in France President Mitterrand had received the co-ordinator of the guiding council of the Government of Nicaragua, that in London Britain intended to maintain "the dangerous seat of tensions in the Southern Atlantic", and that in Brazzaville Jean-Michel Bokamba-Yangouma, member of the Political Bureau of the Central Committee of the Congolese Party of Labour, had received a visiting delegation from the People's Democratic Party of

Afghanistan. It is possible, by turning the news this way and that, to detect a gleam of reality: no one watching television or reading the papers (and millions do, contrary to popular belief in the West) can escape the fact that there is a war on in Lebanon and that Mr Brezhnev has warned America not to send in troops, or that arms talks are going on in Geneva. Or that there may be trouble in Poland, if the Pope goes there. It is all a matter of reading — or watching — between the lines.

But it is also true that, for Russia, the "question of dwelling houses in the countryside" is extremely important, and neither boring nor funny.

Moscow
7 August 1982

Keeping alive the cult of Vysotsky

THEY STAND AT his graveside every day, about thirty people at any one time, tending the blaze of red flowers that lie heaped in front of a simple white headstone inscribed with the words "Vladimir Vysotsky 1939–1980". No one organizes this daily commemoration. It is a spontaneous demonstration — something unusual in the Soviet Union — of the admiration aroused in Russians by the man described by one leading dissident as "the greatest national poet and singer of our time". The second anniversary of Vysotsky's death falls on Sunday, and as with the first anniversary, the police are preparing for the numbers at the graveside to swell to hundreds, if not thousands.

Vysotsky was not strictly speaking a dissident. But in his songs he told the Russians, official and unofficial, how hard their life was, and in lyrics etched in acid openly told the truth about the absurdities and failings of Soviet life.

He sang to guitar accompaniment in the alternately soothing and raucous style of the French *chansonniers* (his wife was the French actress, Marina Vlady), and lived a reckless life of alcohol and drugs which gave his voice its gravelly quality, but killed him at the age of forty-two.

When Vysotsky died, 30,000 people turned up for the funeral service at the Taganka Theatre in Moscow, where he had been the main actor and poet. They were all clutching flowers for the cortège, a seething mass beyond the control even of mounted police. When the coffin had gone, Vysotsky's fans stayed on, singing late into the night.

The crowd on Sunday will not be so ecstatic. The crash barriers erected around the grave last year are still in place, but the cult of Vysotsky has settled into a steady, apparently unshakeable reverence for the balladeer who sang about prison camps, official hypocrisy and arbitrary arrest.

If you believe the stories they tell each other at the graveside, as they pass around dog-eared copies of his lyrics, even the Kremlin has a soft spot for Vysotsky. On the day he died, they say, President Brezhnev was on holiday in the Crimea, just as he is now. His guest on the Politburo's private beach was M. Georges Marchais, the French Communist leader. When the news of the singer's death came, Mr Brezhnev put one of Vysotsky's more biting songs on the record-player, ordered a bottle of cognac, and, to M. Marchais' astonishment, raised his glass in a toast to Vysotsky's memory. It would be nice to think the story was true, and even nicer to think that, on Sunday, Mr Brezhnev will be raising his glass once again.

Moscow
24 July 1982

Musical revolution from the Russian Jazzmen

A COLD DECEMBER Moscow day, with snow and sleet drifting across the grey city. In a bare and chilly suburban cinema, Muscovites are shown to their seats by dumpy ladies in woollen hats. The lights go down and first comes a newsreel in 1950s' socialist realist style, about a steel foundry and chicken farming. And then, suddenly, the screen explodes with colour, exuberance — and music. *Jazzmen* (in Russian *My iz Dzhazza*, or "We are from Jazz") is the exhilarating, lovingly-filmed story of the first jazzband in Russia, formed in Odessa, on the Black Sea, in the 1920s. Partly based on the lives of Russian jazz pioneers (some of whom lived to see jazz flourish, be suppressed and revive), the film sweeps the viewer along on an irresistible stream of music and fun.

The young hero — played with engaging impudence by Igor

Sklyar—is first seen trying out piano rags on an examination panel at the music institute where he is a student. They accuse him of being an "agent of imperialism". Undaunted, he teams up with a pair of itinerant musicians (a kind of Russian Laurel and Hardy act) and a seedy saxophonist they meet in jail after a riotous party. From then on, the band, held together by humour, a kindred spirit and a missionary love of jazz, goes from dizzy success (suites in luxury hotels) to dismal failure (down and out on the streets) in their efforts to have jazz accepted in the young Soviet republic.

Jazzmen, directed by Karen Shakhnazarov, is shot through with wit and enthusiasm and Moscow audiences find the band's antics hilarious as they try to prove that jazz is not a "bourgeois" art-form but "revolutionary" and therefore acceptable in a proletarian culture.

The real history of the jazz pioneers was not in the least funny, since the accusations of "imperialism" which sound so preposterous today were used to persecute musicians and artists in the terrible days of the Stalin terror (none of which is even hinted at in the version of *Jazzmen* passed by the censor). But the film has seized the Russian imagination because it harks back to a "golden age", the 1920s, when there was colour and joy.

For similar reasons, the Anglo-Russian *Anna Pavlova* is proving a popular success.

The film, directed by the Moldavian director Emil Lotianou, depicts the life of the great ballerina from her first steps at the imperial ballet school in St Petersburg to her death in Europe on one of her many strenuous tours.

Soviet critics have panned the film as "superficial" and a "travesty", pointing out (correctly) that the star of the film, Galina Belyaeva, is too lightweight and inexperienced to play the demanding role of Pavlova. *Sovietskaya Rossiya* said that Miss Belyaeva — who happens to be the director's wife — gave a rosy and romantic portrayal of Pavlova "devoid of spiritual content or even interest".

What has really upset officials, however, is that in *Pavlova* the Russian revolutions of 1905 and 1917 are seen as marginal, while imperial Russia appears sparklingly idyllic. The sun always shines in St Petersburg, a city filled with gaiety and plenty. The revolution only intrudes when Pavlova's carriage is held up by a bloodily put-down demonstration on the way to the theatre.

At two and a half hours the film is an hour too long and some of the actors — including James Fox, who plays Anna's lover and manager — look distinctly uncomfortable. The exception is Bruce Forsyth who gives a splendid cameo performance and is even funnier dubbed into Russian.

Most of the ideas put up by the British side of the production team seem to have been jettisoned in favour of an extravagant and unconvincing vehicle for Miss Balyaeva. Diaghilev and Nijinsky merely come across as hysterical.

But for Russians this is beside the point, just as the way *Jazzmen* glosses over Stalinism is forgivable. Like *Jazzmen, Pavlova* fills the screen with colour and excitement, conjuring up a Russia peopled by outstanding individuals against the backcloth of a spontaneous, sparkling Russia long vanished.

Small wonder that Muscovites are queueing up to see both films in preference to standard Soviet cinema offerings such as *Hot Summer in Kabul*, which depicts a positive Soviet hero giving selfless fraternal aid to the Afghan people in their struggle against world imperialism.

Moscow
31 December 1983

A glimpse of the unreachable West

"SOVIET TELEVISION PRESENTS a film made about the United States," is the kind of announcement guaranteed to stir Soviet viewers out of the stupor induced by combine-harvesters, oil production figures and variety shows from East Germany. The film that follows is bound to cast America in a bad light, otherwise it would not be shown. But it comes from "over there", the distant and unreachable West, where streets are simultaneously lined with gold and the bodies of the unemployed. The United States has poverty and a crazed anti-Communist President, but it also has wonders that can be glimpsed on celluloid.

In this case the film, *Run, Simon, Run*, turned out to be an early Burt Reynolds vehicle made in 1970. Mr Reynolds, dubbed into Russian (subtitles are unknown here) played an angry young Red Indian wrongly imprisoned for a murder he did not commit.

Released from Arizona state penitentiary, Simon goes in search of the real murderer — a white man — tracks him down and kidnaps him, only to be shot dead.

As a piece of cinematic art *Run, Simon, Run* is eminently forgettable, except for Mr Reynolds' convincing Red Indian looks and smouldering manner. But it reflects the growing American liberal conscience over the plight of American Indians in the 1960s and therefore was taken out of the archives by Moscow Television to coincide with the Kremlin's current campaign on behalf of Leonard Peltier, a Red Indian leader convicted of murdering two Federal Bureau of Investigation agents. There are growing doubts about the conviction in the United States and the case may be reopened.

The Soviet campaign, however, is also partly designed to counteract Western charges that dissidents — in particular the scientist, Dr Andrei Sakharov — are persecuted in the Soviet Union. Mr Peltier, like Simon, is presented as the victim of capitalist oppression. Or, as the Soviet equivalent of *Radio Times* put it: "This film clearly demonstrates racism in the world's leading capitalist country."

Unfortunately, Soviet viewers tended to be struck not only by the oppression of the American Indian but also by the fact that the Arizona prison seemed remarkably benevolent, the state official administering the Indian reservations was an attractive blond rather than an SS stormtrooper, and the flats inhabited by Arizonans looked spacious and sumptuous. Even Burt Reynolds' cabin seemed fairly luxurious

For more sophisticated viewers there was also the point that the condescension and prejudice encountered by Simon in his search for justice was not dissimilar to the patronizing Great Russian attitude towards ethnic minorities. As the late Yuri Andropov forcefully pointed out, Russians can be arrogant and condescending towards minority nationalities.

On balance, showing selected Western films on television and in cinemas probably benefits the Kremlin rather than the reverse. An ideological point is got across to a mass audience, which in turn is made to feel that it has had a glimpse of Western life.

One of this year's box-office hits across Russia is *Tootsie*, starring Dustin Hoffman. It was shown, according to well-informed Russians, because it combined "the suppression of women in the West" (the Hoffman character encounters male chauvinism when he dresses as a woman) with unemployment (he does so because he is out of work and takes a female role). The film begins, in the original version, with a long sequence which explains why he is out of work. In the Soviet version this opening segment was cut. Most Soviet cinema goers got the message — the West is collapsing socially and economically — while at the same time wondering why an out-of-work actor in New York appears to earn more than President Chernenko and enjoys a life-style beyond the dreams of most members of the Soviet élite, let alone the average worker or peasant.

One or two may also have wondered why Western directors are allowed to make such frankly critical films without being sacked or arrested.

Moscow
27 September 1984

Tass is authorized to state

MOSCOW INTELLECTUALS DISMISS it as crude, but ordinary Russians find it gripping. Night after night for the past two weeks Moscow Television has filled the gap left by the boycotted Los Angeles Olympics with a melodramatic spy thriller called *Tass is authorized to state*. The title is more enticing than it sounds since the phrase always appears over Kremlin announcements of diplomatic expulsions and imperialist plots in the Soviet press.

In this case the story depicts a battle of wits between the Russian KGB and the American CIA in an imaginary African country called Nagonia. Familiar holiday-reading perhaps — except that the KGB agents are clean-cut young men in crisp white shirts and the KGB general who directs them from Moscow is wise, thoughtful and decent. "I must have the facts," he remarked to a subordinate in one of this week's episodes. "The procurator will not let us exhume the body without the facts."

This may have the intelligentsia falling out of their armchairs, but it is all part of a determined and not unsuccessful campaign by the KGB to brush up its image. The 1979 novel by Julian Semyonov on which the series is based is a sell-out and the KGB has even announced a literary competition to encourage further novels and films showing Russian secret agents as scrupulous and honourable men trying to defend Communist Russia against its internal and external enemies. The current film has top Soviet actors to add to its appeal.

The plot of *Tass is authorized* sometimes becomes confused, as the pro-Soviet President of Nagonia enlists KGB help in an attempt to defeat a Western-backed coup against his left-wing regime. But CIA villainy stands out plainly from the intrigue, with American operatives (all speaking faultless Russian) using blackmail, seduction, poison and murder.

The KGB is shown to have a vast computer bank of personal information both in Africa and at the grim Lyubyanka building in Moscow. But as the series repeatedly points out, the KGB — unlike the CIA — is fighting for progressive humanity and uses its powers judiciously.

The series has not entirely blotted out interest in the Olympics in Russia. Moscow has ridiculed the Games, and they have not been shown on television despite official promises that they would be broadcast. But results are announced in the press and followed with fascination and some regret by Russians.

Tass is authorized is supposed to have convinced them by the time it ends on Friday that Soviet fears of trigger-happy Americans in Los Angeles were justified, and that the imperialists are as unscrupulous in the United States as they are in fictional Nagonia.

Moscow
9 August 1984

Rasputin makes a roaring comeback

Mr Mikhail Gorbachov likes films and the theatre, although since he has other preoccupations at the moment it is not yet clear how far he is prepared to go to make the arts in Russia livelier than they were under President Chernenko.

Judging by his remarks as Ideology Secretary last year, Mr Gorbachov is something of a young fogey though with an inquiring mind. "A true artist cannot stand aside from the pressing tasks of the times," the Soviet leader said in a message to the Moscow Film Festival, which ended last week. "He always serves the good and the light and promotes social progress."

Mr Elem Klimov is evidently among the elect, since his film *Go and See*, set in wartime Byelorussia, was the official Soviet entry at the festival.

But there is another side to Mr Klimov, as displayed in his astonishing film *Agoniya* (Agony), about the life and death of Rasputin, the manic holy man who gained a deadly grip on the court just as the beleaguered Tsar was grappling with war and revolution, and who can scarcely be said to have served the good and the light.

Mr Klimov made *Agoniya* over a decade ago, but because of its explosive subject, and its frank scenes, the film has gathered dust in the vaults. It has been screened abroad, whispered about in Moscow, but not shown.

Perhaps because Mr Klimov is now also an "official" Soviet director, it might be embarrassing to have one of his important films banned. Or perhaps this is a liberal gesture by Mr Gorbachov.

At all events, the larger than life figure of Rasputin, physically massive and overpoweringly charismatic, has been released to roar and rampage across the screens of Moscow suburban cinemas, where *Agoniya* played to overflowing houses while cinemas in the centre were commandeered for the festival entries.

Agoniya, even in the heavily cut version finally released, has robust scenes of debauchery and decadence in an atmosphere of eroticism and mysticism, and includes the episode in which a group of young aristocrats put Rasputin to death after a long struggle in which through some diabolic force he survived both poison and bullet.

But it also shows why Rasputin was accepted at court — his influence on the Tsarina, and his ability to heal the ailing Tsarevich — and gives a human portrait of Nicholas II, while blaming him for needless Russian deaths. This is not the Tsar of Soviet caricature: his weaknesses and indecisions are examined sympathetically. (A scene in which he cruelly shoots crows was added later in case the portrait was seen as too benign.)

The *Agony* is not only Russia's agony in war and uprising, it is also Nicholas's.

The Bolsheviks hardly appear at all — not even at the Duma (the National Assembly which was a great deal more lively than the Supreme Soviet), and the only reference to Lenin is in the obligatory quotation at the beginning of the film. Nicholas and the corrupt court are swept away by Russia in the mass.

The release of this stunning re-creation of a lost world — lost above all to the Russians themselves — may presage a revival in the Soviet cinema at last.

The other film showing to crowded cinemas, again away from the festival itself, was Roland Bykov's *Scarecrow*, a painfully honest portrait of a gang of aimless teenagers in a provincial town and their persecution of a newcomer, Lena, and her art-collecting grandfather. A story of adolescent love and betrayal, *Scarecrow* ends with Lena shaving her head to shame her tormentors before being forced to leave town.

Outside the cinema, a group of youths sitting on the steps gave no hint that they had absorbed the moral of Bykov's tale, and indeed looked as if they had just stepped down from the screen. Perhaps, after all, Mr Gorbachov would rather they had been watching Moscow's other current film hit: *Pages from the Life of Yuri Andropov*.

Moscow
16 July 1985

ENDPIECE:

ADVICE TO TRAVELLERS

A guided tour of Russian customs

OUR RADIO CRITIC David Wade recently admitted that despite reading reports from Moscow, in *The Times* presumably, he had no clear idea of what the Russians were really like, never having met one. Since most English people are in the same boat a solution must be found to put matters right — and I have one to hand. It is called *Baedeker's Guide to Russia 1914* (reprinted by David & Charles in 1971 and now out of print again, which is a pity because the original is rare).

Good old Baedeker got it absolutely right as usual, and much of what he had to say in 1914 is still, remarkably, valid. Some of the "advice to travellers" might put potential visitors to Russia off the idea altogether, but it shouldn't. It is simply common sense, and bears a close resemblance to the advice offered nowadays by the Moscow office of American Express.

Take that inevitable introduction to any foreign country, Customs. Here is American Express 1983: "For your own wellbeing, do not attempt to import any article which would obviously be prohibited or which might be considered offensive." Such as? "Such as weapons, ammunition, drugs, political and/or sex literature. Use the broadest interpretation of pornography if in doubt." *Playboy* magazine did not exist in 1914, but Baedeker is on much the same lines.

"Customs examination of passengers' luggage is generally thorough. Books in large quantities are submitted to a censor. Travellers should avoid works of a political, social or historical nature. Gunpowder and playing cards are prohibited." Playing cards, I am glad to say, now seem to be permitted, which I suppose is progress of a kind. You might like a game of rummy at your hotel, while sipping a glass or two of the Moldavian or Caucasian wines which Baedeker recommends, and which are still the dominant wines. Inflation has struck here as elsewhere, alas; in 1914 wine was a rouble a bottle, and is now double that. Still not a bad price rise over seventy years.

Avoid tap water, however: American Express notes that "as in many other countries, care should be taken in regard to drinking water, and it is advisable to use bottled mineral water." Baedeker

1914 said that "unboiled water should be avoided", but suggested tea rather than mineral water as a substitute.

You will then want to have a meal, pausing first to leave your coat in the cloakroom (American Express: "Cloakrooms exist almost everywhere and you are expected to use them", Baedeker: "Overcoats, overshoes and hats must be left in the cloakroom.") American Express describes dining out in Russia as an "interesting experience" with "rather leisurely service", Baedeker was more generous. Russian restaurants, or at least the first-class ones, were "lavishly decorated and furnished" in 1914, and the large number of waiters was a "striking characteristic".

Baedeker does not say whether most of them stood around avoiding your eye, as they tend to do nowadays, but the food offered sounds much the same: "zakuski" or pickled cucumbers, mushrooms, caviar, fish and meat, all washed down with vodka (and very nice too).

No chance of relaxing with a newspaper from home after your meal though: "Newspapers from the west, when available, are up to seven days old" (American Express); and "Foreign newspapers are very scarce, even in the best hotels" (Baedeker).

Never mind, you can go out and take photographs of Moscow sights — provided you are careful. Baedeker warned in 1914 that "the taking of photographs near fortresses is naturally forbidden", adding that even in less important places, "the guardians of the law are apt to be over-vigilant". Similarly, American Express suggest you refrain from photographing military installations, border areas, railways and bridges, adding for good measure that it is probably not advisable to point your camera at "people queueing up, drunks, demonstrations, etc."

Finding your way around should be no problem, provided you take the trouble to master the alphabet. American Express observe that a phrase-book is a useful aid, and that once you can read the Cyrillic alphabet you will be surprised at what you can understand. Baedeker agreed: "Even the slightest acquaintance with the language is a considerable help, and all who visit the country should at least learn the alphabet in order to be able to read street names."

Russians are curious about foreigners, and these days, at least, are keen to show off the broad streets and modern buildings which did not exist in the Moscow of 1914.

You can of course always take a cab to the theatre or ballet, "the excellence of which has been amply demonstrated both in Europe and America" (Baedeker). Be warned, though, that then as now the cabbie "does not always know his way about town and sometimes raises difficulties about giving change" (only sometimes?).

When you come to leave Russia, you will of course need to get your passport back. Baedeker noted that in 1914 the traveller would have to "hand in his passport and obtain a police certificate to the effect that nothing stands in the way of his departure", adding: "As the preparation of this application takes several hours at least, it is advisable to procure the necessary form as soon as possible."

American Express are good enough to warn you of the forms and vouchers you need to fill in, and the passport business, too: "The passport is required for registration. Generally no attempt will be made by the hotel staff to return it to you and therefore please be sure to reclaim your passport in good time before departure."

And long after you have returned home, Baedeker will refresh your memory, describing in clear and incisive prose the ubiquitous samovar and abacus (both still in use), the prevalence of uniforms of all kinds, the church cupolas, dull public buildings and "the sharp distinction" between officialdom and the ordinary people. "Alongside admirable achievements", he writes, "we also find a great deal of merely outward imitation of western forms."

Still, in one area Russia does resemble the West inwardly as well as outwardly: the mass package tour has taken over. In 1914 Baedeker suggested you should bring along with you a pillow or air cushion, linen sheets ("especially useful on long railway journeys and in provincial hotels"), a rug, a small India-rubber bath, and some insect powder. I wonder what the Soviet Customs would make of that little lot?

Moscow
2–8 July 1983